Community, Conflict and the State

Also by Charlie Cooper

HOUSING, COMMUNITY AND CONFLICT: Understanding Resident 'Involvement' (co-edited)

'MODERNISING' SOCIAL POLICY: Unravelling New Labour's Welfare Reforms (co-authored)

RESIDENT INVOLVEMENT AND COMMUNITY ACTION: Theory to Practice (co-edited)

UNDERSTANDING SCHOOL EXCLUSION: Challenging Processes of Docility

Community, Conflict and the State

Rethinking Notions of 'Safety', 'Cohesion' and 'Wellbeing'

Charlie Cooper
University of Hull, UK

First published 2008 by
PALGRAVE MACMILLAN

Palgrave Macmillan in the UK is an imprint of Macmillan Publishers Limited, registered in England, company number 785998, of Houndmills, Basingstoke, Hampshire RG21 6XS.

Palgrave Macmillan in the US is a division of St Martin's Press LLC, 175 Fifth Avenue, New York, NY 10010.

Palgrave Macmillan is the global academic imprint of the above companies and has companies and representatives throughout the world.

Palgrave® and Macmillan® are registered trademarks in the United States, the United Kingdom, Europe and other countries.

ISBN-13: 978–1–4039–9832–3 hardback
ISBN-10: 1–4039–9832–9 hardback

This book is printed on paper suitable for recycling and made from fully managed and sustained forest sources. Logging, pulping and manufacturing processes are expected to conform to the environmental regulations of the country of origin.

A catalogue record for this book is available from the British Library.

Library of Congress Cataloging-in-Publication Data

Cooper, Charlie, 1952–
      Community, conflict and the state : rethinking notions of 'safety', 'cohesion' and 'wellbeing' / Charlie Cooper.
         p. cm.
         ISBN-13: 978–1–4039–9832–3
         1. Communities – Great Britain. 2. Quality of life – Great Britain.
      3. Great Britain – Social policy. 4. Social values – Great Britain.
      5. State, The. I. Title.

HM756.C66 2008
307.0941'09051—dc22   2008020796

10 9 8 7 6 5 4 3 2 1
17 16 15 14 13 12 11 10 09 08

Printed and bound in Great Britain by
CPI Antony Rowe, Chippenham and Eastbourne

For Amélie Rosa and Andrea

Contents

Acknowledgements   viii

Introduction   1

1. 'Community', 'Conflict' and the State – the Historical Field   29

2. Concepts of 'Community' and 'Conflict'   86

3. New Labour, Community Safety, Cohesion and Wellbeing   127

4. Rethinking Community Safety, Cohesion and Wellbeing   172

5. Summary and Conclusions – Community Wellbeing for All?   218

Bibliography   238

Index   255

Acknowledgements

I would like to thank David Shrigley for granting permission to reproduce his cartoon, 'Don't Worry'. I would also like to thank the anonymous reviewer who read my original manuscript and offered some very constructive suggestions; Hazel Woodbridge, Phillipa Grand and Olivia Middleton at Palgrave for their continual support and patience; and the team at Newgen Imaging Systems for managing the completion of this project so expertly.

Introduction

Background

Throughout modernity society has been preoccupied with threats to personal safety and wellbeing. Following the Second World War of the last century, the British state introduced a range of redistributive measures founded on Keynesian welfarist principles which aimed to safeguard the safety and wellbeing of its citizens. Since the late-1970s, however, governments have pursued different ideological aims based on neo-liberalism which claims that it is no longer viable for the state to protect its citizens through redistributive measures (for to do so would erode the profits of enterprise and lead to investment flowing, at the click of a mouse, to more profitable locations). For the past 30 years, governments have increasingly focused on generating a 'stable' environment for the capitalist accumulation of surplus value through the creation of a flexible labour market (via wage constraints, curbs on trade union powers and work-based welfare schemes), cutting taxation and opening up public services to private investment. Increasingly, governments have sought to prioritise the needs of the economy and economic growth – claiming that this is the best means of promoting the wellbeing of the majority. A consequence of this change, however, has been a dramatic transformation in social relations in Britain – characterised by widening social inequalities, increasing community tensions and declining social wellbeing for many people.

At the same time, under the neo-liberal order, social problems have been increasingly redefined as problems of the individual rather than the social, with criminal justice solutions increasingly replacing welfare responses to these problems. A corollary of this has been a dramatic rise in the public's fear of crime, disorder, social conflict and danger. In the first decade of the twenty-first century, restoring community safety and cohesion, and addressing 'anti-social' behaviour, have become the major social policy priorities for government. Buoyed by realist theorists' acceptance of reactionary populist notions of 'crime' and 'disorder' (presented as 'commonsense' – that is, that the fear of 'youth crime' and generalised incivility are the most important social threats of our time and need to be dealt with severely), both Conservative and Labour administrations have competed with each other to appear to be the most authoritarian in their responses to these perceived threats.

Accompanying these developments has been the growing appeal of 'community' as both a site for and agency of policy intervention. Throughout the past few years, there have been notable expressions of institutional support for community involvement in various social and economic programmes. This change in focus is reflected in the current employment market, as evidenced in *Society Guardian* each Wednesday where community-related posts in various social policy areas can often be found advertised – in health and social care, housing, regeneration, criminal justice, youth work, economic development, and so forth. Community involvement has been a consistent theme in urban policy rhetoric since the 1980s. Under New Labour, there has been an increase in political interest in the notion of community involvement through-out a broader range of social policy areas – including crime and disorder prevention. This interest is likely to continue in the foreseeable future. In his first parliamentary speech as Prime Minister (delivered on 3 July 2007), Gordon Brown announced proposals for a new constitu-tional settlement which, he claimed, would change the balance of power between communities and the state in British society. These pro-posals included extending the rights of communities to be consulted on major policy decisions affecting their lives and 'to hold power more accountable... . The right of the British people to have their voice heard is fundamental to our democracy and to holding public institutions to account' (cited in BBC News 2007a). Brown's plans, set out in the Green Consultative Paper *The Governance of Britain*, have been described as a 'potentially dramatic extension of direct democracy' (Wintour 2007: 1). At the time of writing, a new White Paper, *Putting Communities in Control – Empowerment White Paper,* is awaited – previewed in the con-sultation document *Unlocking the Talents of Our Communities* which sets out the government's intentions to involve communities more actively in area regeneration, local democracy, the improvement of public services and local accountability (DfCLG 2008). For many, the readiness of Brown's government to prompt a public debate on the state of British democracy will have been welcomed. David Cameron, leader of the opposition, has also alluded on various occasions to the crucial role communities have to play in tackling social problems.

However, despite the enduring appeal of community, the idea of community itself is contestable and holds different meanings for different people. Ordinarily, the notion of community implies something that is bounded – either geographically (a place or neighbourhood where people live in close proximity) or socially (implying interaction between people holding shared interests or values) (Hillary 1955). In contemporary social policy debates we can identify a clear emphasis on defining communities as places of indigenous people holding shared values and customs (for instance, in relation to 'respectfulness' or 'being British'). This comes close to the communitarian notion of 'community as unity', harmonious and devoid of conflict – a notion which effectively establishes boundaries against the potentially 'dangerous other' who, by failing to conform, poses a threat to the established social order. As we will see at various junctures in this book, community has been used in this way by politicians and the media at various times in history (and particularly under New Labour's period in government) in order to enforce certain desired behaviour (e.g. on 'anti-social youth') or commitments (e.g. from the unemployed to engage in paid work or from foreign nationals to prove their allegiance to the British state). Such rhetorical use of community generates a highly moralising discourse that serves to legitimate both the maintenance of privilege for included insiders and authoritarian sanctions aimed at excluded outsiders unwilling or unable to fit in. Such usages of community in contemporary Britain have invariably served to differentiate between the 'right' type of community (conformist and loyal to 'British' values and middle-England notions of 'decency') and the 'wrong' type (which pose a risk to mainstream social and cultural values – for example, travellers, anti-globalisation protestors, Muslims 'with a grievance' or other black immigrants 'unwilling' to 'assimilate'). Despite the rhetoric of 'empowerment' that generally accompanies community-based policies, the top-down nature of mainstream community involvement approaches in British social policy would suggest that its attraction is, as Crow and Allan have argued, 'less about democratic self-determination and more about managing social tensions and assisting state bureaucracies to accomplish their objectives' (Crow and Allan 1994: 162).

It is with regard to these general themes – dominant notions of social wellbeing, community safety and cohesion, and how these have shaped and are shaping social policy developments; and the contestable nature of community as a concept, and how it has been used by both the powerful (to maintain the existing distribution of privilege and social wellbeing in society) and the disadvantaged (to challenge the existing institutional arrangements for distributing privilege and social wellbeing) – that this book is concerned. In analysing these themes, the book aims to contribute to the contemporary debate on the efficacy of existing societal arrangements in British society for promoting greater social wellbeing, community safety and cohesion. The main argument presented is that enhanced social wellbeing, community safety and cohesion is unlikely to be advanced by a social system whose main objective is the preservation of economic competitiveness in the global market over other goals that include greater social solidarity and more participatory politics. Indeed, it will be argued that it is this very same social system that is the fundamental cause of the decline in wellbeing, the rise in insecurity and the breakdown in community cohesion it purports to heal. This assessment exposes the need to forge alternative institutional arrangements for determining the necessary societal pre-conditions for maximising social wellbeing, community safety and cohesion within wider society, and putting these into effect. Moreover, in considering the viability of realising such a social transformation, attention will be drawn to the emancipatory appeal of community as a site upon which to mobilise solidarity and resistance, and to enhance the capacity of people to engage in collective action for radical social change (in contrast to the mainstream political appeal of community as a means of sustaining the existing social order).

The aim of the book

More specifically, the aim of this book is to interrogate vying concepts in relation to community, social wellbeing, community safety and community cohesion, and to analyse how these ideas have shaped social policy developments in Britain. In offering a conceptually grounded treatment of these themes, the book sets out to encourage the reader to reflect upon what have been the practical and policy-oriented applications and consequences of these ideas over time. The book concludes by revisiting these core concepts and, in doing so, exposes myths and contradictions that commonly accompany such broad-range notions. What becomes apparent from the discussion set out in this book is that the general trajectory of interest in social wellbeing, community safety and community cohesion has focused primarily on threats to wellbeing, safety and cohesion posed by the attitudes or 'misdemeanours' of the least powerful – for example, welfare dependants, youth 'hanging around' public spaces and immigrants holding 'alien cultures'. This focus has served to distract attention away from the more serious social harms caused by the crimes and anti-social acts of the powerful – that is, those carried out by private corporations and governments. Moreover, this glitch in awareness has been aggravated by much of the exiting social policy and criminology literature. For example, in his edited volume on crime prevention and community safety, Nick Tilley, although initially acknowledging that mainstream definitions of crime and deviance largely reflect the dominant values of power-holders, unashamedly goes on to admit that his own treatment of these themes:

> though quite broad, relates only to a subset of crimes and harms that might form the focus of preventative attention. Professional malpractice, corporate malfeasance, terrorism, fraud, environmental crime, traffic offences, political crimes, anger about crime and most victimless crime, for example, are either not discussed at all or are mentioned only in passing. Instead the bias follows that of both literature and most present practice and policy, in homing in on volume property crime, violence, criminality, drugs and fear of crime. ... [T]he selection included here largely reflects dominant assumptions about what matters most for policy and practice, and that is properly a matter for analysis and debate. (Tilley 2005: 7)

By focusing on 'dominant assumptions about what matters most for policy and practice', academics perpetuate distorted and prejudiced understandings of criminality and threats to safety. By focusing on the problems mainly addressed in state-sponsored community safety strategies – 'volume property crime, violence, criminality, drugs and fear of crime' – more serious threats to community safety are not being tackled. This is not to say that theft and street violence should be of no concern to social policy makers and practitioners. It is, however, to argue the case that more serious threats to community safety caused by the activities of the powerful – that is, the social harms to communities caused by pro-market policies (e.g. the effects of welfare cut-backs on life chances) or the actions of major corporations (e.g. environmental pollution) – is equally deserving (if not more so) of analysis and debate. This book seeks to address this lacuna in the social policy and criminology literature by offering a different conceptual understanding of community safety (and threats to social wellbeing and community cohesion) based on a more proportionate understanding of social harms inflicted on communities. More specifically, this book is concerned with the grave threats to community safety, cohesion and social wellbeing caused by the activities of governments and corporations wedded to the neo-liberal social policy agenda since the late-1970s. Richard Wilkinson's (2005) research is illuminating here as it demonstrates how people in more unequal societies (such as Britain) are more likely to experience premature death, greater morbidity, anxiety, suicide and alcoholism, and higher levels of violence. Downes and Hansen (2006) also show that countries with tighter restrictions on welfare rights for the poor have higher imprisonment rates – a trend Britain is emulating. Welfare retrenchment is a consequence of the actions of the powerful – the politicians and policy makers who have presided over (and continue to preside over) social reforms which emphasise the 'power of the market'. Today, British welfare is managed in accordance with market principles and governed by executives rather than via political accountability. In such a context, where the prime motivation is maximising returns or meeting centrally-defined government targets on economy, efficiency and effectiveness, the common wellbeing of society is of little concern. As Avner Offer identifies in his book *The Challenge of Affluence* (2006), the promotion of greater individualism and consumerism in society has been paralleled with a decline in social solidarity and trust – an 'eloquent restatement of Durkheim's sociological critique of anomic and egoistic forms of solidarity, in which the necessary social and moral containment of human aspirations and desires is made weak' (Rustin 2007: 76). As the Canadian law professor Joel Bakan observes, company executives subordinate all considerations to profit, an inevitable consequence of which is: 'the routine and regular harms caused to others – workers, consumers, communities, the environment. This, Bakan notes, makes the corporation essentially a "psychopathic creature", unable to recognise or act upon moral reasons to refrain from harming others' (Edwards and Cromwell 2006: 3).

Such executive-style interventions are now dominating the new forms of welfare organising established to deliver public services in Britain – in particular, the new networks and partnerships set up to deliver the government's crime and disorder and urban regeneration strategies, and also social protection, education, housing and health (see Chapter 4). 'These organisational forms, in practice, make it increasingly difficult to discern what is "public" about public services' (Newman and Mahony 2007: 65) and appear to close down possibilities for engaging in an open public debate within a public realm. In such a context, opportunities for challenging the existing order of things appear to have become increasingly remote.

Despite these concerns, neo-liberal power-holders continue to espouse the 'TINA' mantra – that, in the context of globalisation, *there is no alternative* to market freedom and the liberalisation of all areas of welfare organising. Moreover, under New Labour, government measures aimed at restricting political dissent have been extended. Responding to the 'unprecedented' threat to community safety from 'anti-social behaviour' and 'terrorism' – a threat governments have largely generated themselves – the British state has justified the introduction of a plethora of repressive legislation that is increasingly being used to stifle democratic dissent. 'No act has been passed over the past 20 years with the aim of preventing antisocial behaviour, disorderly conduct, trespass, harassment and terrorism that has not also been deployed to criminalise a peaceful public engagement in politics' (Monbiot 2005a: 27). For example, the 1994 Criminal Justice Act – amended by New Labour in 2003 – was used on 30 September 2005 to convict six University of Lancaster students and graduates of aggravated trespass for protesting:

> against a 'corporate venturing' event involving multinational arms manufacturers and attended by a government minister. The university authorities took the view that their action breached the university's code on harassment and bullying and the ethical thing to do was to inform the police and have the students prosecuted and threatened with prison or antisocial behaviour orders. (MacLeod and Curtis 2005: 12)

The 'harassment' and 'bullying' in question took the form of entering a lecture theatre and handing out leaflets to the audience:

> Staff at the university were meeting people from BAE Systems, Rolls-Royce, Shell, the Carlyle Group, GlaxoSmithKline, DuPont, Unilever and Diageo, to learn how to 'commercialise university research'. The students were hoping to persuade the researchers not to sell their work. They were in the theatre for three minutes. ... [T]hey tried neither to intimidate anyone nor to stop the conference from proceeding. (Monbiot 2005a: 27)

The 1997 Protection from Harassment Act was used by arms manufacturer EDO to keep demonstrators away from its factory gates and by the

Kent police to arrest a woman who sent a drug company's executive two (polite) emails asking him not to test his products on animals (Monbiot 2005a). Furthermore, under the Act:

> In 2001 the peace campaigners Lindis Percy and Anni Rainbow were prosecuted for causing 'harassment, alarm or distress' to American servicemen at the Menwith Hill military intelligence base in Yorkshire, by standing at the gate holding the Stars and Stripes and a placard reading 'George W Bush? Oh dear!'. In Hull a protestor was arrested under the act for 'staring at a building'. (Monbiot 2005a: 27)

Section 132 of the 2005 Serious Organised Crime and Police Act introduced a ban on people demonstrating in any area 'designated' by government. 'One of these is the square kilometre around parliament' (Monbiot 2005a: 27). In addition, Section 44 of the 2000 Terrorism Act allows the police to stop and search people without a need to demonstrate to them that they have 'reasonable suspicion' that they have committed an offence, and to detain them for up to a month without charge. The police have used this power:

> to put peaceful protestors through hell. At the beginning of 2003, demonstrators against the impending war with Iraq set up a peace camp outside the military base at Fairford in Gloucestershire, from which US B52s would launch their bombing raids. Every day – sometimes several times a day – the protestors were stopped and searched under section 44. The police, according to a parliamentary answer, used the act 995 times, though they knew that no one at the camp was a terrorist. The constant harassment and detention pretty well broke the protestors' resolve. (Monbiot 2005a: 27)

More recently, Section 44 of the 2000 Terrorism Act was deployed against climate change protestors converging on Heathrow airport for a week's demonstration in August 2007. Despite climate change being one of the most urgent contemporary social problems facing governments throughout the world, prior to the Heathrow protest the police establishment were already labelling protestors 'criminals':

> The Metropolitan police chief, Sir Ian Blair, has said he fears a minority of protestors intent on breaking the law could cause massive disruption…. Met commander Jo Kaye, in charge of the specialist firearms unit, said some people would 'want to get their message

across using criminal means'. Scotland Yard's plans for handling the protests are revealed in a document ... which was produced by Met commander Peter Broadhurst .... 'Should individuals or small groups seek to take action outside of lawful protest they will be dealt with robustly using terrorism powers'. ... The police report makes it clear that the government has encouraged police forces to make greater use of terrorism powers 'especially the use of stop and search powers under s44 Terrorism Act 2000'. (Vidal and Pidd 2007: 1)

Powers legitimated in the name of 'war on terror' are being used in Britain to stifle and criminalise peaceful political dissent, narrowing possibilities for generating a broad democratic debate on crucial global issues.

Furthermore, prospects for progressive democratic practices in Britain are undermined by the presence of a docile media. In *Guardians of Power: The Myth of the Liberal Media*, Edwards and Cromwell uncover the systematic servility to power of the so-called 'liberal' British media – exemplified in its inability to expose the government's lies about the threat of weapons of mass destruction in the run up to the occupation of Iraq. This duplicity is not the result of state censorship but, as Edwards and Cromwell explain, free market forces – illustrated in the following extract from a related conversation between Andrew Marr (of the BBC) and Noam Chomsky:

Marr ... : 'What I don't get is that all of this suggests ... people like me are self-censoring.' Chomsky disagreed: 'I don't say you're self-censoring. I'm sure you believe everything you're saying. But what I'm saying is, if you believed something different you wouldn't be sitting where you're sitting.' What Marr ... 'doesn't get' is that dissident arguments do not depend on conspiratorial self-censorship, but on a filter system maintained by free market forces – bottom-line pressures, owner influence, parent company goals and sensitivities, advertiser needs, business-friendly government influence and corporate PR 'flak' – which introduce bias by marginalising alternatives, providing incentives to conform and costs for failure to conform. (Edwards and Cromwell 2006: 89)

Further limits on democracy have come about as a result of key decisions affecting social wellbeing now being taken beyond the nation state by unaccountable global institutions – for example, the International Monetary Fund, the World Trade Organisation and the

World Bank. Consequently, Gordon Brown's dramatic plans for extending direct democracy at home, referred to above, would need to extend to the global level.

It is this parallel development in British society – the withdrawal of state support for social and economic wellbeing, alongside the erosion of a public space for expressing legitimate political dissent and engaging in democratic processes – that this book is mainly concerned for it is a development which arguably poses the greatest threat to the welfare of society. In short, the general hypothesis laid out in the pages that follow is that the existing societal arrangements for human relationships to be played out in British society will not lead to sustainable improvements in social wellbeing, community safety and community cohesion. In conclusion, the book offers an alternative perspective on promoting social wellbeing, community safety and community cohesion – one that emphasises the kind of institutional arrangements that are necessary for allowing the societal preconditions for maximising social wellbeing for the many to be put into effect. It is a perspective which recognises that the attainment of universal wellbeing, safety and cohesion in society is more likely to be gained through solidaristic relations with others rather than through individualistic endeavour.

This book will appeal to a wide range of interests including academics, final year undergraduates and postgraduate students from a range of disciplines (history, sociology, social policy, criminology, social anthropology, urban studies, planning, housing studies, public administration and community work), policy makers and welfare practitioners working in the fields of housing, planning, economic regeneration, health care, criminal justice, community safety, youth and community work, community development and so forth, and others interested in community issues. By drawing on current themes in the social sciences – such as theoretical debates on 'community', 'conflict' and notions of 'social harm' – the book will offer a conceptually grounded text for students, academics, policy makers and practitioners that will remain durable over time by retaining its academic and practical relevance. In this way too, the book will encourage reflection about community-related policies in a broader context that emphasises the links between these policies and the social structure. This offers an alternative understanding that encourages students to look beyond community action as a mere practice, requiring the application of technical skills, and to see it as an interesting, lively and contentious subject of social scientific enquiry.

Before moving on to describe the structure of the book, I set out some personal reflections on aspects of my own experience as a welfare practitioner and some of the key changes in social policy I have observed. Many of the post-1970s' changes analysed in this book have coincided with my own time working in the welfare sector. This started in 1976 when I was appointed co-ordinator of a battered women's refuge in Doncaster, more or less the same time Keynesian welfarism was starting to be abandoned in Britain when James Callaghan's Labour government converted to monetarism. My reflections therefore offer something of a benchmark in which to gauge some of the effects of social policy changes since that time – at least from the perspective of my own experiences. These observations are also consistent with feminist thinking which argues that the way in which the researcher is affected by the context of the research should be revealed. It seems honest to disclose that I am far from dispassionate in respect of the issues discussed in this book (although this may be obvious to the reader already!) and that my views have – to a significant extent – been shaped by my own biography. As May argues, the biography of the researcher is important:

> Both the researcher and those people in the research carry with them a history, a sense of themselves and the importance of their experiences. However, personal experience is frequently devalued as being too subjective, while science is objective. ... Researchers should be aware of the ways in which their own biography is a fundamental part of the research process. It is both the experiences of the researched *and* researchers which are important. (May 2001: 21 – emphasis in original)

By setting out a brief autobiography of my work and some of the changes I experienced, I aim to situate my general thesis within a more engaged style of argument. Whilst I endeavour to present a robust thesis, some readers may find my critique polemical in tone. I do not apologise for this as I feel it offers a much needed antidote to the so-called 'balanced' accounts of social policy development which dominate the literature and which presuppose, as Durkheim did, the existence of a benign constitutional framework within which to conduct the debate on how best to promote human wellbeing. This book argues that such a framework does not exist and that the institutional arrangements for promoting human wellbeing in Britain are fundamentally flawed, corrupt and illegitimate. Perhaps one of the most salient illustrations of this is the ability of the establishment to not only 'move on' from its participation in a gross war crime – the war in Iraq – but also to reward one of the chief architects of this crime with a vast pay-off.

The International Military Tribunal at Nuremberg ruled that 'to initiate a war of aggression...is not only an international crime; it is the supreme international crime'. The tribunal's charter placed 'planning, preparation, initiation or waging of a war of aggression' at the top of the list of war crimes. (Monbiot 2008: 24)

Instead of being called to account by the International Criminal Court for a crime that (to date) may have killed over a million people: 'The press and parliament appear to have heeded Blair's plea that we all "move on" from Iraq. The British establishment has a unique capacity to move on, and then to repeat its mistakes. What other former empire knows so little of its own atrocities?' (Monbiot 2008: 24).

Moreover, on top of his earnings as Middle East envoy for the US, Russia, EU and the UN, his £500,000 from speaking engagements and £5.8million deal with Random House for his memoirs, Tony Blair is appointed part-time adviser to JP Morgan Chase – the bank selected to operate the Trade Bank of Iraq, created by the US to manage billions of dollars to finance imports and exports – on another estimated £500,000 per annum (The New York Times 2003, Woodward 2008). More recently, Blair has been touted as the first full-time president of the EU council – effectively, 'president of Europe' (Wintour 2008a: 1). The fact that so little attention is directed at the crimes and lack of accountability of the powerful reflects the stranglehold of neo-liberal hegemony over policy making, practice and research in Britain, and the rise in selfish opportunism within the academic community. Here I share David Byrne's observation that 'Social science has been, rightly, accused of adopting a posture of palms up to the rich for the receipt of funding and eyes down to the poor as part of the surveillance necessary for their control' (Byrne 2006: 5). Certainly, the recent emphasis in mainstream social policy research has been about 'what works best' for treating, regulating, resocialising or punishing 'problem' individuals and dysfunctional communities – a research agenda that serves to maintain the privileges of the status quo. Unless we first acknowledge the need for acute structural change, the quest for universal community wellbeing will remain a futile one.

Personal reflections on a life in English 'welfare'

The themes addressed in this book are in part inspired by a life working in English social welfare – initially as a housing practitioner then latterly in higher education – and my concerns in respect of the effects of social policy changes on my own experience of changes in social relations in England. A central concern throughout my working life has been the concept of 'social justice' (in terms of my own and other people's social wellbeing) and the importance of engaging in collective action in pursuit of this notion whenever possible – often in defiance of mainstream policy and practice.

As mentioned above, I worked for Doncaster Women's Aid in the mid-1970s – a job I was always ambivalent about given the tension that existed between the radical and welfarist branches of feminism at the time (the former arguing that women's movements should work separately from men). This voluntary sector post was funded through Urban Aid, a stream of government funding which allowed a number of important and alternative social projects to set up and become established in local communities. After a year I moved into the voluntary housing sector, initially in Portsmouth and then, in the 1980s, in London which included periods with two housing associations actively engaged in promoting radically different and (what we believed to be) more humane ways of living and working 'in community'. Both associations identified themselves as 'community-based' and were organised as workers collectives (where each worker received equal pay and were jointly and severally responsible for day-to-day decision making). The associations' residents and other members of the local community – including representatives from black organisations, women's groups, squatting campaigns and other social movements – were encouraged to participate in the association either as members of the management committees or through partnership working. Both associations were funded by the Housing Corporation (the body responsible for funding and monitoring the activities of housing associations – to be reconstituted in 2009 as the Homes and Community Agency), the London Boroughs and the Greater London Council – the latter described at the time as 'the flagship of municipal socialism' (Lansley et al. 1989: 47). Despite the election of a Conservative government committed to welfare cutbacks in 1979, generous support (at least in London) for alternative community-based initiatives was still available in the mid-1980s.

One of the associations, Patchwork Community, specialised in the provision of communal living in mainly short-life properties (mostly due for rehabilitation or redevelopment) licensed from public authorities. In the majority of cases, the properties licensed were adjacent to each other – thereby presenting possibilities for building a spatial 'Patchwork community'. People in housing need would be allocated their own room and share the use of communal areas with other residents. Each house would also have someone described as having 'special needs' (e.g. a single parent, someone with 'mental health problems', an ex-offender, a young single homeless person or someone escaping domestic violence) allocated to it and the other residents would be expected to provide informal support if needed. In addition, all Patchwork workers were expected to live in a Patchwork house and provide an additional source of support. Patchwork's philosophy came close to that of such thinkers as R.D. Laing (1960), Ivan Illich (1977) and Erving Goffman (1963, 1968) – advocates of the anti-psychiatry movement. Laing himself had established a community psychiatric project at Kingsley Hall in the east end of London where the patients and therapists lived together. The three were all concerned with the disabling effects of institutionalised social care and the activities of 'experts' who practised within these establishments. Patchwork offered a genuine alternative to such institutions and, in recognition of this, qualified for Housing Corporation hostel deficit grant – a revenue subsidy towards the care costs of these schemes. Capital grants were also available for essential repairs to ensure that the properties licensed were habitable.

Writing about Patchwork in 1982, David Donnison described it as 'one of the best organised communes' he had come across, run by people who 'believed they had found a better way of living' (Donnison 1982: 100–101). By the late 1980s, however, Patchwork had lost its collective status and, in the 1990s, its management committee became increasingly manipulated through Housing Corporation interference. In January 2006, the ownership of the association's assets was transferred by the Housing Corporation to Community Housing Group in Camden. Around the same time, the Housing Corporation also enforced the take-over of the other collective I had worked for – Solon Wandsworth Housing Association (SWHA – which had retained its collective management structure to the very end). One of the stated reasons for SWHA's take-over was its 'failure' to exploit its 'commercial opportunities' sufficiently or – in the words of a Housing Corporation appointee to SWHA's management committee – in a sufficiently 'aggressive manner' (cited in Beckmann and Cooper 2005a: 9). However, the main criticism of SWHA was reserved for its management structure. The Inquiry Report conducted under powers contained in the 1996 Housing Act claimed that: 'Solon's real weakness flows from the ineffective working of its collective institutions, which have proved ineffective and inefficient…. Because the meetings endeavour to operate by consensus they take a very long time…[and] implementing decisions is a matter of negotiation' (cited in Beckmann and Cooper 2005a: 9).

Clearly, negotiation, deliberation and consensus no longer have a place in the model of welfare organising urged by the new managerialism – indeed, they are seen as values that constitute a threat to organisational efficiency.

The character of the housing association movement was to profoundly change following the implementation of the 1988 Housing Act and the introduction of a new financial regime for development programmes. Since 1974, the development costs of associations' housing schemes attracted generous government subsidies which allowed rents to be kept well below the 'market' rate. Indeed, rents were fixed by the government's Rent Officer in advance of the completion of a scheme and based on the size of accommodation and amenities provided (a 'fair rent' not based on market value). After deducting an allowance for management and maintenance costs from this 'fair rent', an amount available to pay for the development costs would be calculated – usually coming to around five per cent of the total scheme cost. The remaining 95 per cent of costs would be covered by a one-off grant payment. The effect of this system was that the rents were generally affordable – particularly for people in paid work but on low incomes. The 1988 Act changed this system by forcing associations to rely more on private capital finance and commercial interest rates. Instead of the rents being determined in advance now the grant payment would be pre-determined (at a much lower rate) and the rents calculated on completion of the scheme. Rents rose dramatically (towards market levels) due to the reduced grant rate and higher interest payments. The culture of associations changed and came to resemble the commercial sector with a greater emphasis on risk and cost control: for example, less risky developments were pursued (such as new build schemes on sites in less costly locations – at the cost of inner-city rehabilitation); standards were reduced (to cut costs) and greater emphasis was placed on whether or not a prospective resident would pay the rent when allocating homes (increasingly, applicants who qualified for housing benefit would be chosen because direct rent payments could be guaranteed – at the cost of applicants in paid work and earning just above the threshold for claiming housing benefit). A major effect of these changes was that associations in the 1990s increasingly housed poorer households on benefit in poorer quality housing – generating, as some of us working in the housing association movement had predicted – a 'residualised' (Malpass 2000) housing sector. At the same time, housing officers increasingly found it difficult to offer the 'care' element they had traditionally provided as part of their role – a part of the role that had initially attracted many people into housing work. 'Care' has little value within the market paradigm. One colleague at Solon at the time believed that the housing officer of the future would become more like a robot. Whilst it could be argued that this denies agency, certainly the marketisation and fragmentation of social housing provision that followed from the 1980s made resistance to the imposition of a business culture more difficult.

Developments within the voluntary sector in Britain since the late 1980s have been eloquently analysed by Andy Benson, the founder of the National Coalition for Independent Action (NCIA). Benson believes that the voluntary sector in that time has been co-opted by government, with the complicity of large multimillion-pound national charities acting as businesses. Moreover, this has had profound negative consequences for the sector:

> Over the last 22 years, I've seen the voluntary sector being deliberately co-opted by the state…. It is the role and right of the voluntary sector to take independent action, to pursue divergent interests and to hold the state to account, and this is what is under threat.…This is about our collective belief to identify our own perspectives and pursue them. This is about our collective liberties. (Cited in Kelly 2008: 5)

The closing down of the voluntary sector's space to engage in radical alternative action has been achieved, Benson argues, through the government's use of 'regulation, quality assurance standards, managerialism and punitive social policies' (cited in Kelly 2008: 5) – and 'commissioning' voluntary organisations to meet an agenda defined by central government.

> Small and medium-sized charities providing public services won't have the freedom to look downwards to their communities; they'll have to look up to their commissioners, who will be the ones deciding which services are the most appropriate. … By trying to take over this space, the government is launching an attack on our freedom to take any kind of positive voluntary action to address needs we consider important. They're taking every last bit of power away from communities, because they don't trust the public to do anything on our own. (Cited in Kelly 2008: 5)

Because of such imminent changes in the voluntary housing sector in the late 1980s – changes I really did not feel I wanted to engage with – I left the housing association movement in 1989 to move into higher education – joining (the then) South Bank Polytechnic as a senior lecturer in housing studies (primarily teaching day-release students from housing organisations enrolled on a vocational postgraduate diploma validated by the Chartered Institute of Housing – the CIH) – with the expectation that this would provide me with a better opportunity to critically engage with the housing debate. To the uninitiated, housing studies may be thought of as merely concerned with the production and consumption of housing. Whilst it does relate to these issues, it is also an area of study that reflects housing's interdependence with major relationships of power. So, for instance, housing (or rather, our residential experience) is both a reflection and source of social advantage or disadvantage – that is, housing both reflects wealth or social status (based on class, 'race' and gender) and presents opportunities (or not) for further benefits gained through wealth accumulation (via the increase in value of the property) and access to local amenities (such as better schools or a healthier environment).

Housing has also been important for protecting dominant interests in capitalist societies – in Britain, for instance, subsidised council housing in 1919 was seen as a 'bulwark against bolshevism', while the 'Right to Buy' legislation in 1980 helped to break working-class solidarity by dividing the interests of the affluent, skilled working class (who gained most from the sale of council housing) from those of the unskilled and unemployed (who invariably remained left behind in the least desirable council housing estates). At the same time, housing has also been a site for resistance and there is a rich history of urban social protest based around housing campaigns – for instance, the 1915 Rent Strikes, squatting movements and the more recent Defend Council Housing campaign. Much of my own teaching and research has been concerned with these struggles, particularly through the work I have done on the CIH's *National Certificate in Tenant Participation* – a day-release course aimed at tenant activists and housing workers committed to user involvement. This work also influenced my research agenda in the 1990s which included a couple of co-authored/ co-edited books on tenant participation and community action (Cooper and Hawtin 1997, 1998) – work which highlights the utility of participation and community for both facilitating the agenda of governments (e.g. privatising council housing or management efficiency gains) and mobilising community resistance (e.g. against the privatisation of council housing). The lessons from this work filtered back into my teaching with tenants and activists. In particular, introducing students to approaches to community development based on Freirean pedagogy helped some on the course to address their own internalised disabling notions of 'failure'. Other students applied lessons from the course to their own local campaigns for improved housing conditions – such as one organised by Stephen Wyatt (a tenant activist) and described in 'The Pugilist's Guide to Tenant Participation' (see Cooper and Wyatt 1997).

Also in the 1990s, I developed an interest in comparative housing studies and exploring the policy implications of successes and failures evident through cross-national comparative research. This included an EC-funded TEMPUS project researching and designing a Masters Programme in Comparative Urban Planning and Housing with a university in Sofia in 1995 – a course aimed at architects and planners interested in understanding the options for transforming the Bulgarian housing and planning system following the fall of communism. This involved applying a comparative research framework designed by James Barlow and Simon Duncan (Barlow and Duncan 1994) – based largely upon Esping-Andersen's (1990) typology of welfare capitalist systems – to an assessment of the efficacy of different capitalist planning systems. Comparing the systems of Britain, France and Sweden, this study suggested that the more regulated planning systems of Europe (i.e. Sweden and France) produced greater production and consumption efficiencies in terms of the quality, cost and affordability of the housing developed, and the wider choices of tenure available (with lower levels of social polarisation between tenures). There was also lower volatility in housing production over time. In 1996, I received a British Council grant to conduct a further study on tenants' democracy in Sweden. This work demonstrated the benefits gained by social housing tenants in Sweden from having firmly established autonomous resident movements which allowed them a greater say over substantive areas of housing policy (Cooper 1998). More generally, because of its strong welfarist tradition, extensive political rights and relatively egalitarian share of income distribution, Swedish society achieved a more distinctive balance between freedom and solidarity with relatively high levels of self-assessed social wellbeing (Jordan 2006). Through comparative housing studies, therefore, it was possible to expose the harmful effects of neo-liberal social policy reforms in Britain in relation to the stability of the housing market and social solidarity, cohesion and wellbeing – harms which have recently been acknowledged by Gordon Brown's government.

In the late 1990s, I worked on a co-authored evaluation of New Labour's 'modernisation' agenda for social policy (Burden et al. 2000).

This research exposed the exclusionary effects of New Labour's third way welfare discourse including, in particular, its focus on 'social inclusion' through 'paid work' – a flawed concept given that wages in today's casualised labour market remain far too low to guarantee full social participation. Moreover, it is an idea that discounts other ways of 'being' in society such as caring for others or being active within the local community. As Bill Jordan argues, despite the rhetoric of inclusion and autonomy in New Labour's welfare discourse:

> [T]he main thrust of the Third Way notion of autonomy – independence through employment, earning and property – tended to devalue both those who needed care (who were therefore by definition 'dependent') and those who looked after them without pay (who qualified for benefit as carers, but only if they withdrew from full participation in the labour market). The liberal individualism of a political philosophy built upon the choices of free-standing property owners relegated care to the shadows, and supported it with reluctance and stigma…. In this approach, responsibility was primarily towards the self, for realizing potential through paid work and ownership, and only very secondarily towards mutuality in family and kinship groups…. (Jordan 2006: 164)

Under the terms of the new social order constructed by neo-liberalism, it became clear to us that little value is placed on showing commitment and loyalty to others. More generally, as John Clarke has observed, much of the care work in social welfare has been lost – 'beyond the contract', irrelevant to 'performance' (Clarke 2004: 122). This is borne out by comparing today's housing assistant job descriptions with those of the late-1970s when I first worked for a housing association – the former stress the role of dealing with 'anti-social behaviour' whilst the latter underlined the role of 'welfare support'. Bauman (2001) explains this change in terms of the absence of community in late modern times – that is, community in the sense of the collective provision of social solidarity and security. Put simply, a lack of care. All this, in turn, corrodes community cohesion and social wellbeing – a situation that has important policy implications: if rampant individualism wrought by years of neo-liberal reforms has eroded the societal preconditions needed for collective social wellbeing, how do we establish the conditions for community cohesion and social wellbeing to be restored? As Wright argues, if the existing institutional arrangements for social organising are generating harms, we need 'to formulate *alternatives* which mitigate those harms, and to propose *transformative strategies* for realising those alternatives' (Wright 2007: 26 – emphasis in original). In our own critique of New Labour's welfare reforms we argued the case for a Basic Citizen's Income (BCI) – an unconditional (i.e. non-means tested and with no work requirement) cash payment payable to every individual as of right and throughout their lives. The level at which this BCI would be set would be sufficient to meet people's basic human needs – defined in accordance with prevailing social norms (Burden et al. 2000). We justified this on the grounds that it would ensure that everyone would have the capacity to make autonomous choices in relation to their life plans by supporting people's financial inclusion; and it is affordable. As David Purdy argues, a BCI would:

> ... enhance people's freedom in the sphere of work. It would provide the flexibility to move in and out of paid work as needs and circumstances change. If it was set at or above subsistence level, it would offer protection against exploitation, and a lever for improving pay and conditions at the lower end of the labour market. It would also provide an opportunity to pursue activities that are financially unrewarding, but intrinsically gratifying. In effect, [BCI] would subsidise activities in the household and voluntary sectors of the economy, thereby countering the current bias in favour of getting and spending. (Purdy 2007: 59)

A BCI 'would help to initiate a long-term, gradual process of socio-cultural transformation ... and facilitate the transition from boundless economic growth to balanced social development' (Purdy 2007: 59) and, as a consequence, enhanced social wellbeing. Wright lends support to the BCI concept on similar grounds:

> [F]irst, it facilitates the expansion of non-commodified productive activity in a wide range of domains – care-giving, artistic production and performance, community building – by guaranteeing the participants in such activities a basic standard of living unconnected to market earnings, and second, it shifts the balance of power from capital to labour by giving workers greater bargaining power both individually (because of the option of quitting given jobs or exiting the labour market altogether) and collectively (because [BCI] functions as a permanent unconditional strike fund). (Wright 2007: 30)

In addition to the importance of financial security for individual and collective social wellbeing, it is also important for people to feel that they can have some influence on policy decisions affecting their lives. As in the case of Sweden:

> [A] political culture of democratic membership, where all citizens are treated with equal respect and feel able to influence the decisions of their government, might be expected to lead to high and rising rates of happiness. ... Among the countries with the highest levels of self-assessed well-being are Denmark, Norway, Finland and Sweden ... , all of which have very stable political systems with social democratic institutions .... (Jordan 2006: 177)

In order to rejuvenate the political engagement of disadvantaged communities – that is, those communities effectively marginalised and disenfranchised in British society – our own analysis of New Labour's welfare reforms sought to identify ways of establishing a new political environment in which active citizenship could thrive. To enable this, we argue the case for radical community development based on the principles of Paulo Freire (alluded to earlier) and his emphasis on empowering disadvantaged people to engage collectively in political action (Burden et al. 2000). We will return to this later in the book but, briefly here, the aim of radical community development is to rebuild collegiality and social solidarity against oppression and alienation, and to support collective strategies that seek to improve the wellbeing of all communities – for instance, instead of communities dividing in their search for the 'best' school for their child, a search which leaves the poorest communities left with the 'worst' performing schools, communities could, as an alternative strategy, organise collectively around campaigns demanding a more humane and quality education system for all – benefiting society more broadly.

The form an alternative education system might take is an issue I have explored over more recent years. Certainly, there are increasing concerns being expressed about British state education – particularly with regard to the relevance of the curriculum, the value of the testing regime and the implications of divisions within the school system for social inclusion, community cohesion and personal wellbeing. My own research has raised serious concerns about the capacity of the existing education system to be inclusionary and, as a corollary, to be socially just (Cooper 2002). This systematic failing can be conceptualised within the context of Foucault's (1976) observations on the utility of education systems for the production of docile bodies and the maintenance of existing power relations. Those who dare challenge education's disciplinary regime – not just pupils, but parents/carers and teachers alike – risk censure from its strict practices. The intensification of market forces and the new managerialism in schooling since the 1980s has worked against education's role in promoting humanistic values. The relentless focus on testing, targets, league tables and competition is causing disaffection and unhappiness amongst many children. Many pupils feel under pressure from a curriculum they consider to be meaningless and from teachers who treat them with disrespect. Meanwhile, many teachers feel they have lost autonomy over their work and are unable to care for pupils as they would wish. This has serious consequences for social policy as many children excluded from school have special educational needs which are not being catered for (Cooper 2002). Alan Smithers (key adviser to the Commons Education Select Committee) argues that 'schools have been reduced almost to factories for producing test and exam scores' (cited in Guardian Unlimited 2007: 1). A report submitted to the Commons Education Select Committee in June 2007 by the General Teaching Council (the professional body for teaching) called for all national exams for under-16-year-olds to be banned because:

> ...the stress caused by over-testing is poisoning attitudes towards education.... [E]xams are failing to improve standards, leaving pupils demotivated and stressed and encouraging bored teenagers to drop out of school.... [T]eachers are being forced to 'drill' pupils to pass tests instead of giving a broad education. ... Psychologists have reported going into schools at unprecedented rates to tackle exam stress, with children as young as six suffering from anxiety. (Asthana 2007: 1)

Predictably, Alan Johnson, then Secretary of State for Education, countered with the managerialist defence that scrapping tests 'would be "profoundly wrong". ... [T]hey had helped raise attainment and provided a transparency and accountability that parents valued' (BBC News 2007b). Meanwhile, many teachers continue to 'fear to speak out' (Cooper 2004: 17) against the harms caused by the school system – closing off the prospect for an open and free dialogue on how to generate a more humane education system. The liberalisation of the education system is increasingly threatening education's purpose for facilitating critical thinking, respect and empathy. This has clear implications for the kind of society we are creating.

Since the late-1970s, education's role has been increasingly defined in terms of its relevance to the needs of commerce and industry – with a correspondingly reduced emphasis on its role for preserving a more just, caring and democratic set of social relations (Beckmann and Cooper 2004, 2005b). A theme initially introduced by Labour Prime Minister James Callaghan in October 1976 (in his Ruskin College Speech) – that is, that the educational establishment was failing to prepare young people for the world of work – remains with us under New Labour Prime Minister Gordon Brown in 2008. Shortly after becoming Prime Minister, Brown announced the establishment of a new Department for Innovation, Universities and Skills (DIUS) which would have a remit to ensure that higher education played a key role in improving the skills base needed for economic growth. (Pre-19 education becomes the responsibility of a new Department for Children, Schools and Families). This continued emphasis on university involvement in developing skills perceived as economically valuable in an increasingly unstable labour market discounts the wider social benefits from a higher education system that, as Bob Brecher argues, challenges dominant conventions and helps people develop critical understanding and intellectual self-confidence (Brecher 2007). According to Brecher, university lecturers are being driven to become little more than 'time-serving, low-level learning managers in a degree factory' (Brecher 2007: 42). As Henry Giroux warns:

> [H]igher education is aggressively shorn of its utopian impulses. Undermined as a repository of critical thinking, writing, teaching, and learning, universities are refashioned to meet the interests of commerce and regulation. In the current onslaught against non-commercial public spheres, the mission of the university becomes instrumental; it is redesigned largely to serve corporate interests whose aim is to restructure higher education along the lines of global capitalism. (Giroux 2000: 115)

These personal reflections and observations illustrate some of the deeply-felt changes in the nature of welfare organising in England that I have experienced since 1976 – particularly in the fields of housing and education (themes that reappear later in the book in support of the general thesis argued). Failings in the housing and education systems in particular have been fundamental to the exacerbation of spatial and social exclusion in Britain – with profound consequences for community safety, cohesion and social wellbeing. In particular, democratic accountability in welfare organisations has been lost as spaces for collective action and critical dissent have been closed off. Socially and residentially, we have become increasingly polarised whilst notions of social justice have been corroded. As a result, the ways we live and work together in British society have been dehumanised. Our lives appear increasingly fraught with danger as the collective provision of social protection and care is diminished. The main reason for this situation lies in the (flawed) assumptions about social wellbeing in neo-liberal thinking.

Challenging the assumptions of neo-liberal philosophy

According to neo-liberal philosophy, social wellbeing rests on allowing individuals 'free choice' – unhampered by state interference. It emerges in a context where people are encouraged to be more responsible for themselves and their dependants – on being independent, autonomous beings, free to explore their full potential and, in doing so, contribute to the prosperity and progress of society as a whole. Human wellbeing relies on individual liberty and freedom from the coercion of others (particularly state authorities). Accordingly, neo-liberal ideology assumes that: 'well-being is most reliably sustained and improved by the actions of ordinary individuals, because these are co-ordinated by processes beyond the imaginative scope or political control of governments. In other words, *well-being relies on the unintended collective consequences of individual choices*' (Jordan 2006: 127 – emphasis in original).

However, neo-liberalism in practice does not serve the interests of individual free choice nor enables individuals to take responsibility for their lives. Neo-liberal practices do not assist individuals to become autonomous beings nor achieve human wellbeing. Moreover, neo-liberalism does not free us from the political control of governments. Indeed, since the late-1970s in Britain, the converse has happened. In the interest of freedom, progress and human wellbeing, neo-liberal states have intervened *against* the interest of many people's social wellbeing. For example, neo-liberal states:

> saw the loss of manufacturing sites as a necessary process of adaptation; they regarded bankruptcies and redundancies as aspects of 'creative destruction'; they facilitated the firing of workers and the weakening of trade unions; and they cut benefits and services to encourage unemployed people to be more mobile, motivated and self-reliant. ... At the same time, some of the least skilled members of the workforce – especially those in one-earner families and lone

parents – lost ground relative to the mainstream. Members of minority ethnic groups were more polarized than the white majority; the poorest fell into destitution…. (Jordan 2006: 64–66)

According to Jordan, under neo-liberalism, the social wellbeing of many citizens – not just the poorest – has become extremely precarious. As mutuality and collective bonds disappear, we all have to become more self-reliant and develop our own personal and material resources to cope with all eventualities of risk at whatever stage of our life cycle. For many of us, this has involved getting into increasing personal debt to pay for the cost of housing, health insurance, education, pensions and social care needs. Meanwhile, work for many of us has become increasingly unsatisfying, stressful and insecure. These changes are leading, as writers such as Robert E. Lane and Richard Layard suggest, to a general decline in happiness and social wellbeing in society (see Jordan 2006). A concern for the powerful is that these same changes are posing a threat to community safety and cohesion in British society. Because of welfare retrenchment over the past 30 years, the state can no longer counter these threats effectively without finding alternative sites of social control. Hence, the New Labour government's appeal to the institutions of civic society – families and communities – to become more responsible for their own wellbeing and more proactive in generating mutual aid and restoring social cohesion. This appeal, however, is founded on flawed assumptions based on communitarian values which idealise 'community' itself as unproblematic – unified, cohesive and compliant.

In reality, communities are made up of different and diverse interests that invariably come into conflict with each other (e.g. based on 'race', class, gender, age and sexuality). This book interrogates these mainstream 'commonsense' notions and assumptions about community more deeply and, in doing so, offers a more nuanced, critical assessment of the effects of community-focused social policy reforms on community safety, cohesion and wellbeing in Britain. It will do this by revisiting the way concepts and discourses of community, safety and cohesion have been used over time, how these have shaped social policy developments, and what have been the effects in relation to community safety and social wellbeing. The book will conclude by offering a different reading of community safety, cohesion and social wellbeing, and the role community might play – as a site of *conflict* and *resistance* (i.e. where human agency is played out in practice) – in realising an alternative, egalitarian vision of social wellbeing. To a significant extent, we share many of the concerns of the left-of-centre pressure group Compass and its vision of the good society – a vision of ways of social organising that counteract the social harms reaped by neo-liberalism:

> We have become a more unequal and divided society. Levels of personal debt are unprecedented, and we are time-poor, working long hours either to make ends meet or to buy the ever-changing trappings of success. Alongside economic insecurity a new set of social problems has emerged – widespread mental illness, systematic loneliness, growing numbers of psychologically damaged children, eating disorders, obesity, alcoholism and drug addiction. (Shah and Rutherford 2006: 28)

The presence of such harms in our society means that a wider debate about the kind of society we want – one involving a broad constituency – is now essential.

> Progressive politics is impossible without a vision of what could be. We need to create a society based on the freedom of everyone to flourish. This requires that we all have the resources, time and political recognition to live our lives to the full. We want a culture that understands that humans are interdependent, social and emotional beings, fundamentally oriented towards, and dependent upon, other people. Such a society must have at its core social justice, environmental sustainability and quality of life. (Shah and Rutherford 2006: 28)

It is this search for an alternative vision of society – one that promotes the safety and wellbeing of all (social justice) – that this book is principally concerned.

The structure of the book

The analysis explored in this book is structured into five chapters. Chapter 1 places the themes community and conflict into historical context. It traces the changing social, political and economic context within which community relations and tensions have been played out throughout modern times, and the dominant discourses that emerged in relation to these themes. What this coverage reveals is that community relations in modern Britain have largely been shaped within the context of a deeply divided society, socially and spatially, and that an enduring symptom of this fissure has been communities in conflict. What it also illustrates is that whilst the language and emphasis of these discourses may have changed over time, what they are addressing or talking about is largely the same thing – or, as Foucault termed it, 'the same field of battle' (Foucault 2005: 142) – that is, from the perspective of the powerful, the need to protect the interests and safety of the privileged by managing risks posed by 'dangerous communities' (be they the 'residuum', 'underclass' or 'socially excluded') within a divided society; and from the perspective of the oppressed, the need to assert their own needs and demands through engaging in community action and conflict.

Chapter 2 then explores different conceptual understandings of community and conflict in order to illustrate the contestability of these ideas. This examination focuses on two meaningful competing notions of community and conflict – one which sees community as the solution to social conflict (where conflict is interpreted in negative terms – something bad) and a counterweight to threats posed by 'dangerous' people; the other which sees community as a potential site for mobilising social conflict (where conflict is interpreted in positive terms – something good) as resistance or in pursuit of positive social transformation. The former offers an understanding of the utility of community and conflict for the state and how these concepts have been exploited to legitimise social policy interventions aimed at ensuring compliance and domination – an understanding more recently associated with communitarian thinking. In contrast, the latter offers an assessment of the utility of these same concepts for understanding possibilities for generating a transformative community politics in the interest of social justice. This chapter, therefore, establishes the analytical framework that will be used to scrutinise the utility of the concepts community and conflict for legitimising social policy interventions by the powerful and for mobilising collective action in pursuit of social justice by radical social movements.

Chapter 3 analyses the community-focused policies pursued since 1997 under the administrations of New Labour – particularly in relation to community safety, urban regeneration and community cohesion. This analysis will illustrate the way New Labour's discourse on community and safety is heavily rooted in communitarian ideology. According to this position, community safety, cohesion and wellbeing will be enhanced through people interacting with each other as neighbours, families and friends ('in community'). Interacting together in this way will lead to a strengthening of civic society in which people will experience improved social, political and economic wellbeing. However, this notion of community is problematic – based, as it is, on a naïve assumption that individuals can be socially engineered into homogeneous communities characterised by shared social values. As commented on above, this is rarely the case as communities invariably consist of different and diverse interest groups – some of whom will feel isolated and alienated from the mainstream values that inevitably dominate the agenda within the new networks and partnerships that have been set up to oversee the delivery of 'community-focused' local services. It is argued here that New Labour's policies will not succeed in generating their stated aims on community cohesion and wellbeing because they continue to fail to acknowledge these power differentials and structured inequalities in society – focusing instead on the communitarian preoccupation with the 'cultural deficit' of 'failed communities'. This also raises questions about whose interests are being met through these community-focused social policies.

Chapter 4 revisits the core concepts of community safety, cohesion and wellbeing in order to expose a number of myths and contradictions that are evident in mainstream social policy discourse around these three themes and to present a different reading based upon a more proportionate understanding of threats to social wellbeing. In particular, this chapter looks beyond dominant interpretations that focus on the relatively minor misdemeanours of the least advantaged to focus instead on the destructive effects of the 'anti-social' policies and practices of government and private corporations. This exposure illustrates how economic change and the social policy choices of the powerful since the 1980s have contributed to the emergence of a less supportive society and, as a consequence, increasing exposure to risk for many people.

In the final chapter of the book, we revisit the core concepts of community and conflict again in order to assess the utility of these notions for facilitating the development of a broad constituency of critical understanding and support for a more progressive vision of community wellbeing – one that is advantageous to all. Here, we draw on critical theories of community and conflict, described in Chapter 2, to stress these concepts' transformative capacities and the possibilities for transcending the established order of things in order to generate the societal preconditions whereby all people can share in opportunities to achieve their aspirations and attain a sense of social wellbeing – effectively, an alternative vision of comprehensive community wellbeing for all.

1
'Community', 'Conflict' and the State – the Historical Field

Background

Community is a vague and contested concept. For some it has no meaning at all whilst for others it describes a self-contained collection of people living in the same neighbourhood and sharing a sense of belonging. Throughout modernity, community has often been used to describe collections of 'dangerous' people living in 'dangerous' places who are a threat to the 'natural' order. Such descriptions – from politicians, policy analysts, the media and academics alike – have largely served to legitimise a range of punitive policies aimed at maintaining social cohesion and wellbeing in the 'national interest'. This focus on communities set apart has also allowed public attention to remain focused on a limited understanding of 'dangerousness' and 'crime' – a corollary of which is that other more serious social harms (caused by the actions of the powerful) have escaped public scrutiny. Throughout the same time, however, the notion of community has also been embraced by the disadvantaged as a site for mobilising collective engagement in social activism and conflict. For disadvantaged groups, community has served as a symbol of human agency around which collective struggles of resistance have been (and can still be) organised. It is because of its utility as a concept for both the powerful and the disadvantaged that community has remained a fascinating and enduring notion in social policy discourse.

The discussion that follows will consider the political ramifications of the structural changes brought about with industrialisation for communities in Britain. It will highlight the powerful structural continuities that have shaped community relations and experiences throughout modernity. In particular, it reveals the way these relations and experiences have, throughout industrialised and post-industrial Britain, been played out within the context of acute social and spatial divisions. Moreover, by exploring the role notions of community and conflict have played in the modern history of social policy, it is possible to reveal clear tendencies about the utility of these concepts both for the powerful (for maintaining social control) and the disadvantaged (in relation to understanding the conditions under which successful collective struggle for positive social change might be possible). This will show the way the binary relationship between community as social structure (a site for social control) and human agency (a site for mobilising resistance) has influenced developments in social policy. This includes examining how discourses of the powerful have served to construct the threats of 'dangerous communities', and how these constructions served to legitimise state interventions to counter these threats, as well as the way disadvantaged communities themselves have engaged in social action in pursuance of their own interests.

The discussion that follows takes the turn of the eighteenth century as its starting point – a period when the social consequences of the industrial revolution and the political foundations for community relations in modern Britain became firmly embedded. It is during this period that the structural context for social relations in modern Britain, with its deep-rooted social and spatial divides, was firmly established. It is therefore fitting that this stage in time marks the starting point for this trawl through the historical field of community relations, conflict and state action in Britain.

It finishes in the late-1990s when the legacy of Thatcherism on community relations, and the severity of the challenge facing Labour on being returned to power after 18 years in the political wilderness – details of which are addressed in Chapter 3 – had become clear.

The direction of the chapter follows a chronological approach whilst, at the same time, highlighting key themes relevant to an understanding of critical power influences on community experiences – in particular, the effects of ideological positions (classical liberalism, socialism, Keynesian-welfarism and Thatcherism/neo-liberalism), Methodism, social class and the social constructs of 'race' and 'gender' on social relations. The chapter shows how popularist concerns about the threat from 'dangerous' communities set apart have persisted throughout modern Britain. However, the way the state has responded to these concerns has varied at different moments in time – responses which are distinguishable by their emphasis either on social welfare solutions (where the wellbeing of working-class communities significantly improved) or criminal justice sanctions (the preferred option prior to the post-Second World War welfare state and increasingly since the late 1970s). What has been a consistent feature of state intervention in modern Britain has been its failure to repair the structural flaws of capitalism – despite the long history of community struggles for social improvement. As a consequence of this failure, issues that preoccupied Victorian Britain – social and spatial divisions, and community breakdown and conflict – remain with us today.

Industrialisation, urbanisation and social transformation

The industrial revolution represented a major turning point in economic, social and political relations in Britain. As E. P. Thompson observes, 'In the years between 1780 and 1832 most English working people came to feel an identity of interests as between themselves, and as against their rulers and employers' (Thompson 1991/1963: 11). As Stuart Hall argues:

> What makes us distinctive is indeed the particularities, the specificities of our historical and other experiences. There's a phrase by Marx ... that, of course, people are all unified in the fact that they are all human, but that what matters more are the different social categories into which people are divided: slave and slaveholder, worker and capitalist. ... That's where the trouble begins. That's where the conflict over wealth or interest arises. (Hall 2007: 154)

Whilst some people chose to move to the new industrial centres – 'lured from the countryside by the glitter and promise of wages' (Thompson 1991/1963: 486) – many had little choice due to the decline in the rural economy. The process of industrialisation was particularly brutal for the working classes – pushed through 'with exceptional violence' (Thompson 1991/1963: 486). This was largely due to the upper- and middle-classes' fear of revolution spreading amongst the new urban proletariat in Britain in the years following the French Revolution, as well as the military threat from Napoleon at the turn of the century. The 1790s to 1820s was one of the most formally repressive periods in British history with the suspension of *habeas corpus*, the arrest and imprisonment of dissenters without trial, the prohibition of constitutional and reform societies, the taxation of newspapers to a level beyond the means of working-class people, and the employment of 'Church and King' mobs and government informers.

The counter-revolutionary panic of the ruling classes expressed itself in every part of social life; in attitudes to trade unionism, to the education of the people to their sports and manners, to their publications and societies, and their political rights. ... In the decades after 1795 there was a profound alienation between the classes in Britain, and working people were thrust in to a state of *apartheid* whose effects ... can be felt to this day. England differed from other European nations in this, that the flood-tide of counter-revolutionary feeling and discipline coincided with the flood-tide of the Industrial Revolution; as new techniques and forms of industrial organization advanced, so political and social rights receded. The 'natural' alliance between an impatient radically-minded industrial bourgeoisie and a formative proletariat was broken as soon as it was formed. (Thompson 1991/1963: 194–195)

The model of capitalism wrought by industrialisation in Britain – classical liberal capitalism – was, therefore, one fraught by new forms of class antagonism 'unrelieved by any sense of national participation in communal effort. ... Its ideology was that of masters alone' (Thompson 1991/1963: 486) and opportunities for the owners of the new machines to accumulate wealth through the unbridled exploitation of labour power – a form of exploitation that has persisted throughout modern times. Moreover, as Orum observes,

As the wealth of the owners grew, it appears that the poverty of the laborers also grew. They generally were paid small wages, often for piecework (work paid for by the piece or quantity). ... By and large, the industrial growth was accompanied not only by poverty among the laborers but also by increasing amounts of disease and illness in the expanding urban areas. Houses were tightly packed together and were overcrowded with tenants. ... The sewer systems were primitive, and human excrement was left on the street. (Orum 2003: 652)

Industrialisation in Britain led to the emergence of new forms of social relations in newly urbanised areas. Archaeologist Gordon Childe referred to this as an 'urban revolution' characterised by a 'shift from simple tribal communities with largely village-based agricultural systems to complex urban-based production systems' (Kumar 2003: 1434). The old pre-urban social order broke down as urbanisation advanced: '[T]he city became the site of conflicting cultures and divergent ways of existence. ... There was a distinct lack of social cohesion. ... The community became fragmented' (Kumar 2003: 1434). Popular notions of community that emerged in the nineteenth century reflected this concern about the perceived breakdown in social cohesion. The focus of attention was largely a romanticised concept of 'rural community' – an idealised way of living together that had been destroyed by rapid industrialisation and urbanisation. As Taylor suggests, throughout modernity policy debates concerning community have largely focused on community deficit – 'communities that are considered to be deficient in some way' (Taylor 2003: 17) and not like they once were.

Social-spatial divisions and the threat of the 'dangerous Other'

With industrialisation and urbanisation in Britain emerged different (largely segregated) socio-spatial arrangements and, simultaneously, the emergence of the middle-class nightmare – the 'Other' ('dangerous' people) in 'communities set apart' ('dangerous' places) who threatened the safety of the 'respectable':

> What was seen as a breakdown in the natural order led to a developing sense of alarm and crisis amongst the members of the new ruling elite, described as a 'fear of the town or dangerous classes'; there arose a search for new ideas and new attempts to create within the mass of ordinary people the need for self-discipline, order and a respect for lawful authority. (Robson 2000: 45)

The 'threat' took the form of dangers to public health (from the 'diseased' slums) and political cohesion (from socialism and class conflict), and to the moral and legal order (from vice and crime). To some, these dangers posed an overall threat to social progress, illustrated in the work of Henry Mayhew who believed that the health of the economic body was threatened by parasites in the social body – those unproductive 'vagabonds' who prey 'upon the earnings of the more industrious portions of the community' (Mayhew 1861/1967: 90). Working-class communities were invariably characterised as the 'residuum', a 'community' left behind by industrialisation, or 'alien', a 'race apart' (comparable to the way explorers to 'Darkest Africa' described their journeys abroad) (Charlton 2000).

In response to the identification of 'communities set apart', various multi-faceted social interventions emerged in the nineteenth century aimed at regulating and reforming the lower orders. These included public health measures, the criminalisation of certain 'street life' (casual trade, begging, prostitution, 'hanging about'), policing, and philanthropic and charitable endeavours aimed at promoting more regulated leisure – these latter ventures including activities organised by the temperance movement, youth work (Graham and Clarke 2002), the Charity Organisation Society and university settlements (Craig 1989, Popple 1995). At the heart of these activities lay a strong desire to impose a 'middle class morality' (Robson 2000: 45) on lower-order communities and instil compliance with the contemporary order of things. 'The emergence of charitable institutions at the same time as the creation of social reforms was seen as an attempt to "dull" the minds of the working class, making them less amenable to radical or revolutionary solutions' (Robson 2000: 64).

The influence of Methodism (and football?) on community relations

An important influence on community life in Britain from the late eighteenth century onwards was Methodism. The Methodist Church, with its elevation of such virtues as social order and moral discipline, appealed to both mill-owners and manufacturers, and the working classes. As E. P. Thompson observes:

> Methodism obtained its greatest success in serving *simultaneously* as the religion of the industrial bourgeoisie ... and of wide sections of the proletariat. Nor can there be any doubt as to the deep-rooted allegiance of many working-class communities (equally among miners, weavers, factory workers, seamen, potters and rural labourers) to the Methodist Church. (Thompson 1991/1963: 391 – emphasis in original)

As Thompson argues, Methodism 'acted most evidently as a stabilizing or regressive social force' (Thompson 1991/1963: 50) – inculcating in the worker: '... "the first and great lesson ... that man must expect his chief happiness, not in the present, but in a future state". Work must be undertaken as a *"pure act of virtue* ... inspired by the love of a transcendent Being, operating ... on our will and affections"' (cited in Thompson 1991/1963: 398 – emphasis in original).

Thompson offers three explanations for Methodism's hold over so many working people: indoctrination; Methodism's sense of community; and its palliative effect. First, Methodist Sunday schools, established from the late eighteenth century, adopted the Wesleyan notion of the 'sinful child' whose character and conduct required moulding (indoctrinating) from an early age. The poet and author Robert Southey, writing in 1890, cites Wesley's argument for the need to:

> Break their wills.... Begin this work before they can run alone, before they can speak.... Let a child from a year old be taught to fear the rod and to cry softly.... Break his will now, and his soul shall live, and he will probably bless you to all eternity. (Cited in Thompson 1991/1963: 412)

The main purpose of 'education' in Methodist Sunday schools was to indoctrinate children into accepting their unworthiness – as 'wretched slaves to sin' – and to find 'moral rescue' in the virtues of duty, obedience and industry (Thompson 1991/1963).

Second, at the same time, Methodism 'did offer to the uprooted and abandoned people of the Industrial Revolution some kind of community to replace the older community-patterns which were being displaced' (Thompson 1991/1963: 416–417). The Methodist chapel, with its open doors, would particularly appeal to the lonely migrant worker new to town – a place to meet and find a sense of mutuality in an otherwise hostile world (Thompson 1991/1963). Third, in the context of a counter-revolutionary mood of the new millennium – many working-class communities had seen their aspirations for a better future frustrated with the collapse of the political reform movement in the 1790s – many working people turned to Methodism as a 'consolation'. As Marx famously stated, 'religion is the opium of the people' (Marx 1844: 1) – something to relieve their pain 'at the point where "political" or temporal aspirations met with defeat' (Thompson 1991/1963: 428).

As society became more secular, association football was considered by some to have had a similar influence to that of Methodism (on working-class men at least). In the nineteenth century, the character of football went through various transformations – initially, from being a folk ritual of urban 'undesirables'; then a pastime of public schoolboys; and then, by the 1870s, to being the national game for working-class men (as players and spectators – though not the owners of football clubs!). To some observers, the function of football was similar to Marx's notion of the function of religion: for Karl Kautsky, a German Marxist theorist, 'football functioned as an opiate, pure and simple – a diversion from the more pressing tasks of industrial organization and revolutionary politics' (Goldblatt 2006: 52). Goldblatt, however, contests this notion, arguing that the British proletariat had never been a revolutionary animal anyway (due, perhaps, to Methodism). 'Football mania did not create a reformist Labour Party and a cautious economistic trade union movement; it merely reflected these institutions and their outlook' (Goldblatt 2006: 52).

The emergence of a radical labour movement

At the same time, however, the nineteenth century did witness the emergence of a radicalised labour movement comprising trade unions and political parties. Out of this movement grew a strong network of self-help welfare organising – for example, friendly societies, savings clubs, health societies and food co-operatives – which helped poor communities fend for themselves at a time when, other than the Poor Law system, the state would not provide. The working-class movement also developed its own education system ranging from miners schools to night classes, Sunday schools, Chartist schools and reading rooms. As Jones and Novak observe: 'Fiercely independent of the attempted influence of the established church, philanthropists, and later of the state, they were to embody the essential belief, as one advocate put it, that "a people's education is safe only in a people's own hands"' (Jones and Novak 2000: 43).

Radical class consciousness within working-class communities was greatly influenced by this education system and people would read the work of such figures as Karl Marx, Frederick Engels, Charles Dickens and Elizabeth Gaskell – who all drew attention to the harsh reality of urban life for the working class. 'From the time of the Industrial Revolution onwards, a growing working class had recognised, in the words of the masthead of one of the most popular (and, after their suppression, illegal) of working-class newspapers, *The Poor Man's Guardian*, that "Knowledge is Power"' (Jones and Novak 2000: 43).

Indeed, in 1854, at a time when different religious bodies were in dispute about what type of education system should be established, *The Times* newspaper had called for the state to intervene urgently in education to counter a perceived threat of working-class militancy:

> While we are disputing which ought to be the most beneficial system of education, we leave the great mass of the people to be influenced by the very worst possible teachers. ... In 1850 Harney's Red Republican has published in full 'The Communist Manifesto' supporting every revolutionary movement against the exiting social and political

order of things. ... The National Reform League is campaigning for the nationalisation of land .... Cheap publications containing the wildest and the most anarchical doctrines are scattered, broadcast over the land. ... Only in one way can this great danger, this great evil be counteracted. The religious sects must bury their differences. Let prudent spirit of conciliation enable the wise and the good to offer to the people a beneficial education in the place of this abominable teacher. (Cited in Jones and Novak 2000: 44–45)

Some time later, in 1870, the state introduced the Elementary Education Act which established an elementary system of schooling for the working class which, by the 1880s, had become compulsory. This intervention is seen by Jones and Novak as an attempt 'to replace "dangerous knowledge" with "useful knowledge", and thus subvert the radical potential that working-class self-education threatened' (Jones and Novak 2000: 45). It is seen as an example of the way social reform served as a political strategy to counteract the rising revolutionary consciousness within working-class communities. This view is shared in John Charlton's account of how working-class campaigns at the end of the century led to a series of social welfare reforms in the years preceding the First World War. Widespread strikes and violent conflict between employers and the working class erupted throughout the country from the mid-1880s into the 1890s – involving craft workers, miners, dock workers, tailors, gas workers, iron workers, rubber workers, blast furnace workers, engine workers, chain makers, firemen, seamen, cotton workers and labourers. Many of these strikes were led by the Social Democratic Federation (SDF). The SDF grew out of the Chartist tradition and represented the first Marxist political group in Britain (established in the early 1880s). Amongst its membership were prominent trade unionists (such as Tom Mann and John Burns) and other radicals (such as Eleanor Marx – youngest daughter of Karl – and William Morris) (Charlton 2000).

By the end of the century, the élite were becoming increasingly fearful of the threat from working-class communities to the established order. In 1885 Samuel Smith, in reference to the proletariat, commented 'I am deeply convinced that the time is approaching when this seething mass of human misery will shake the social fabric, unless we grapple more earnestly with it than we have done' (cited in Charlton 2000: 55). C. F. G. Mastermann described labouring communities in 1909 as:

shabby figures .... The multitude of the unimportant gather together having hopes. With incredible rapidity appear among them the criminal, the loafer .... There is a note of menace in it ... the evidence of possibilities of violence in its waywardness, its caprice, its always incalculable mettle and temper ... the smile may turn into fierce snarl or savagery. ... Humanity has become the Mob. (Cited in Charlton 2000: 58)

In parallel with these fears, by the end of the nineteenth century the dominant orthodoxy shaping social policy in Britain – *laissez faire* political economy – was coming under strain due to increasing social problems both at home and abroad. Charles Booth's study of poverty in East London identified that 35 per cent of the population was living in poverty. In addition, reports on recruitment for the Boer War at the end of the century identified that a significant proportion of working-class men were in an unfit physical state to fight (Charlton 2000). On top of this, class conflict and community protest was intensifying. These factors threatened economic production and social stability at home, as well as Britain's imperialistic ambitions abroad. Britain faced increasing trade competition at this time from developing international markets, particularly those of the US and Germany. The state had to become more interventionist.

During the early part of the twentieth century, class conflict intensified with an increase in working-class campaigning. 'Between 1900 and the outbreak of the First World War there was a mounting tide of militancy and dissatisfaction with governments and trade union leaders' (Grayson 1997: 28). Conflict between the labour movement and their employers and landlords took the form of radical campaigns organised around strikes, withholding rent, rioting and collective resistance against evictions (Grayson 1997). In response, the British state began to depart from its *laissez-faire* stance. As Popple explains, as the turn of the century approached, the 'already alarmed bourgeoisie' began:

> to question the extent to which *laissez-faire* doctrines could effectively deal with persistent and worsening social conditions. The threat to Britain's superior trading position similarly moved the government of the time to examine collectivist solutions to its economic and social dilemmas. In response the Conservative governments of the turn of the century, and the 1906–14 Liberal government, implemented a number of social and educational reforms which were intended to head off class conflict, and to benefit the long-term interests of British capital by equipping its workforce to compete both militarily and economically with its foreign rivals. (Popple 1995: 9)

However, the failure of government to take adequate measures to tackle housing problems had, by the First World War, fuelled further tenant militancy and, throughout communities of munitions production, there were calls for strikes.

> [O]ne of the earliest recorded forms of community action was in the city of Glasgow. During the early part of the twentieth century there were a number of struggles in Glasgow against the Munitions Act and for the campaign demanding a 40-hour working week. In 1915 both working-class and lower middle-class people demonstrated against increases in rents and the lack of attention to slum housing. (Popple 1995: 11)

In October 1915, 15,000 Glaswegians were on rent strike including five Labour councillors. Women were at the forefront of this campaign, organising rent strikes through the Women's Housing Association and assaulting bailiffs by pelting them with rubbish and flour. By November 1915, 20,000 people were on strike. The government had established the Hunter Committee in the previous October to review the situation, but the rent strikes continued to escalate – particularly around the trials of rent strikers. A General Strike was threatened after a mass demonstration on 17 November and eight days later, on 25 November 1915, a Rent and Mortgage Interest Freeze Bill was introduced, becoming law in four weeks flat, receiving the Royal Assent on 25 December (Grayson 1997). The impact of rent controls eroded the role of the private landlord in British housing – a role that was already in decline by the end of the previous century due to the availability of more profitable investment opportunities overseas – which in turn put pressure on the state to intervene in the housing market when the war ended. This intervention took the form of exchequer subsidies for council housing for the very first time – introduced under the Housing and Town Planning Act 1919 (Daunton 1987). Some commentators on this period agree that the British establishment lived in genuine fear of a social revolution, and saw the need to concede to working-class demands. The state also needed to ensure that the now organised and enfranchised working classes were incorporated into the post-war reconstruction effort. This represents a significant shift from the housing campaigns of the nineteenth century, largely led by elements from within the unskilled labouring classes. Now, the 'threat' to the established social order was different, coming as it did from the organised and skilled working classes. Consequently, the government's response was different – 'homes for heroes' or, more specifically, the provision of subsidised council housing for the skilled working classes. As Harloe observes:

> The first mass programmes of social rented housing were, therefore, not a simple response to housing needs but a response to *strategically important* housing needs, in brief the needs of those sections of the population – the skilled, organised working class and part of the middle class – whose continuing disaffection posed the greatest threat to the re-establishment of the capitalist social order. (Harloe 1995: 101 – emphasis in original)

Community conflict and 'race'

Alongside the fear of the militant multitude in the nineteenth century emerged a dread about 'alien' immigrant communities. Jewish arrivals, many of whom had fled the pogroms of Eastern Europe, were accused by one commentator of importing the principles of 'secret socialistic or foreign revolutionary societies' (cited in Charlton 2000: 59). The Jewish community was also blamed for unemployment, poor housing conditions and the spread of disease (Charlton 2000). Throughout modernity, immigrants have been perceived as presenting a drain on scarce urban resources. At the same time, 'race' was to become a metaphor of 'danger' – partly reflecting the concerns of the eugenics movement (Graham and Clarke 2002). In the nineteenth century, Irish communities were considered a threat to the social order: 'Asa Briggs' analysis of the growth of Chartism in the middle of the nineteenth century referred to the potential for revolution amongst the mass of Irish "navvies" who had entered cities such as Liverpool, Birmingham and Manchester "of which it was estimated one fifth were Irish"' (Robson 2000: 46).

There had been skirmishes between Irish and English workers in direct competition for jobs in the building industry or in the docks back in the 1830s and 1840s, and in parts of London anti-Catholic and anti-Irish feeling was particularly strong at this time. However, according to E. P. Thompson, Irish communities generally settled peacefully in England (Thompson 1991/1963).

By the twentieth century the focus of concern became 'black' immigrants. Sections of the trade union movement, Conservative politicians and extra-parliamentary action groups such as the British

Brothers League campaigned for restrictions on entry, leading to the enactment of the Aliens Order 1905 under the then Conservative government.

> This was the first of a series of restrictive measures in the early part of the twentieth century.... The most important provisions of the legislation were (a) that aliens could be refused permission to enter Britain if they did not have, or did not have the means to obtain, the means to subsist in adequate sanitary conditions; and (b) that an alien could be expelled from Britain without trial or appeal if he or she was found to be receiving poor relief within a year of entering Britain, was found guilty of vagrancy or was found to be living in insanitary conditions due to overcrowding. Other provisions of the order were that the home secretary would have the power to expel 'undesirable' immigrants.... (Solomos 2003: 42)

Further powers of restriction on entry were contained within the Aliens Restrictions Act 1914 which gave greater authority to the government to decide who could be prohibited from entry and who could be deported. Although it was argued that this legislation was a temporary measure in the interest of national security at a time of war, it was later extended under the Aliens Restriction (Amendment) Act 1919 (which repealed the 1905 Order) despite the war now being over.

Clearly, the early years of the twentieth century proved to be an important period in terms of the way immigrant communities were represented in public discourse and political debate, and the impact these representations had on social policy developments (Solomos 2003). For example, a major theme that emerged in the political debate on black communities in the inter-war years was 'the supposed social problems to which their presence gave rise' (Solomos 2003: 44). Hence, after the war, efforts were made under the 1919 legislation to restrict further immigration. At the same time, white seamen unions campaigned to restrict employment to 'alien others'. 'In the resulting competition for work, Indian, Chinese and Caribbean seamen who had settled in Britain became the victims of racist violence in Cardiff, Liverpool and Glasgow' (Solomos 2003: 45–46). The National Archives report that in June 1919:

> In Cardiff, in particular, white ex-servicemen, including Australians stationed in the area, headed lynch mobs that terrorised the city's black community during a week of violence that left three men

dead and dozens more injured. In the aftermath the government repatriated hundreds of black people (600 by mid-September). (The National Archives 2007: 1)

In 1920, the government passed the Aliens Order allowing immigration officers to refuse entry to an 'alien' considered unable to provide for their own support. The Home Secretary also gained powers to deport an 'alien' 'whose presence was not considered to be "conducive to the public good"' (Solomos 2003: 43). Lastly, 'aliens' wishing to work in Britain were required to have a work permit from the Ministry of Labour. This would only be issued where it could be shown that no British worker was available to do the job in question. In 1925, the Special Restrictions (Coloured Alien Seamen) Act was passed. This applied to colonial seamen – previously entitled to sign off from a ship in a British port and to seek residence there – who did not have adequate documentation to prove they were subjects. These seamen now had to obtain the permission of an immigration offer to land and were subject to removal from the country (Solomos 2003).

> [I]n practice the police, the Aliens Department and immigration officers also forced 'coloured' British subjects who did possess the required documents to register under the Order, an action that deprived them of their legal status of British subject and thereby rendered them subject to... [registering] with the police, to whom they were required to report any change of address... and to the possibility of deportation. (Solomos 2003: 46).

It was clear that the Order was designed particularly to restrict the entry of black colonial British citizens.

> The response of the state, at both the local and the national level, was dual-faceted. It was responding to local racist agitation and violence against those defined as 'coloured seamen'.... The two most common responses to black immigration and settlement in this period were political debates on the need to control their arrival and calls for the repatriation of those who had already settled in Britain. Partly because of the violent conflicts that occurred with some regularity in some of the port towns, but largely because of the mobilisation of an image of black enclaves as seats of social problems, even the relatively small communities that developed in the interwar

period were perceived as 'alien' and a possible threat to the British way of life. (Solomos 2003: 47)

In explaining societal and state responses to black colonial immigrants at this time, reference needs to be made to the way Eurocentric perspectives on 'White Supremacy' and imperialism, and the characterisation of 'coloured races' as 'savages' (Freud 1919, Lombroso 1968) or 'primitive' (Jung 1950, cited in Robinson 2004), will have shaped attitudes. As Les Back argues, throughout history, 'European racisms have...insisted that the distinction of the European be established and maintained in the face of barbarism and inferiority of the native, the immigrant or the ethnic minority' (Back 2004: 28), with profound consequences for the experiences and social wellbeing of 'black communities'.

Women's activism and 'gender'

The early twentieth century also witnessed an increase in women's activism. Women had participated in political agitation throughout the previous century. E.P. Thompson identifies protests involving women in the textile districts in the years following the Napoleonic War. In particular, women were demanding employment opportunities in the spinning-mills and at the hand-loom. In 1818 and 1819, the first Female Reform Societies (FRSs) were founded, and between 1815 and 1835 women workers engaged for the first time in independent trade union action. Such action was greeted with alarm in a society where 'the woman's status turned upon her success as a housewife in the family economy, in domestic management and forethought, baking and brewing, cleanliness and child-care' (Thompson 1991/1963: 455). The social reformer, John Wade, commenting upon a strike of 1,500 women card-setters in the West Riding in 1835, remarked 'Alarmists may view these indications of female independence as more menacing to established institutions than the "education of the lower orders"' (cited in Thompson 1991/1963: 454). A correspondent of Jabez Bunting, a Wesleyan minister, with reference to the FRSs, 'lamented the default of the "pious sisterhood" who were embroidering reform banners' (Thompson 1991/1963: 454). Although the actual role of the FRSs had largely been restricted to offering 'moral support to the men...even these forms of participation called forth the abuse of their opponents' (Thompson 1991/1963: 456). The *Courier* described members of the FRS in Manchester as ' "degraded females", guilty of "the worst prostitution of the sex, the prostitution of the heart", "deserting their station" and putting off the "sacred characters" of wife and mother "for turbulent vices of sedition and impiety"' (cited in Thompson 1991/1963: 456).

If the experiences and identities of black communities in Britain have been (and are being) shaped in the context of a 'White Supremacist' hegemony, then women's experiences and identities have been shaped by essentialist notions of 'gender' based on biological and psychological determinations founded on anatomy and brain chemistry. However, 'gender' holds social and cultural meanings, and 'appropriate' definitions of 'male'/'female', 'masculinity'/ 'femininity' are social constructs which vary from society to society, within societies over time and within different social categories (Robb 2007). There are in essence different types of 'masculinity'/ 'femininity', linked to 'race', class, sexuality, age and ability, and we therefore need to talk of 'masculinities' and 'femininities'. At the same time, nevertheless, at any one period there will be dominant definitions of 'gender' (culturally preferred versions) held up as ideal models against which we will all be measured in that particular society (the hegemonic definition). This implies a hierarchy of masculinities/femininities, with further implications for power relations. In some respects, the social construction of 'gender' is evident in the way women's activism has been played out since the nineteenth century – it being invariably focused not merely on housing and employment issues (as we have seen) but also child care, education and health. Such activism is exemplified in the work of Sylvia Pankhurst who, with her group the East London Federation of Suffragettes, set up: 'a cooperative toy factory to provide employment, with a crèche based on progressive theories of education through play. The Gunmaker's Arms was transformed into a health clinic for mothers and babies, renamed The Mother's Arms' (Ledwith 2005: 9).

It can be argued that women's activities in communities are largely shaped by their predetermined 'gender' role as 'carers'. As Dominelli has observed, for women 'organizing in the community often resolves around family life and entails: stretching scarce resources to their limit through self-help networks; providing day-care facilities; getting access to decent, affordable housing; preventing school closures; securing rights to minimum incomes; and a host of other issues linked to women's caring roles' (Dominelli 1995: 134).

Significantly however, as Fiona Williams has observed, the contributions of women (and black people) in the social struggles of the nineteenth and twentieth century have largely been overlooked in the 'grand narratives' of social policy (Williams 1989).

The emergence of the 'urban problem' and 'community work'

As cities expanded in the early part of the twentieth century socio-spatial segregation intensified – particularly with the development of new transport technology. This led to the emergence of the 'urban problem'. The affluent middle classes moved outwards to the suburbs, leaving behind twilight 'zones of transition' – areas characterised by older, low-cost housing close to factories near city centres and occupied by transient populations with a so-called propensity to engage in 'crime' and 'deviance' (Graham and Clarke 2002). The theories that emerged within the inter-war years and into the immediate post-war period were dominated by the assumption that the poor populations of the inner-city were inherently flawed in some respect and that this was the primary cause of the urban problem (which must be repaired through therapy).

In the US, such developments had attracted the attention of the Department of Sociology at the University of Chicago, established in the late nineteenth century. The 'Chicago School' was particularly interested in patterns of urban growth and population distribution, and the way these configurations were shaped by competition and conflict between different communities over land-use. Specific areas of research interest included such Durkheimian preoccupations as what binds people together as social groups and what values do these groups hold? A particular focus of concern was social segregation in modern cities and the social pathology of transient and 'deviant' communities. Researchers at the School used ethnographic techniques such as participant observations to assess the motives and attitudes of different urban communities. Their work included Thrasher's 1927 study of gangsters; Andersen's 1923 study of migrants and tramps; Cressey's 1932 study of women who danced with men for payment; and Zorbaugh's 1929 study of slum dwellers (see Cooper 2005). They were particularly concerned with the breakdown of traditional forms of social bonding (the family, rural economies) in modern industrial cities and in finding ways of generating new forms of social cohesion (through political associations and community organisations). This breakdown was largely explained by reference to the constant movement of urban populations and the consequent absence of 'cultural integration'. In contrast to suburban areas, the 'zones of transition' left behind were places conducive to the development of a criminal sub-culture and delinquency. 'Criminal communities' are effectively the product of the ' "ecology" of the inner city – its inability to provide integrative mechanisms that could link inhabitants to the wider social order' (Graham and Clarke 2002: 165).

Similar concerns emerged in Britain around the same time founded on similar assumptions – that is, that there was an emerging urban problem and that this was largely due to internal deficiencies within poor communities themselves. By the late 1940s, the idea of 'community work' – in the form of working to fix 'broken' communities (in contrast to social work focused on individual or family needs) – was beginning to be mooted. However, it was Murray G. Ross, in the 1960s, who became the first theorist to advocate a wider role for community work beyond the specialist discipline of social work. For Ross:

> community work was a social tool to be used in a wide variety of contexts – agriculture, education, etc. ... [T]he primary objective was undoubtedly that of social control – what he called 'community integration'. Stability and equilibrium were the important things, to be achieved, he argued, through a strategy of consensus. (Corkey and Craig 1978: 37)

Ross clearly saw community work as a means of incorporating marginalised communities into the existing power structures of society – without the need to question the legitimisation of those structures. Here, class antagonism is seen in negative terms (as divisive) – a view shared at the time by Irving Spergel who believed that class conflict 'contributes to isolation and stigmatisation ... as working people isolating themselves from the rest of society, and thereby suffering bad social conditions' (Corkey and Craig 1978: 38). T.R. and Madge Batten, also writing in the 1960s, argued that 'many of our current political, economic and social problems ... would have been avoided, or would be solved more easily if only more people were more mature' (cited in Corkey and Craig 1978: 37) – therefore, the main purpose of community work should be to develop these people's maturity (through group-work exercises).

The assumption that people's problems are primarily due to their lack of maturity is not borne out by history – as we have already seen from our discussion of the strong network of self-help welfare organising that emerged within the working class during the last century when the state did not provide. The Battens and other social theorists in the 1960s would also have been aware of the successful community campaigns around housing in the immediate post-war years. The lack of an adequate housing supply had led to direct action in the form of squatting campaigns – campaigns which had gained much public sympathy, including from the most unlikely source the *Daily Mail* which 'praised the squatters for their "robust common sense" and their ability when governments fail them "to take matters quietly but firmly into their own hands"' (cited in Grayson 1997: 43).

However, the idea that the flawed pathology of disadvantaged communities was at the heart of the urban problem, requiring a therapeutic response through group work (rather than structural adjustment), came to dominate community development practice in the post-war period. The Calouste Gulbenkian Foundation Community Work Group (CGFCWG) was influential here with its emphasis on group work within existing power structures, and the need for individuals to contribute to the life of the community and to develop good relationships. The CGFCWG comprised:

> highly influential academics and administrators…. [T]he essence of community described in their first book is a 'sense of common bond, the sharing of an identity, membership in a group holding some things physical or spiritual, in common esteem, coupled with the acknowledgment of rights and obligations with reference to all others so identified'. (Cited in Corkey and Craig 1978: 40)

The policy prescription here is that poor communities need to find consensus and work together in harmony within existing power structures to overcome their marginalisation. Critic Tom Woolley described this line of thinking as: 'an attempt to contain and direct working-class discontent, and that it must be seen in the context of British reformist tradition whereby Britain has in effect avoided revolution for over two centuries by introducing enough reforms to dispel protest without altering the power relationships which cause discontent' (Corkey and Craig 1978: 41–42).

Shaw and Martin are sympathetic to this position – arguing that the central premise of the CGFCWG's perspective was 'to provide a means by which diverse demands could be mediated and managed' by encouraging 'participative democracy in a pluralist society' (Shaw and Martin 2000: 402). According to Shaw and Martin, the CGFCWG considered that,

> [C]ertain people were disabled as citizens in relation to the exercise of their democratic rights/or responsibilities. The solution was

two-fold: first, to integrate deficit/disaffected individuals and groups into the mainstream; second, to make providers of services more sensitive to their needs.... In short, community work sought, in Seymour Martin Lipsett's celebrated phrase, to 'tidy up the ragged edges of the good society'. (Shaw and Martin 2000: 402)

Whilst such an approach to community work may extract small gains for disadvantaged communities, these will be little more than crumbs from the table of capitalism and do little to challenge the foundations of a system that continues to exploit and alienate. The CGFCWG's perspective, however, came to shape the early Community Development Projects (CDPs) of the 1960s, established (alongside other state interventions of the time such as slum clearance and redevelopment) to tackle the effects of persistent poverty and urban tensions in the inner city.

Keynesian welfarism and the post-war political 'consensus'

The political situation changed in post-war Britain as a consequence of the landslide election victory of a Labour government in 1945. Immediate post-war policy developments were shaped within the context of Keynesian welfarism – a so-called social-democratic consensus committed to state intervention in social and economic affairs (largely to achieve the renewal needed after the war). This 'consensus' surfaced in the context of a prosperous British economy and a long economic boom stretching to the early 1970s – 'reflected in rising levels of output and living standards, low unemployment, and expanded trade' (Popple 1995: 13). It was a period of optimism 'about the potential capacity and desirability of the state to engineer social change and to usher in an end to poverty, deprivation and discrimination by direct state intervention' (Hughes and Edwards 2005: 16). It was also a period (albeit brief) which heralded significant gains for working people – particularly in the shape of the welfare state (Craig 1989). There was a political consensus at the time that a primary goal of government was to manage 'potentially damaging and wasteful conflicts of interest between the classes' (Jordan 2006: 52). Welfare states were one mechanism for achieving this goal:

> They aimed to use democratic means to resolve conflicts, restrain economic competition, and redistribute the benefits of more cooperative relationships between the classes. They drew on the theories of the economist John Maynard Keynes...to show how the state

could, by its management of interest rates, taxation, redistribution, investment and public spending, smooth out the 'cycles' of inflation and deflation, boom and bust, which had afflicted liberal democratic versions of capitalism. In this way, financial, business and trade union organizations could be drawn into systems which allowed reliable economic growth, and citizens could have their human development needs met through social security, health-care, education and welfare services financed out of contributions from all the three elements in the 'social partnership'. (Jordan 2006: 52)

For the theologian Küng, the post-war welfare state experiment in western Europe represented a desire to establish a 'third way' between totalitarian-state economic command systems and free-market liberal economies – one that would use the power of the state to regulate the economy in the interest of wider social and political goals (Byrne 2006). Whilst the Keynesian-welfare state system was inherently controlling – representing what Amin describes as 'a series of political compromises, social alliances and hegemonic processes of domination which feed into a pattern of mass integration and social cohesion, thus serving to underwrite and stabilise a given development push' (cited in Byrne 2006: 45) – it did, in parallel with trade union rights, lead to relative gains for the working classes (although these gains were differentiated in terms of 'race', class and gender). In particular, it was a system which:

> channelled accumulation away from absolute surplus value expropriation which depended on the exploitative emmiseration [sic] of workers and towards relative surplus value expropriation which involves the use of technology and labour process organization to increase the volume productivity of workers. This latter was the essence of Fordism. It was the basis of a general raising of all metropolitan sector incomes during the Fordist era. The owners got more absolutely but wages still rose. (Byrne 2006: 45)

Workers saw their wages rise not only in terms of their pay packets, but also in terms of the social wage – that is, increased state investment in education, health care, subsidised housing provision and social protection.

The other mechanism used by the state for regulating conflict was community development. One problem area where community development was seen as the solution related to council housing. A major challenge for urban policy in the immediate post-war period was the replacement of unfit or war-damaged housing (again, to house the 'heroes'). One response to this was the prioritisation of new town projects and new-build peripheral council estates. These developments came to be seen as one of the major causes of the breakdown of the kind of traditional community network such as the one identified by Young and Wilmott in their famous examination of community life in Bethnal Green. Their study challenged the notion that 'community' had been undermined by industrialisation and urbanisation, and identified strong forms of social bonding in what they conceptualised as an 'urban village' (Young and Wilmott 1962).

One solution to the problem of community breakdown in the new public housing developments was 'community development' in the form of encouragement for tenant participation (Grayson 1997) and the establishment of community centres to encourage social activities and a sense of 'community spirit' (Craig 1989, Popple 1995). A key aim of these initiatives was to incorporate council tenants – many of whom had been rehoused 'from the slums' – into an established moral order. The National Council of Social Service (NCSS) supported this approach to community work – declaring in 1950 that the appeal of 'community' was its 'undertones of order, cooperation, the harmonious working and development of an established system' (cited in Craig 1989: 6). This fascination came close to that of Raymond Williams around this time who, in *Culture and Society*, spoke of the 'warmly persuasive' attractiveness of community (Williams 1958). It was also a mode of working consistent with the British labour movement's reformist approach to social change at this time:

> Collective community action of this period was...never fully in the revolutionary mode. The ideology of self-help, which was a feature of the Victorian middle class, was also an aspect of working-class life, with the development of the co-operative movement, adult education (the Workers' Educational Association was established in 1903), friendly societies as well as trade unionism reflecting an 'ameliorative rather than revolutionary social philosophy'. (Popple 1995: 12)

The rise and fall of the Community Development Project experiment

As we described earlier, community work's ameliorative role in mainstream service provision had been theorised from the late-1940s in

Britain and, from the late-1960s, various reports appeared – not only the Calouste Gulbenkian Foundation Report (1968), which identified community work's importance for improving service provision in schools, social work, health care, planning and housing, but also the Seebohm Report (1968), which recommended a key role for community development in social work, and the Skeffington Report (1969), which recommended stronger public participation in urban planning (Ledwith 2005). At the same time, in 1968, the government established the Urban Aid Programme (UAP) and, in the following year, the national CDP. The UAP and CDPs were Home Office initiatives involving initially four (extended later to twelve) local projects in different parts of Britain with high levels of multiple deprivation. These reports and initiatives were aimed at addressing a number of particular concerns that had emerged by the end of the 1960s.

First, by the beginning of the 1960s the 'dominant complacent view that the British economy was delivering the affluent society to all its citizens was being challenged' (Popple 1995: 13). Prior to this period, urban problems were largely seen as physical problems – to be tackled through urban redevelopment, regional planning or new town development. The social aspects of urban problems were largely ignored, reflecting the belief that the establishment of the welfare state and Keynesian-managed full-employment had eradicated poverty. In his third social survey of York in 1950, Seebohm Rowntree had reported a steep decline since his previous study of 1936 in the percentage of households living in poverty. He attributed the bulk of this decline to government welfare reforms enacted during and after the Second World War. In addition, in 1956 Labour MP Anthony Crosland had argued that further wealth redistribution would have 'made little difference to the standard of living of the masses' (cited in Robson 2000: 98) – so successful had been the welfare state. However, by the mid-1960s these perspectives on the success of the welfare state were coming under increasing scrutiny.

In academic circles, the first to raise doubts publicly about Rowntree's claims was Peter Townsend in his article 'Measuring poverty', published in the *British Journal of Sociology* in 1962, and later in a booklet *The Poor and the Poorest*, published in 1965 with Brian Abel-Smith (which estimated that 7.5 million people were living in or close to the poverty line) (Abel-Smith and Townsend 1965, Townsend 1962). For Townsend and others, the welfare state had failed to eradicate poverty due to low wages, persistent unemployment and flaws in the social security system (benefit levels were set too low, whilst the stigma of social assistance means-testing had created a disincentive to claim). In terms of shaping the mind-set of the British public more generally, one of the most vivid and enduring images of social deprivation of this period was a television drama-documentary film called *Cathy Come Home*, first shown in 1966. At the time there were only two television channels – the BBC and ITV – and the majority of households with televisions would have watched this programme. The film exposed the harsh reality of poverty and homelessness, and the insensitive way state agencies responded. Its initial airing led to a public outcry and the foundation of Shelter, the housing charity. Despite the welfare state, poverty, squalid housing conditions and the housing shortage had not been tackled.

> This rediscovered poverty was initially interpreted in the light of the prevailing theory of *social pathology*. This perspective contended that, given the far-reaching nature of welfare state policies, the causes of any residual poverty had to be the 'pathological' behaviour of the people or communities who remained in poverty. This effectively directed attention away from systematic failures and structural inequalities and on to the more limited issue of how to deal with the individuals/groups still living in poverty. (Atkinson and Moon 1994: 33 – emphasis in original)

This growing recognition of the persistence of poverty and squalor prompted the social programmes set out in the various government reports and initiatives of the 1960s – which were largely: 'designed to reach further "into the community" (by which was meant, though never explicitly stated, working class neighbourhoods, thus paralleling in some ways the concern of the upper classes in the Victorian era about the possibilities of social unrest amongst a disenfranchised minority)' (Craig 1989: 8).

Second, the rediscovery of poverty coincided with public concern for growing urban unrest and 'racial' conflict. Black immigration had risen after the war due to the recruitment of many African-Caribbean and Asian workers to British industry, the expanding National Health Service and other public services at a time of labour shortages. After the war, many Afro-Caribbeans arrived on the SS Empire Windrush in 1948, and in 1956 immigration from the Caribbean peaked with 30,000 making the journey (Craig 1989, Race in Britain Special Edition 2001, Williams 1989). However, 'Successive British governments…failed to accept any major responsibility for properly meeting the needs of various black communities: when, as one observer put it, laissez-faire discrimination gave way to overt racialism which was then institutionalised in the discriminatory provision of jobs, housing and social services' (Craig 1989: 10).

Throughout the 1950s, the British media focused on the need to control 'black' ('coloured') immigration – seen as a problem in relation to housing, welfare, employment, crime and the 'national identity' (Solomos 2003). In August and September 1958, street fights broke out between Afro-Caribbean and White youth in Notting Hill, London, and St Anne's, Nottingham – portrayed in the media as 'race' or 'colour' riots. The media portrayal failed to acknowledge the reality of the tensions which had largely been caused by Teddy boys terrorising the immigrant community – partly due to their outrage that young black men were going out with *their* White women. As various commentators have observed, sexuality has been a significant theme in the way black people's identities have been constructed in western societies. Angela Davis for example, in 'The myth of the black rapist' written in 1981, demonstrates how African-American men have been constructed as a violent sexual threat to White women (Bhattacharyya and Gabriel 2004). A *Times'* report on 3 September 1958 summed up the resentment against young black men in Notting Hill at the time:

> There are three main causes of resentment against coloured inhabitants of the district. They are alleged to do no work and to collect a rich sum from the Assistance Board. They are said to find housing when white residents cannot. And they are charged with all kinds of misbehaviour, especially sexual. (Cited in Solomos 2003: 55)

The government response to the conflict between white and black people included the 1962 Commonwealth Immigrants Act which brought in restrictions cutting 'black' immigration – marking ethnic minority immigrants from others of white skin. Further restrictions were introduced in 1968, 1971 and 1981. In the election of 1963, the Conservative campaign in Smethwick in the West Midlands was accused of adopting the mantra 'If you want a nigger for a neighbour, vote Liberal or Labour'. In contrast, a more temperate attitude to 'race' was shown by the Labour government – who passed the first Race Relations Act in 1965. In 1966, Roy Jenkins, then Home Secretary, defined 'integration not as a flattening process of conformity, but cultural diversity, coupled with equality of opportunity ...' (Race in Britain Special Edition 2001: 3). However, urban tensions were exacerbated further by Enoch Powell's 'Rivers of Blood' speech in April 1968 – when Powell declared

'I am filled with foreboding. Like the Roman, I seem to see "the River Tiber foaming with much blood"' (cited in Race in Britain Special Edition 2001: 3–4). It is suggested by Popple (1995) that these growing racial tensions were also partly responsible for the establishment of the UAP in 1968 and the national CDP in 1969. Whilst the UAP had been planned before Powell's speech, the 1960s had witnessed so-called 'race riots' in US inner-city areas – putting pressure on politicians at home to take the urban question seriously.

A third problem the initiatives of the late-1960s were aiming to address was economic. The government were becoming increasingly concerned about the cost of welfare – a concern that had been reflected in the Seebohm Report's recommendations on the need for integrated social service departments – recommendations 'informed by the notions of rationalisation, merger and productivity which were common currency in the private sector' (Corkey and Craig 1978: 44–45). Additionally, in setting up the national CDP, the Home Office were quite clear that cost-effectiveness was to be a key concept in its implementation. In its general outline on the CDP in 1969, circulated to participating local authorities, the Home Office stated that:

> In the past, official efforts to analyse and meet social needs…were largely compartmentalised. Nowadays, however, the number of compartments is gradually diminishing (e.g. through developments like Seebohm); and their degree of separation is also lessening (e.g. through improvements in the techniques of planning and management). The CDP seeks to identify and demonstrate, by reference to the problems of selected small local communities, some practical ways of taking this trend further, through consultation and action among the separate departments of central and local government and voluntary organisations and the people of the local communities themselves. (Cited in Corkey and Craig 1978: 45)

On the one hand it could be argued that the shift towards community engagement in the 1960s reflected a concern in some quarters about the impersonality and institutionalisation of some social services – particularly social care in hospitals, and also in relation to other services and themes out of which a range of social movements emerged around campaigns relating to welfare rights, anti-racism, women's health, sexuality, rights for disabled people, housing, and alternative ways of living and working such as the 'utopian' communities and workers' collectives promoted by Patchwork Community and Solon Wandsworth (referred to in the introduction) (Cooper and Hawtin 1997, Creed 2006a and 2006b, Price 1983, Taylor 2003). At the same time, amongst the political left, the idea that 'class could be replaced by community as a model for change' (Robson 2000: 67) was beginning to take hold. By the late-1960s, 'community became the battlefield on which new banners were to be struck' (Robson 2000: 68–69). For many, 1968 is seen as a watershed in terms of both world-wide developments and radical community activism:

> 1968 was a year of revolt, rebellion and reaction throughout the world, with a catalogue of events which included: the student and worker struggles in Paris during May; student demonstrations and occupations at universities in several countries, including Britain; the Vietnamese Tet Offensive against American imperialism; world-wide protest and demonstrations against US involvement in Vietnam; racial riots in the United States; the assassinations of Martin Luther King and Robert Kennedy; the US Civil Right's Bill; the invasion and occupation of Czechoslovakia by Warsaw Pact troops; civil rights activists in Derry defying the government's ban on their marching; and the first mass open-air concert in Britain. It was a year of turmoil and change and, to quote one commentator, 'a year after which nothing could ever be the same again, a year which divides epochs, and a year which branded a generation for life'. (Popple 1995: 15)

In this environment, many advocates of radical community development saw genuine possibilities for their projects to achieve significant social transformation. However, in terms of the state's interest in community development, there is little doubt that its cost-saving potential was the key attraction. Significantly,

> From the politicians' point of view, although they appeared to be doing something... the initiative didn't actually cost much (the cost of the Urban Programme as a whole was not expected to exceed £25m). And while there was no commitment actually to act on the findings of CDP, it gave central government an opportunity to look more closely at the social problems of the inner city. (Corkey and Craig 1978: 46)

To a large extent, therefore, the establishment of CDP was an expedient response to a broad set of social welfare concerns, community tensions and economic imperatives at the time – indeed, its establishment can be seen as more important than what it did (Corkey and Craig 1978).

For Craig, what was significant about CDP was that for the first time domestically 'the state…was attempting to use community work as an instrument of social control' (Craig 1989: 11). Each CDP was established for a period of five years and had an action team (linked to a local authority), and a research and evaluation team (based in a university or polytechnic). Twenty-five per cent of the funding for action teams was provided by local authorities and 75 per cent by central government through the UAP. The research teams were funded 100 per cent by central government through the UAP.

The projects were based at Batley, Benwell (Newcastle), Canning Town (London), Clarksfield (Oldham), Cleator Moor (Cumbria), Glyncorrwg (West Glamorgan), Hillfields (Coventry), North Tyneside (North Shields), Paisley (Glasgow), Saltley (Birmingham), Southwark (London) and Vauxhall (Liverpool). A central team was established to co-ordinate the entire scheme and deduce its lessons for future policy making (WCML 2005: 1). 'When initiated, the projects supported a community pathology model of poverty that argued that people in disadvantaged communities failed to compete in the marketplace because of internal community or personal problems rather than structural inequalities' (Popple 1995: 18). An Inter-Project Editorial team was also established and produced three publications in 1977. One of these, *Gilding the Ghetto: The State and the Poverty Experiments*, described the initial purpose of the CDPs:

> Their brief rested on three important assumptions. Firstly that it was the 'deprived' themselves who were the cause of 'urban deprivation'. Secondly, the problem could best be solved by over-coming these people's apathy and promoting self help. Thirdly, locally-based research into the problems would serve to bring about changes in local and central government policy. (Cited in Robson 2000: 100)

The title 'Gilding the Ghetto' was inspired by the minutes of a conference called by Prime Minister Harold Wilson in 1969 to debate British and US poverty initiatives.

> Miss Cooper, chief inspector, children's department, Home Office, said: there appeared to be an element of looking for a new method of social control – what one might call an antivalue, rather than a value. 'Gilding the ghetto' or buying time, was clearly a

component in the planning of CDP and Model Cities. (Cited in Robson 2000: 100)

However,

> Things did not go to plan! Many, though not all, CDPs developed radical critiques of the economic and political policies underlying poverty and deprivation. Some came into conflict with the local authorities because of their involvement in tenants and other local community groups which opposed council policies on housing and other issues. (WCML 2005: 1)

In 1974 some CDP members formed the Political Economy Collective (PEC). The PEC applied a Marxist framework of analysis in its research on poverty, drawing attention to structural changes in the inner city brought about by economic processes beyond it. This Marxist analysis highlighted the link between local neighbourhood problems and the global processes causing them – in particular, the International Monetary Fund's (IMFs) restrictions on public finance (with implications for housing investment) and the disinvestment by multi-national corporations shifting finance capital abroad to cheaper locations (with implications for job prospects). This radical CDP approach identified 'the need therefore to build international and global alliances to combat these processes' (Craig, pers. comm.). This analysis directly challenged mainstream thinking at this time – the PEC case was that urban disadvantage was caused by structural constraints external to the area rather than psychological motivations internal to it. This assessment highlights one of the major failings of area-based policy interventions – that is, that they fail to address the systematic causes of social disadvantage which are largely structured around inequalities (e.g. based on class and ethnicity). However, as we saw above, this analysis led to a rift within the CDP movement with some of the projects adopting the radical critique – where urban problems were viewed as 'an inevitable by-product of uneven capitalist development' (Atkinson and Moon 1994: 49) – whilst others focused on 'the need to exert some influence on the "decision-making structures" of local government' (Robson 2000: 101).

In the case of those CDPs accepting the critical diagnosis, these projects now focused more on mobilising local populations to resist the activities of the capitalist state which were seen as working against their interests – for example, organising resistance against the Housing Finance Act 1972, which introduced 'fair rents' (a euphemism for 'quasi market rents') and a new rebate system for council tenants (effectively, making the less poor subsidise the poorest); and campaigns for better local services. However, as Atkinson and Moon explain:

> This exacerbated the problems of conflict between the teams and the local authorities and it hardly needs to be said that the adoption of such an approach also made the CDPs extremely unpopular with central government. It is perhaps one of the greatest of ironies that the Home Office found itself funding a bunch of Marxists. (Atkinson and Moon 1994: 50)

Radical community workers increasingly found themselves located in a contradictory position, seeing themselves as activists working alongside disadvantaged communities in campaigns *against* the same state agencies employing them – effectively, working 'in-and-against' the state.

In 1976, funding for CDPs ceased altogether (WCML 2005). As Robson puts it, 'In spite of the lip-service it pays to community initiative, government is really not interested in creating a monster which might lead to its own downfall' (Robson 2000: 83). Still, the 1960s and 1970s were considered by many as halcyon days for community development – a reflection of both the state's fear of social unrest and the radical mood of the time. However, the CDP experiments failed to produce sustainable, bottom-up community-led alternatives to state-led service provision. As Robson explains:

> The principal common factor in the separate initiatives outlined is the dominant role of the state, first of all, in initiating the projects from above and secondly in attempting to influence their subsequent development. All of those who were actively engaged in those initiatives enthusiastically adopted what they all described as a 'community development approach' to the specific social problems identified as their reason for being involved. However, almost all of the projects collapsed in an atmosphere of distrust and disillusionment. The CDP report [*Gilding the Ghetto*] was to claim that 'the state's fight against urban deprivation has been exposed like the "emperor's new clothes" as empty rhetoric'. (Robson 2000: 102–103)

This perhaps reflects the basic dilemma of the entire CDP enterprise – how could the projects meet the demands of deprived communities whilst, at the same time, satisfy the needs of the capitalist system that initiated them? It is clear that these experiments were never intended to address the real underlying causes of social disadvantage and deprivation but were, rather, expected to defuse the growing social turmoil of the period (caused by sustained social inequality and racism) whilst retaining the legitimacy of the state. This proved frustrating for many involved in the CDPs at the time. 'Community workers and researchers on the ground in Britain were having to come to terms with the philosophical and ideological constraints of locating their practice within what could be described as a piecemeal and a reformist tradition' (Robson 2000: 104). Community workers faced the prospect of either pursuing an approach based on the structuralist critique of social disadvantage (working as a revolutionary against the state, but ultimately not changing very much) or one based on pragmatism (working as an agent of and with the state, but ultimately having a minimalist effect on social disadvantage).

Robson is cautious about being overly optimistic about community development's radical possibilities, suggesting that it is naïve to think that it ever had 'the potential for the creation of a new counter-hegemonic project' (Robson 2000: 113). Indeed, he suggests that some would consider such a position to be socially irresponsible, neglectful of the possibility of at least ameliorating certain aspects of deprivation in a way that would enhance the wellbeing of disadvantaged communities. 'The poor could not wait for the structures to make adjustments or for the political changes to take place before their needs were addressed' (Robson 2000: 73).

Keynesianism 'in crisis' and the rise of the New Right

By the end of the 1970s the so-called social-democratic consensus that had shaped social policy and community relations in the post-war period came to an end. The seeds of the decline of this consensus had been planted in the mid-1970s. By this time, the conditions that had enabled the Keynesian model to work effectively – that is, the need for state investment in economic production and social capital (particularly housing) due to wartime destruction and the declining quality of existing provision, and the aggregate demand for this – were coming to an end. On top of steep rises in oil prices in the aftermath of the 1973 Arab-Israeli war – which caused inflation to escalate and economic growth to go into reverse – productivity gains in manufacture (based largely on the introduction of machinery and reliance on less skilled labour) generated a real decline in the demand for skilled manual labour (Byrne 2006). At the same time,

> the 'product mix' of the global capitalist economy has moved away from the heavy engineering products which were the main locus of skilled manual employment towards both light electronic goods and a range of services. These changes in the nature of the real economy are part of the story of the weakness of classic Keynesian policies over the last two decades. Another important factor has been the globalisation of finance capital based on new communications technology. For nationally based Keynesian policies to be effective, the political forces vested in nation states had to be able to control capital flows. (Byrne 2006: 37)

From the 1970s onwards, therefore, the Keynesian-welfare model became increasingly exposed (Jordan 2006). In response, Edward Heath's Conservative government attempted to cut public spending by restraining wage increases. This led to a national miners strike in 1973 and mass picketing of coal deliveries to power stations. The shortage of fuel led to a three-day working week for most industrial workers (Popple 1995). The conflict between government and trade unions at this time was described as 'a scene of industrial bitterness perhaps unparalleled since the General Strike of 1926' (Sked and Cook 1984, cited in Popple 1995: 23). 'These extraordinary events were to herald the beginnings of a decline in the post-war social-democratic consensus and to create the foundations for the rise of the New Right within the Conservative Party' (Popple 1995: 23). The Conservatives declared a State of Emergency in 1973 and a general election for February 1974 – which Heath lost.

In power, Labour had to tackle the highest recorded balance of payments deficit, rapidly rising unemployment (around 1.5 million by 1977) and inflation above 24 per cent. In doing so, they instigated further significant cuts in public expenditure (Popple 1995). It was James Callaghan, who succeeded Harold Wilson as Labour Prime Minister, who effectively converted to monetarism and heralded the end of the social-democratic consensus when, responding to pressure from the IMF, he declared an end to the era of tax-and-spend (Burden et al. 2000). The IMF, a brainchild of Keynes, had, by the 1970s, abandoned its original role and now insisted on lower balance of payment deficits, higher taxes and higher interest rates as conditions for its loans to governments. Slower economic growth and high rates of inflation in the

1970s provided an opportunity for right-wing economists critical of Keynes' theories 'to come to the fore as influences on political leaders, especially in the USA, and later in the UK' (Jordan 2006).

> An important part of the argument for the new model [of economic policy] was...that decisions about the funding of business investments should be made by commercial banks, and not by governments. Money could only go to its most efficient uses if bankers were free to make loans to those they judged to have the best prospects of being profitable. All this should happen within an overall supply of money which increased only in line with the growth in production. (Jordan 2006: 60)

Similarly, the new model of social policy from the late-1970s criticised state welfare for eroding:

> the freedom and independence of individuals by encouraging them to look to the state for *collective* decisions about their well-being, and generalized provision for their needs, based on the manipulation of aggregates. It wanted to restore the primacy of individual liberty, markets and a form of government which saw the preservation of these as its first task. (Jordan 2006: 61 – emphasis in original)

Callaghan's drive to cut Britain's deficit by cutting public spending – in line with the IMF's insistence on restructuring – led to further conflicts between government and trade unions (including public-sector worker strikes and the 'Winter of Discontent' 1978–1979), and ultimately the election of the Conservatives under Margaret Thatcher in 1979.

Thatcher's election paved the way for a new consensus in British politics. Her policies built on the monetarist economic model embraced by Callaghan and focused on meeting the needs of neo-liberal global market forces and restraining the scope of the public sector (Jordan 2006). Her policy initiatives drew largely on the neo-liberal notion of 'freedom of choice' and allowing individual consumers to make 'rational' choices in unfettered markets. Market forces were restored to prominence in political discourse, and in economic and social arrangements for organising people's lives. In relation to economic and social welfare, 'According to the neo-liberal narrative, exposing practices to market forces will ensure effective allocation of resources, efficient delivery of service and an economical production of commodities' (Smart 2003: 33). This account reflects the rise to prominence of Public Choice theory in

British politics, an idea built on a critique of public-sector welfare bureaucracies as not only inefficient and wasteful but also coercive in terms of enforcing uniformity in service provision. Neo-liberals claim, in contrast, that 'the market "permits wide diversity" and promotes economic freedom' (Smart 2003: 93). The neo-liberal response to the economic problems of the late-1970s was to abandon Keynesian welfarism and promote market-led reforms. This revival of the 'free market' philosophy in British politics led to a number of shifts in social policy emphasis: 'These include a reduction in some aspects of the role of the state, an increasing accommodation of social policy to the values of the free-market economy, a revalorization of individualism, an erosion of collective provision and an undermining of the public sector' (Smart 2003: 71).

From 1980, some services provided directly by the state were privatised – particularly council housing, initially through the right-to-buy and then later through stock transfer. At the same time, 'policies ... restricted the capacity for replacing and maintaining the social housing stock' (Taylor 2003: 69) – leading to the 'residualisation' of social housing as accommodation for those with least choice in the 'market'. This strategy divided working-class communities by separating the more affluent (those who could afford and bought the better quality council houses) from the least affluent (those who could not afford to buy and remained in the least desirable council stock).

In other areas of provision – such as health and education – 'efficiency' gains were to be achieved through the 'discipline' of quasi- or internal markets (Burden et al. 2000). Increasingly, more and more areas of social life were to become subjected to the discipline of market forces (Smart 2003). Additionally, in an effort to break the 'dependency culture' created by the welfare state, greater emphasis for social problems was to be placed on individuals and their families (Atkinson and Moon 1994).

> [T]he broader political objective of the Conservative governments of the 1980s was a moralisation of individuals in ways that were not dissimilar to the UP [Urban Programme], or the policies that have been put into place by the current Labour government. Pre-empting the pronouncements of Tony Blair, Margaret Thatcher argued that society is not an abstraction, 'but a living structure of individuals, families, neighbours and voluntary associations' .... She claimed that 'it is our duty to look after ourselves, and then to look after our neighbour ...'. (Imrie and Raco 2003: 10–11)

The 1986 Social Security Act in particular resulted in devastating hardship for the poorest communities in Britain by cutting benefit entitlements. Children were becoming the most vulnerable to poverty, whilst the number of people living in poverty increased by around 50 per cent between the 1980s and 1990s (Ledwith 2005).

Thatcherism in conflict

However, the Conservatives could not rely entirely on the free operation of market forces. The election of Mrs Thatcher coincided with one of the severest economic slumps in the post-war period. A major recession alongside deindustrialisation in the British economy led to a significant rise in unemployment. National unemployment figures were estimated at between 3million and 4million by 1985, with those working in traditional manufacturing industries in metropolitan areas hardest hit. Britain in the 1980s came to be characterised as a more sharply divided society based on class, ethnicity, gender and locality (including the emergence of a North–South divide and rapidly declining inner-cities) – a consequence of the combined effect of economic restructuring and social policy choices (Atkinson and Moon 1994). These changes were to provoke further hostilities in the inner-cities.

In 1984, class conflict erupted in the guise of the coal miners' strike. For Thatcher, the miners were 'the enemy within' – a danger to liberty. For Arthur Scargill, the National Union of Miners (NUM) President, the miners' action was not simply against an employer, the British Coal Board, but against a government aided and abetted by the judiciary, the police and the media. The strike was effectively a battle of ideals between a government (keen to close down 'uneconomic' mines and resist 'excessive' trade union powers) and a union (keen to save mines from closure in the interest of sustaining the mining communities). Effectively, this was class conflict.

The height of the conflict occurred on 18 June 1984, at the British Steel coking plant, Orgreave, in South Yorkshire. A significant watershed in the early 1980s was a change in the way the state police responded to conflict:

> Following serious public disorder in Toxteth and Brixton at the start of the '80s [discussed below], the police had secretly refined new techniques, effectively 'softer' versions of colonial riot tactics as used, for example, by the Hong Kong Police, which in turn featured remarkable similarities to classic Roman military tactics with shields, lines

of 'foot soldiers' and 'cavalry'. These would now be used against pickets where deemed necessary. (Giles 2002: 1)

5,000 to 6,000 pickets converged on Orgreave to blockade 'scab' labour and coke lorries attempting to leave the plant. Police from ten counties were deployed in 181 Police Support Units (PSUs) – at least 4,200 policemen, although some accounts claim up to 8,000. 58 police dogs were deployed and between 42 and 50 mounted police (Giles 2002).

> Unlike previous demonstrations, where pickets had been prevented from reaching their intended 'target' through use of road blocks and diversions, this time the police actually escorted them to Orgreave and into a pre-determined holding area in a field in front of the 'Topside' of the coke plant. Looking around, pickets could see a solid line of police to their front and mounted police with dog handlers loosely containing them to the left, right and right rear. About half a mile to their rear, the Sheffield to Worksop railway line ran at the bottom of a steep embankment, forming the fourth side of a rough rectangle, with only a narrow road bridge into Orgreave village offering a way out. Was this a prepared 'battleground'? Most pickets and even one of the police recently interviewed believe that it was, and that the police were under instructions from the government to take a tough line with demonstrators…. (Giles 2002: 2)

The police were commanded by Assistant Chief Constable Anthony Clement. In addition to the ordinary police officers, Clement was also authorised to use new policing formations with crash helmets and short shields, and trained in the then new arrest 'snatch squad' or dispersal tactics – although these had never been used before on mainland Britain.

> Particularly when combined with mounted police, they represented a potent tactical force easily capable of defeating rioters…. Most important of all, their use would represent a major turning point in British police tactics, i.e. a deliberate change in emphasis from defensive to offensive tactics, something that until now had not been thought to be acceptable to the British public. (Giles 2002: 2)

Tactically, the police's strategy of preparing the 'battleground' and deploying new policing formations never before used on mainland Britain was clearly successful in terms of defeating the miners and aiding Thatcher's purpose of closing 'uneconomic' mines and restraining trade union powers – again, a major watershed in terms of the future wellbeing of working-class communities. It remained a style of policing throughout the Thatcher era to deal with the 'enemy within' perceived as a threat to the economic and social order – for example, against marchers in support of the miners' strike in London (February 1985); against travellers at the 'Battle of the Beanfield' (June 1985); against print workers picketing 'scab' labour and lorries at Rupert Murdoch's News International site at Wapping in London (1986–1987); and in Trafalgar Square during the poll tax demonstration (1990). This was a ruthless style of policing that the British media deliberately tried to disguise. As Neil Goodwin observes when comparing Orgreave and the Battle of the Beanfield:

> There were many similarities between Orgreave and the Beanfield. Both the travellers and the striking miners were considered to be 'an enemy within', a threat to democracy and the economy. Both were depicted in the right-wing press as an invasion force – the 'other' – a marauding army intent on occupying private land, abusing local people, and openly flouting the law. Both provided the Thatcher government with the ideal public order situations with which to manufacture and sell increasingly draconian police powers to an increasingly gullible British public – in both cases, laws preventing movement and congregation. Both Orgreave and the Beanfield involved a preordained police operation, the cooperation of several neighbouring county forces, and an increasingly para-militarised style of policing, which was pro-active rather than responsive. Finally, both the Battle of Orgreave and the Battle of the Beanfield involved a media cover up – ITN's cover-up at the Beanfield [film footage was censored], and the BBC swapping the order of events during their coverage of Orgreave, where a police baton charge provoked a stone-throwing incident, and not the other way around as reported on the BBC news. (Goodwin 2005: 178–179)

Arguably, Orgreave and the Beanfield represent a defining moment in respect of post-war civil rights – not only in terms of the state violence inflicted, but also in terms of paving the way for the punitive legislation that followed (from the 1986 Public Order Act, which imposed strict restrictions on public gatherings, trespass and civil protest, right through to the more recent legislation aimed at restricting people's movements and styles of political agitation).

Despite the increasing draconian nature of Conservative legislation on civil rights, political protest continued to flourish in the 1980s. A particularly important contribution to the campaigns of this period include forms of organising influenced by radical feminism and reflected in such campaigns as 'Reclaim the Night' (marches against street violence and rape), anti-pornography campaigns (including the firebombing of a bookshop in Leeds) and the Greenham Common Women's Peace Movement (GCWPM) (Cooper and Hawtin 1997). The GCWPM in particular highlighted important lessons for community action. As Dominelli argues: 'By compelling community workers to re-examine traditional positions, Greenham Women became a catalyst for changing the nature of community work to promote more egalitarian organisational and less stigmatising forms of participation' (Dominelli 2006: 202).

The 'Greenham Camp' was established in 1981 to protest the siting of US cruise missiles in Britain and maintained a presence until 2000. The women organised spontaneously (without community workers) and decided to exclude men to prevent patriarchal ways of working – hierarchies, male domination and aggression – from impeding the campaign. They illustrated how women could work collaboratively in the political arena. Their way of working involved collective, egalitarian relations and non-oppressive practices which allowed women to personally determine the extent of their own contribution to the struggle (Dominelli 2006).

The central attack on municipal socialism

Another source of the 'enemy within' for Thatcher was municipal socialism – which required her government to embark on a concerted effort throughout its time to impose strict constraints on local government powers.

> [I]t began to be clear that the Conservative's social and economic policies were not only responsible for a rapidly deteriorating situation within the urban centres, but that the legal and financial ability of local government to respond to this situation was also to be severely curtailed.... By increasing financial and legal constraints on local councils, the government sought to diminish the scope of collective services provided by them. (Craig 1989: 14)

The neo-liberal Conservative's dominance within central government in the 1980s had determined the resolve of the new urban Left to operate within Labour-controlled authorities from where they could spearhead their opposition. From 1982, a number of Labour-controlled councils were guided by councillors representative of the new urban Left, particularly in London (initially with the Greater London Council (GLC), Lambeth, Southwark, Lewisham, Hackney, Greenwich, Islington and Camden, but later Haringey, Brent, Hammersmith, Ealing and Waltham Forest), Sheffield and Manchester (Lansley et al. 1989). The activities of these councillors succeeded, to a significant degree, in improving the quality of life for many local communities. 'Many interesting and important initiatives were developed which reflected a new and more open form of community emphasis across the whole range of council services (the Greater London Council being the example *par excellence* with its women's campaigns, police monitoring unit and anti-racist and anti-sexist policies.)' (Craig 1989: 15).

Under Ken Livingstone, the GLC invested *inter alia* in specific support services and cultural activities for gays and lesbians. 'In a small way, by providing social events, information, concerts and venues, but also by relaxing and changing the prevailing ethos, the GLC made London a better place to live for many lesbians and gay men' (Lansley et al. 1989: 163). Thatcher became increasingly distrustful of municipal authorities – seeing their potential for becoming power bases of socialism. She therefore continued to find ways of reducing their spending powers, particularly in relation to housing, education and social services:

> The attacks on town hall spending served [Mrs Thatcher's] wider political objectives – to weaken the power of local councils and reduce the grip of collectivism .... The subsequent cuts can therefore be seen alongside other initiatives – the forced sale of council houses, restrictions on direct labour organisations, privatisation and the introduction of enterprise zones and urban development corporations – as part of a political strategy to weaken the role of the local state and, as she later put it, 'to roll back the frontiers of socialism'. (Lansley et al. 1989: 24–25)

Under the 1980 Local Government, Planning and Land Act, the old system for supporting local government finance was replaced with a new Block Grant which was to be based on centrally-determined assessments rather than local assessments of what was needed to be spent. The Act also introduced new controls over local authority capital expenditure. Despite these measures, government ministers remained dissatisfied at the level of cuts, leading to the introduction of a system of targets and penalties in 1981/1982. If an authority chose to spend over target its Block Grant would be cut. Under the 1982 Local Government Finance Act, the Conservatives established the Audit Commission to monitor local authority spending for 'value for money'. This Act also stopped local authorities raising additional revenue by abolishing supplementary rates (Stoker 1991). A significant feature of central government's withdrawal of support for local government, however, was the emergence of a number of decentralisation and 'partnership' initiatives led by local authorities 'keen to re-establish their credentials as providers in the face of the privatisation agenda of the Thatcher government' (Taylor 2003: 23).

Assessing the effects of Thatcher's neo-liberal social and economic reforms in the 1980s, some commentators see this period as a time of 'indifference and, in some instances, outright antagonism towards poor families and the social services on which they depend' (Walker 1987, cited in Popple 1995: 25). Increasing poverty, unemployment and social inequality in Thatcher's Britain provoked major conflict and violence.

Inner-city tensions and the re-emergence of 'race'

Inner-city tensions in the form of 'riots' flared up in a number of urban areas during the summers of 1980, 1981, 1985 and 1986 – areas with significant African-Caribbean residence. In response to these troubles and a perceived rise in the fear of crime more generally, 'community safety' emerged as a central urban policy issue in the 1980s. '[T]he community safety agenda followed the discovery of apparently disproportionate fear in the British Crime Surveys, and the left realist rejoinder which found the lived realities of fear of people in high crime areas to be most definitely proportionate' (Gilling 1999: 2).

The question of effective crime control came to dominate the political agenda, particularly following the 'riots'. For the Conservative political right, such tensions have traditionally been perceived as an immigration issue – exemplified by Enoch Powell's 'rivers of blood' speech in Birmingham (mentioned earlier) and Margaret Thatcher's assertion in 1978 about the possibility of Britain being 'swamped by people with a different culture' (cited in Hasan 2000: 174).

Racial tensions had been simmering during the latter years of Callaghan's Labour administration – fuelled largely by the activities of the National Front (NF) and racist proclamations by 'celebrities' of the time. For instance, in August 1976, rock musician Eric Clapton called on people to 'Vote for Enoch Powell' and 'Stop Britain from becoming a black colony' (cited in Vulliamy 2007: 23). David Bowie had previously pronounced that Adolf Hitler was 'the first rock star' and Britain needed a 'right-wing dictatorship' (cited in Vulliamy 2007: 23). These incidents partly contributed to the rise of 'Rock Against Racism' (RAR) in 1977 – a counter anti-racist movement that demonstrated 'how music and youth culture could activate and energise' (Vulliamy 2007: 27). In 1976, the NF gained 120,000 votes at local elections across London, 44,000 in Leicester and, with the British National Party, 38 per cent of the vote in Blackburn. The NF's political perspective then can be summed up by the views of one of its leaders at the time – John Kingsley Read – who gave a speech in 1976 berating 'wogs and coons' and reacting to the death of a young Sikh with 'One down. One million to go' (cited in Vulliamy 2007: 27). On 13th August 1977, an NF 'anti-mugging' march through Lewisham – an area with a significant black population where some police operated a tactic known as PNH ('Police Nigger Hunt') – was confronted by around 10,000 anti-racists. The incident marked the first occasion of the use of police riot gear on mainland Britain and running battles erupted in New Cross. The march was ultimately stopped by the counter demonstration. 'By the end of the year, the umbrella group had been formed which would harness these energies against racism and fascism and leave its symbol, the arrow, forever indented on the epoch: the Anti Nazi League' (Vulliamy 2007: 23). The Anti-Nazi League built support from a wide constituency that included football managers (e.g. Brian Clough and Terry Venables), religious leaders, politicians and musicians (including the Clash, Steel Pulse and Tom Robinson) (Vulliamy 2007). The general election campaign of 1979 saw a major demonstration at an NF meeting in Southall – an area of significant Asian presence – on 23 April. A police riot erupted around dusk at which a Special Patrol Group officer struck and killed schoolteacher Blair Peach (Vulliamy 2007).

The 1979 election saw the NF poll less than one per cent of the vote and later they all but disappeared. Vulliamy suggests the reason for this was because:

> much of the NF's rhetoric on immigration had been adopted and repackaged by the emergent force and resounding victor at the polls, Margaret Thatcher, picking at the bones of a failed Labour Party so that the disaffected Labour vote that had drifted to the Front now swung behind the Conservatives. (Vulliamy 2007: 31)

Despite the demise of the NF, a media-induced focus on a 'race problem' in the early 1980s continued to fuel a hostile political rhetoric on 'race'. For example, following the summer riots of 1981 – riots provoked partly by press indifference to black deaths in custody and oppressive policing (Race in Britain Special Edition 2001) – the *Daily Mail* carried the headline 'Black War on the Police' (6 July 1981, cited in Solomos 2003: 146) – depicting the events in racialised terms. Sir John Stokes, then MP for Halesowen and Stourbridge, referred to the riots as an indication of 'something new and sinister in our long national history' (cited in McGhee 2005: 19). Lord Scarman, in his report of the inquiry into the Brixton disturbances of 1981, denied the role of subjective or institutional racism in British society (particularly within the police force – despite their heavy deployment of the 'sus' law, and stop and search powers disproportionately targeted at black youth) and pointed instead to problems within the African-Caribbean community. Riots broke out in Brixton in April 1981 after the London Metropolitan Police launched 'Operation Swamp 81' to tackle burglary and robbery – in six days, police officers stopped 943 people and arrested 118. Similar violent disturbances followed in Toxteth in Liverpool where the police used CS gas for the first time in mainland Britain. Further disturbances followed in other parts of the country and continued sporadically throughout the first half of the decade – including the 1985 disturbance on Broadwater Farm estate in Tottenham when PC Keith Blakelock was violently killed (Race in Britain Special Edition 2001). For Scarman, however, these disturbances were largely due to a toxic mix of social disadvantage and an undisciplined African-Caribbean 'family culture':

> [W]hat did exist in Brixton (although exacerbated by flawed and unimaginative policing practices) and elsewhere in the country were African-Caribbean communities blighted by 'racial disadvantage'…. Thus, Scarman managed to turn the inquiry away from the legal and political questions of institutional racism and discrimination by the police against the African-Caribbean community, to a focus on the social problems associated with racial disadvantage, as being the root of the problems in Brixton. (McGhee 2005: 22)

Effectively, the Scarman Report provided:

> the official seal to the definition of the origins and extent of African-Caribbean crime through tying these to distinct patterns of protest and family life that were presented as being characteristic of

African-Caribbean culture. This shift in emphasis in the Scarman Report, as depicted by Gilroy, was evident in the media reporting of police and Conservative politicians' statements in the summer of 1981, which focused on violent street rioting and the alleged weakness of the family unit in West Indian communities…, which was viewed as being incapable of disciplining young people. The Prime Minister at the time, Margaret Thatcher, was quick to place the responsibility for the riots with the families of the 'rioters'. She was reported in *The Times* on 10 July 1981 as saying that if the parents concerned could not control the actions of their children, what could the government do to stop them. (McGhee 2005: 22)

Given the 'incontrovertible evidence that the British riots of the 1980s…were multiracial' (Hasan 2000: 185), the unrest could not be described as 'race' riots. However, this description had 'symbolic significance' for the powerful in that it 'appeared to forge a new link between "race" and inner-city disorder. There was a new "enemy within" and it was black' (Graham and Clarke 2002: 172). Such impressions led to some new calls for stricter immigration controls and repatriation, although less extreme Conservatives viewed the 'rioting' as a law and order issue – as irrational criminal violence requiring a firm police response: 'the centrality of the law and order theme and the expressed fear that disorderly street violence would become an established part of British life reflected the fact that the re-establishment of order was the main topic of concern in official political disclosures during this period' (Solomos 2003: 149).

Liberal/social democrats, whilst continuing to view the riots as 'irrational acts', did acknowledge a link between the conflict and urban deprivation, suggesting the need for better resource redistribution to deprived areas. This is reflected in Roy Hattersley's contribution to the parliamentary debate on the 1981 civil disturbances when he outlined four common themes: inadequate housing; a lack of social amenities; a failing education system; and high levels of youth unemployment. A similar analysis appeared in the Scarman Report published in November 1981 – although this also highlighted feelings of alienation and disempowerment (Solomos 2003). Despite this, whilst the 'government had carried out many changes in relation to the police after 1981 it had done remarkably little in respect of political, social and economic problems' (Solomos 2003: 153).

In response to the riots, the government appointed a Cabinet committee to review inner-city policy and the Urban Programme – 'so offering the overall appearance that it was dealing with the issues raised by them' (Popple 1995: 27). As Popple observes: 'Throughout this period the Urban Programme and the Inner City Partnership schemes were used to fund local community projects in areas that experienced unrest. Community work was again employed as a palliative when the substantial resources needed to overcome the major injustices were not forthcoming' (Popple 1995: 27).

Community development techniques were being used at neighbourhood level – to quash any further discontent in these troubled places – within a wider context of cuts in public expenditure on health, housing and social services. At the same time, unemployment continued to rise after 1981 (Burden et al. 2000).

Thatcherism, urban policy and the exacerbation of social divisions

Thatcher's Conservative administration diagnosed the urban problem as the lack of appropriate infrastructure to facilitate inward economic investment. 'Regeneration, Thatcher-style, was characterised by the use of public subsidies, tax breaks, and the reduction in planning and other regulatory controls, as mechanisms to create a context to encourage corporate capital to invest in cities' (Imrie and Raco 2003: 3). In addition, the government's urban initiatives were based on the premise that the economic benefits of these private-sector, property-led economic regeneration schemes would 'trickle down' to all members of the population. Because of Thatcher's distrust of municipal socialism, discussed earlier, the role of local government in these ventures was largely bypassed through the establishment of non-elected quangos (such as the Urban Development Corporations and Task Forces) to manage them (Atkinson and Moon 1994).

The Conservative's urban initiatives in the 1980s are largely perceived to have failed economically and socially. In particular, the expected trickle-down effect did not materialise and social disadvantage was exacerbated. As Taylor argues:

> Most evaluations of the economic development programmes of the 1980s were lukewarm about their achievements. Economic development in its 1980s incarnation led to a decrease in the number of unskilled and semi-skilled jobs, an increase in part-time and casual jobs which did not provide a living wage, and a benefit system that provided the most minimal income but discouraged claimants from

increasing this through casual work…. Notably, economically-driven urban initiatives failed to deliver jobs or housing to the indigenous population…. Wealth did not trickle down. Jobs went to outsiders and new housing brought in a more affluent population which either displaced the indigenous population or, through a process of gentrification, pushed it to the margins. (Taylor 2003: 28)

Imrie and Raco share this assessment of the Conservative's urban policy failings:

Regeneration projects tended to encourage gentrification and rising land values, but did little to tackle an endemic shortage of affordable housing, job insecurity, and the proliferation of low-waged employment. In particular, the persistence of social fragmentation and the intensification of social disadvantage in 'sink estates' were cited as evidence of policy failure and of the difficulties for poorer people to exercise their citizenship through Thatcher's preferred route – as dutiful consumers. (Imrie and Raco 2003: 11–12)

At the same time, and in response to increasing anxiety about the police's capacity to maintain law and order in light of the riots – effectively, a 'crisis in legitimacy' (Gilling 1999: 3) for policing – the government stressed the need for partnership working, involving various agencies and the community at large, in crime control; effectively, this represented 'the abrogation of sole responsibility for the crime problem by state criminal justice agencies' (Gilling 1999: 3). The combination of a legitimacy crisis in policing and retrenchment in welfare spending meant that, as far as poor communities were concerned:

if the fear of these people…was to be tackled, it was going to have to come mainly from their own efforts: hence the first prong of the government's dual strategy around the mid-1980s was an active citizenship drive in crime prevention, especially through the vehicle of neighbourhood watch and the promotion, through publicity, of 'practical ways to cut crime'. (Gilling 1999: 4)

The second prong in this dual strategy was to make community safety an integral objective of urban policy more generally and urban regeneration in particular. Community safety (as opposed to crime prevention) had been adopted by many local authority led partnerships set up in the 1980s to tackle neighbourhood crime – even though such initiatives received little support from a Conservative government ideologically hostile to the idea of giving local government a stronger role in crime control. The Conservatives rejected the recommendation of the Home Office Standing Conference on Crime Prevention Report 1991 (the Morgan Report) that local government should be given a stronger coordinating role for community safety. They had, however, established the Safer Cities Programme in 1988 to support local initiatives in 'creating a safer environment in which enterprise, community activity and personal responsibility can flourish' (Home Office Press Release, cited in Gilling 1999: 5). The priority was to create a more attractive urban environment for business and commerce. 'The community to be made safer by community safety was the frightened (business) community, not the disadvantaged community' (Gilling 1999: 6). Consequently, it is therefore no surprise that research on local government community safety activities, published by the Local Government Management Board in 1996, showed that the most common strategy deployed was town centre security with CCTV systems predominant. Summarising the situation of that time, Gilling states:

> [T]he main point to emerge is that local authorities are constrained with regard to how far they can resist the logic of community safety set at the wider national level. Their involvement is often on terms which limit the degree of local autonomy which may be shown. Thus, whilst many local authorities are now Labour-controlled, and many of these would take a more liberal interpretation of community safety which presented it as a means of addressing some of the problems of disadvantaged communities where crime and fear of crime are normally higher, they can not necessarily go that far down this path, although ... this is not to say that they do not make attempts in this direction, or that such attempts are not, on occasion, successful. There is, however, strong pressure, some of which may be from the private sector and some of which may indeed be populist, which forces them in another direction. (Gilling 1999: 8)

The main thrust of government policy was largely in response to populist and media fuelled anxieties about 'dangerous people' exporting 'their roguish trade beyond the neighbourhood' (Gilling 1999: 9) and threatening the interests of the 'respectable'. It is an agenda 'which has become increasingly intolerant of disorder and its negative consequences for the local economy, housing management and, obviously, the community's sense of safety' (Gilling 1999: 1). As such, it is an agenda that undermines possibilities for more constructive policy responses in meeting the needs of those suffering the worst fears and the most severe social harms – that is, those people:

> [W]ho have been left on other occasions to the vagaries of the market and the beneficence of the 'trickle down effect', to exclusion from the labour market, and to cutbacks in welfare benefits and social services…. State agencies have not been especially accommodating of this group's interests in other policy areas, and there is no reason to suppose that community safety, or at least the state-sponsored version of it, is any different in this regard. (Gilling 1999: 4)

It is evident, therefore, that the advancement of 'market principles' in social policy throughout the 1980s in Britain was not to the benefit of the most disadvantaged communities. Many public services and welfare entitlements have been lost whilst what state provision has remained is increasingly directed at programmes which continue to deliver central government's agenda – that is, facilitating the interests of the business community and protecting the powerful from threats posed by 'dangerous Others'.

The combination of John Major replacing Thatcher as Prime Minister in 1990 and a slow-down in economic growth led to a slight change in urban policy in the early 1990s with greater emphasis on community participation and partnership working through City Challenge and the Single Regeneration Budget (SRB) Challenge Fund. However, many saw this change as little more than tokenistic – with little happening in terms of genuine community empowerment in urban policy decision making (Imrie and Raco 2003).

The emergence of the British 'underclass'

The New Right's social policies coincided with Britain's transformation to a post-industrial capitalist society and were largely driven in anticipation of the changing interests of business given the changing economic context – in particular, their desire for labour market flexibility. A major consequence of this was heightened social inequality and what has become referred to as 'social exclusion' – reflected in widening income differentials and spatial segregation (Byrne 2006). For the New Right, this development represented the emergence of a new 'dangerous' community – the 'underclass', a sub-terrain of the lower social order who displayed a culture of dependency that had been encouraged by the welfare state. 'Lone mothers' and their 'feral' offspring ('problem youth') were particularly singled out as being responsible for this situation – in particular, the absence of 'respectable fathers ... is [seen as] the causal element for a life course of deprivation and deviance' (Byrne 2006: 24). This account was applied to the British context by the American sociologist Charles Murray, in collaboration with *The Sunday Times* and the Institute of Economic Affairs (Murray 1990). The cause of poverty was seen to lie in the obduracy of poor people themselves – their refusal to work and to be morally 'responsible'. Poor and disadvantaged communities were seen as dysfunctional – unable to integrate in the world of paid work or society's values more generally.

> The underclass has come to carry exactly the mixture of 'horrible fascination' that characterized nineteenth-century investigations into, and reportage of, the dangerous classes. They are in, but not of, the city, representing an exotic and unregulated other way of life. As in the nineteenth century, the underclass plays across our concerns and fears about class, 'race' and gender. (Graham and Clarke 2002: 175)

The underclass thesis had important implications for the way 'youth' were perceived at the time. Whilst Stanley Cohen (2004) had identified the emergence of a 'moral panic' in relation to aspects of youth subcultures back in the 1960s, by the 1990s this had developed into a more generalised anxiety about the state of youth in Britain – or, more specifically, the state of white working-class and black youth (perceived as victims of the economic recession and a threat to community wellbeing) (Campbell 1993). In 1991, 'rioting' had broken out on some of the most disadvantaged peripheral housing estates in England and Wales – Ely in Cardiff, Blackbird Leys near Oxford, and Meadowell, Elswick and Scotswood on Tyneside – rather than the inner-cities. These events appeared to confirm the New Right's notion of an emerging 'underclass' in British society.

This focus on an underclass legitimated a range of punitive social policy measures aimed at 'curing' this 'breed' of their welfare dependency and taming their 'incivility' (particularly through cuts in benefit entitlement). Young working-class women in particular were to become the target of such reforms and, since the 1990s, there has been a particular intensification in hostility towards their children. As recently as the 1970s, some politicians in Britain subscribed to the notion of the existence of a degenerate underclass whose breeding should be regulated – with some calling for sterilization as a solution.

Keith Joseph, in a speech at Edgbaston, Birmingham on 19 October 1974, set out his project for the remoralisation of British society in the build up to the then Conservative party's leadership contest. In this, he maintained:

> The balance of our population, our human stock, is threatened ... [by a] ... high and rising proportion of children being born to mothers least fitted to bring children into the world and bring them up. They are born to mothers who were first pregnant in adolescence in socio-economic classes 4 and 5. Many of these girls are unmarried, many are deserted or divorced or soon will be. Some are of low intelligence, most of them of low educational attainment. They are unlikely to be able to give children the stable emotional background, the consistent combination of love and firmness which are more important than riches. They are producing problem children, the future unmarried mothers, delinquents, denizens of our borstals, subnormal educational establishments, prisons and hostels for drifters .... Yet what shall we do? ... Proposals to extend birth control facilities to these classes of people ... evokes entirely understandable moral opposition .... But which is the lesser evil, until we are able to remoralize whole groups and classes of people ... ? (Cited in Trombley 1988: 30)

This speech reflects the degree to which Malthusian notions of population control have retained an attraction for the extreme political right.

Whilst the notion of an underclass is a highly contested one, it is an idea that has held significance for the way dangerous people and dangerous places have been perceived and treated by policy interventions since Victorian times: 'Fears about the underclass bear a remarkable similarity to the nineteenth-century anxieties about the dangerous classes .... Once again it is claimed that the city contains a virulent threat to the social order, and one that is a volatile cocktail of immorality, criminality and political instability' (Graham and Clarke 2002: 176).

The underclass thesis encouraged a sharper focus on the notion of 'local criminals intimidating poor communities' (Lea 2002: 161) and arguments for welfare retrenchment. With declining welfare support – 'to the detriment of poor communities too fragmented to sustain much notion of collective security' (Lea 2002: 162) – grew increasing public anxiety about how to manage the victims of welfare retrenchment and their 'undesirable and risky' (Lea 2002: 162) behaviour.

The punitive turn – the criminalisation of social policy

Since the 1990s, the policy solution to the threat from the underclass has increasingly been about resorting to stricter criminal justice resolutions rather than social welfare measures – effectively, the criminalisation of social policy:

> [C]riminalisation as a way of managing an increasing variety of socio-economic problems and behaviours is increasing…. [T]he advance of criminalisation is an obvious result of the relative decline of mechanisms of collective negotiation and planning characteristic of the Keynesian welfare state. Social problems are increasingly seen as individual problems of behaviour and responsibility rather than as collective political issues of resource allocation, while the state turns to criminal law rather than to social planning as the preferred form of intervention and regulation of social processes…. The result is the general criminalisation of the socially excluded poor, the new 'dangerous class'. (Lea 2002: 162)

This punitive turn in British social policy, whilst initially influenced by New Right realist discourse, was soon to be applauded by Left realists – academics from 'the Left' who argued that the fear of crime represented the lived reality of many disadvantaged city residents and that this should be acknowledged and taken more seriously by the Left. In arguing this way, Left realists were accepting (and ultimately promoting) a socially-constructed and populist view of 'crime' as those acts committed by 'dangerous people' in 'dangerous places'. Meanwhile, the crimes of the powerful remain largely immune from interrogation:

> What is striking in this process of crime definition and the connections between crime and the city is that it never includes white-collar or corporate crime. The 'City', with its crimes of fraud, corruption, illegal trading and misuse of funds (such as pension funds) is never included as a 'criminal' place, even though the personal consequences of its crimes can be devastating and are intimately bound with urbanism as a way of life. (Graham and Clarke 2002: 177)

What is significant about the rise to predominance of the realist discourse in social policy from the 1990s and its emphasis on 'blaming the poor' for the social tensions of the time is that it further marginalised more meaningful critiques that highlighted the more deep-rooted structural changes that had occurred in British society and which were having a profound effect on the way community relations were being played out.

The legacy of Thatcherism for communities in Britain

Lipietz characterises the effects of neo-liberal reforms on the shape of the social structure of society as a shift from a hot-air balloon (where most people shared a standard of living somewhere in the middle) to an hourglass (representing increasing inequality between those at the top and those at the bottom of society). The widening social divide witnessed in hourglass societies is largely explained by reference to increasing disparities in earned incomes, cuts in welfare redistribution and reduced opportunity for social mobility (Burden et al. 2000, Byrne 2006). There had been some attempt during the Keynesian-welfare era to reduce income inequalities – benefiting some of the poorest communities in relative terms. However, 'In postindustrial capitalism economic restructuring and changes in policy have interacted to produce more unequal and excluding societies' (Byrne 2006: 85).

A key indicator of this change is data on childhood poverty. In terms of the percentage of children in the UK living in households with less than 60 per cent of the median household income, 'In 1979, 12 per cent of children in relation to total income and 14 per cent of children after housing costs had been deducted fell into this category. By 1991–92 the respective figures were 26 per cent and 31 per cent' (Byrne 2006: 88). Child poverty had doubled as a consequence of Thatcherism. The incidence of rising inequality and poverty in Britain is experienced differently – not only in relation to social class, but also 'gender' (particularly with regard to households headed by female single parents who are likely to be poor – not so much because of welfare dependency, but due to the low wage levels within the service sector economy), 'race' (with Pakistanis and Bangladeshis particularly disadvantaged) and age (particularly with regard to the increasingly limited job opportunities for traditional early school leavers) (Byrne 2006).

The deeply-divided social and spatial landscape developed by industrial capitalism and recorded by Engels in 1845 (Engels 1987) was still evident in the 1990s – with profound consequences for social mobility and community wellbeing. As Engels observed, with the rapid extension of industrial manufacture in the nineteenth century, the population was reduced to:

> the two opposing elements, workers and capitalists.... In the place of the former masters and apprentices came great capitalists and working men who had no prospect of rising above their class. ... [T]he destruction of the former organization of hand-work, and the disappearance of the lower middle class, deprived the working man of all possibility of rising into the middle class himself. Hitherto he had always had the prospect of establishing himself somewhere as master artificer, perhaps employing journeymen and apprentices; but now, when master artificers were crowded out by manufacturers, when large capital had become necessary for carrying on work independently, the working-class became, for the first time, an integral, permanent class of the population, whereas it had formerly often been merely a transition leading to the bourgeoisie. Now, he who was born to toil had no other prospect than that of remaining a toiler all his life. (Engels 1987: 62)

As alluded to above, evidence suggests that opportunities for social mobility had been improved by policies based on the Keynesian-welfare consensus.

> During the golden years of Keynesianism, the combination of full employment and strong trade unions with a considerable growth in household earnings, derived in large part from increased economic participation by married women, meant that most households could reasonably access a material standard of living which was that of the general social norm. For example, most council housing estates in the UK were occupied by working-class people with steady jobs and a standard of living comparable with that of those living in owner-occupied areas. Movement from council housing to owner occupation was often the product of quite small incremental gains in income. Upward social mobility was general. ... There were very poor people living in appalling conditions in the industrial cities, but for most people the middle range of experience was the norm and most people saw a prospect of upward mobility for themselves or their children. (Byrne 2006: 170–171)

However, by the 1980s the dynamics of personal mobility had changed due to the loss of skilled manual jobs, erosion of trade union power, pitiful service-sector wage levels and increasing job insecurity

(Burden et al. 2000, Byrne 2006). These financial difficulties were exacerbated by polarised residential experiences (Cooper 2005). This is not solely a matter of housing position but residential location: '[S]patial location determines access to crucial social goods, in particular to different kinds of state education, which matter for future life trajectory. ... It is also extremely important for health' (Byrne 2006: 117).

'Race' is less a factor in relation to spatial segregation than class – with the exception of Bangladeshis in poor quality social housing estates in East London, and Pakistani Muslims segregated from white working-class people in West Yorkshire and East Lancashire (Byrne 2006). In respect of 'gender', residential segregation is significant for female-headed lone parents who are generally poorer. 'Such households form a much larger proportion of all households with dependent children in the poorer halves of divided cities' (Byrne 2006: 123) – concentrated in 'social housing' which has become a residualised housing sector mainly for the 'poor, non-employed, aged under 29, and single parents' (Byrne 2006: 124).

Widening social and spatial inequality has also being exacerbated by the increasing role of the 'market' in the regulation of social order. Whilst notions of power and social control in society have invariably focused on the role of the state, since the 1970s increasing attention has been given to the role of the market in operationalising social control. As Spitzer argues, there was a: 'Tendency to overestimate the role of the state and underestimate the role of the market in interpreting how social control actually operates in capitalist societies.... [T]he advanced capitalist societies are more likely to rely on the market and private mechanisms [to achieve social control]' (cited in Robson 2000: 54).

The dynamism of market forces has intensified in some western societies – particularly Britain and the US – since the 1970s, leading Spitzer to claim that, in these cases, the operation of social control 'is much more effectively pressed implicitly through "free enterprise" than through the explicit organs of the state.... [F]ree enterprise "has penetrated everyday life far more effectively and thoroughly than the state"' (Robson 2000: 55).

The increasing intrusion of market forces and consumerism into social policy developments since the 1980s is undeniable. In urban policy in particular, over the past 20 years there has been a growth in the development of 'gated communities' ripe for consumption – be they areas regenerated under Thatcherite urban planning (such as London Docklands, gentrified for 'yuppies'); out-of-town shopping malls such as Meadowhall near Sheffield (designed to keep out the 'flawed consumer'); or 'edge cities' containing all the work, social and leisure amenities needed by 'the respectable' (Graham and Clarke 2002) – and all 'heavily guarded, electronically surveyed…to keep their distance from the "messy intimacy" of ordinary city life' (Bauman 2001: 54). These developments represent the creation of ' "communities" in name only' (Bauman 2001: 54) – they are effectively 'closed communities' and 'zones of exclusion': 'The development of these new urban spaces has been accompanied by forms of social exclusion: processes through which people are systematically disadvantaged, marginalized and subordinated. These processes combine economic, spatial, cultural and political divisions, producing deepening structures of social inequality' (Graham and Clarke 2002: 180).

They also lead to greater opportunity for prohibiting certain activities in the public realm in favour of consumption. In the case of shopping malls:

> Once privatized, they become subject to new exclusions ranging from the closing of the centre after shopping hours because it is 'too expensive' in terms of security to keep open, to controlling anything and everything that is seen as a potential threat to the task of maximising returns. That this can take some curious forms was illustrated in…[a] *File on 4* programme [BBC Radio 4, 1 March 1994], which documented the banning of preaching by the Salvation Army (too 'political'), the advertising by a Women's Institute of homemade jam (a threat to established businesses), and primary school children with clipboards (too intrusive). Even sitting was discouraged by making the seats less comfortable, and in one case was justified by reference to market research which purported to demonstrate that the general public was 'particularly distressed' by the sight of old people sitting down. The underpinning purpose was that nothing should hinder people's willingness to part with their money. As one centre manager put it, he didn't want people disturbed by contentious issues, so 'we don't allow people to come in an uncontrolled manner'. (Graham and Clarke 2002: 180–181)

As Bauman has explained, neo-liberalism's emphasis on market forces has led to the demonisation, criminalisation and exclusion of those deemed 'failed consumers' (Bauman 1998). A corollary of this is the increasing protection afforded 'successful consumers' through the intensification of gated private spaces.

> The built environment has become less and less *accessible* as traditional 'transitional' areas between public and private space such

as street-level shops have been replaced by blank walls, dark glass frontages and curtained offices. Remaining public spaces contain 'ingenious deterrents' against 'undesirables'. (Graham and Clarke 2002: 182 – emphasis in original)

Whilst these developments might reflect a more crucial role for 'free enterprise' and 'market forces' in British urban policy – the state remains the 'prime agent' (Robson 2000: 62) of the dominant, ruling elite, and retains a highly instrumental role in preparing the ground for 'market' exploitation with minimal disruption from social conflict. That is, the state remains the central agency in the regulation of social control.

Conclusions

Popularist perceptions of community, conflict and threats to safety – fostered mainly by the media, politicians and academics, and largely reflecting middle-class concerns – have influenced social policy interventions in Britain throughout modernity. These ideological constructions have systematically sustained socio-spatial differentiation and disadvantage by representing particular lifestyles as pathological – thereby legitimising the imposition of social control techniques over marginalised (yet 'dangerous') communities. These symbolic representations of 'dangerous communities' largely reflect the broader logic at work in western capitalist societies – namely, the perpetuation of the interests of the established order through disciplinary power and control. Meanwhile, nuisances and dangers experienced *by* communities, and caused by the actions of the powerful (e.g. social harms from environmental pollution, corporate crime and regressive social policies) remain largely hidden from public scrutiny.

The persistence of acute social and spatial divisions throughout 200 years of modernity raises important doubts about the ability of a capitalist system founded on classical liberal beliefs to deliver social cohesion and community wellbeing. As Byrne suggests, the perpetuation of social and spatial segregation in Britain reflects the intellectual power of the Marxist critique and its core idea 'that if the objectives of solidarity are to be achieved, then capitalism will have to become something else' (Byrne 2006: 9). More specifically, this requires attending to the structural causes of social problems and community tensions founded on unequal and exploitative power relations.

Whilst the emphasis and language relating to community and conflict may have varied over time, a common theme evident throughout has been the utility of these terms for both the powerful (in terms of maintaining privilege through managing threats posed by 'dangerous communities') and the disadvantaged (in terms of promoting their own needs through engaging in conflict). As we have seen, since the nineteenth century, the 'respectable' classes have continually feared for their safety due to threats posed by the 'dangerous Other' – those identified as 'aliens' or 'communities apart' (initially by their lowly class status and more lately by their ethnicity). These identities legitimated a range of state interventions aimed at regulating the activities and behaviour of these 'dangerous communities'. The stress of these interventions has varied in time between a greater criminal justice emphasis (e.g. the criminalisation of certain ways of behaving, stricter law enforcement sanctions and more proactive forms of paramilitary policing) and more supportive welfarist approaches (e.g. through community and youth work interventions, more generous social protection, and improvements to health and housing services). The former emphasis has largely been deployed at times when state intervention was targeted at a perceived 'underclass' or 'undeserving' lower social order – evident in the Victorian era and more recently under neo-liberal reforms. In contrast, the latter emphasis has largely been deployed at times when state intervention was largely planned to secure the co-operation of the 'respectable', 'skilled' working classes – evident in the two immediate post-war periods of the last century.

   At the same time, the language of community and conflict has also been embraced by the oppressed to mobilise communities of resistance and, throughout history, we have witnessed various successful campaigns for justice spearheaded by trade unions, political movements, women's groups, anti-racist movements, housing activists and so forth. Whilst for many these campaigns may have achieved little more than crumbs from the table of capitalism, there was a period between the end of the Second World War and the late-1970s when working-class communities saw significant improvements in their wellbeing thanks to improved housing conditions, better health care and educational opportunities, enhanced employment prospects and collective social protection. Whilst acknowledging that gendered and racist inequalities persisted throughout this period, the post-war Keynesian welfare state did reduce social inequality more generally in Britain. This all ended in the late-1970s, however – initially due to external pressures following the global economic crisis after 1973 and the requirement to conform to IMF demands, and then later following the rise to predominance of the New Right in British politics and the abandonment of the Keynesian welfare model as the driver of social and economic policy.

Throughout the 1980s and early 1990s, Britain became an increasingly divided society, with conflict around class, gender and ethnicity intensifying. In the context of neo-liberal domination at the heart of state ideology, the government's solution to these rising tensions was to adopt a particularly punitive turn – an approach that characterised the victims of its own economic restructuring stratagem as a 'dysfunctional underclass' whose improvement required stricter criminal justice measures and less welfare support. Once weaned off their welfare dependency, these people should be able to reintegrate into mainstream society – a society whose future wellbeing would be assured by allowing the dynamism of free market forces to flourish. This was the vision of society that New Labour inherited in 1997. In Chapter 3 we explore how New Labour has dealt with this inheritance by examining, in particular, its community-focused policies. This analysis will investigate some of the key ideas shaping New Labour's discourse on community – and how this discourse has translated into social policy measures and practices. It will also include an assessment of the outcomes of these initiatives in terms of who has gained, and who has lost out. However, before we embark on this analysis, the next chapter offers an examination of different conceptual understandings of community and conflict in order to illustrate the contestability of these ideas. More specifically, this assessment provides an analytical device for probing the utility of these concepts for (on the one hand) legitimising social policy interventions aimed at countering threats to social wellbeing from 'dangerous Others' and (on the other hand) for radical social movements seeking to mobilise fragmented communities to engage in conflict in pursuit of social justice. As such, this framework offers a conceptual toolbox for unravelling how notions of community and conflict have, throughout modernity, shaped both social policy developments *and* aided the activities of radical social protest movements. We will revisit this framework to aid analyses set out in later chapters of the book.

2
Concepts of 'Community' and 'Conflict'

Introduction

The previous chapter illustrated modern Britain's enduring fascination with notions of community, conflict and safety. Throughout modern (and post-modern) times, various theorists, concerned that the shared beliefs and customs which held traditional (pre-modern) societies together could no longer be assumed, have pondered the nature of social cohesion in industrial (and more recently, post-industrial) society. Traditional forms of association ('community') were seen to have been destroyed by industrialisation and urbanisation, a consequence of which appeared to be radical changes in the nature of social relations and the generation of new sites of community conflict. These changes were the concern of classical sociologists such as Durkheim, Weber, Marx and Tönnies.

As Durkheim argued in *The Division of Labour in Society* (1933/1893), the 'mechanical solidarity' that held people together in pre-industrial society – a solidarity founded on shared beliefs and functions (the 'conscience collective') – had been eradicated with modernity. Modern society was more complex, with people holding different beliefs and more specialised occupational functions. As Plant observes, over the past 200 years: 'the notion of community has been used almost universally by social and political philosophers to point up some of the drawbacks and baneful characteristics of urban industrial society and to point the way toward new and more humane forms of social relations' (cited in Creed 2006a: 26).

This chapter presents an overview of key perspectives relating to community and conflict in modern industrial society, and the extent to which these positions have been adopted by both the powerful (i.e. to legitimise state-sponsored social policy interventions aimed at countering threats to social wellbeing from 'dangerous Others') and the less powerful (i.e. social activists seeking to mobilise disadvantaged communities to engage collectively in conflict in pursuit of social justice). The purpose of this analysis is to generate a theoretical grounding for understanding the utility of these key ideas for both the powerful (keen to maintain social cohesion and existing power relations) and the less powerful (in terms of informing the make-up of struggles of resistance and campaigns in pursuit of social justice). We will return to this device in Chapter 3 in our analysis of New Labour's community-based social policies; again in Chapter 4 in revealing various myths and contradictions evident in mainstream social policy discourse on the themes of community safety, cohesion and wellbeing; and again in Chapter 5 in our reflections on the kind of contextual social framework necessary for a more universalistic and egalitarian vision of community wellbeing to become realisable.

A fundamental assumption underpinning the analysis set out below is that any attempt at establishing an absolute definition of community is futile. Various authors have endeavoured to do this: some equate community with feelings of connectedness and belonging to people, place or interest cluster – a source of support, security or enjoyment; others associate community with disconnectedness and exclusion – a basis for the 'Othering' of outsiders (see Christensen and Levinson [2003] for a comprehensive overview of the way community has been conceptualised). However, as Margaret Stacey (1974) argues, there are so many different and competing definitions of the term that these have become almost meaningless and are best avoided. What does remain significant, however – particularly in relation to social wellbeing – is how the idea of community has been utilised by various individuals and interest groups to pursue an ambition or vision (more specifically, in respect of this book, how community has been used by different interests at different spectrums of social policy discourse). To address this utilisation, therefore, the chapter is organised into two substantive sections – each characterising the essence of two contradictory positions.

The first section examines standpoints stressing the need to foster social cohesion by improving the regulation of existing social arrangements and, thereby, enabling the contemporary social order to be preserved. Here, conflict is seen as harmful for society whilst community serves as a means of governance. These positions focus attention on the perceived threat to social cohesion and safety posed by 'dangerous Others' (invariably found in 'dangerous places'). Such viewpoints emphasise either the *lack* of community or the *wrong type* of community – that is, something that has either been lost or infected – and the failure of people to take responsibility for meeting their obligations and performing their civic duties. To address this lack or these failings, these positions invariably prescribe area-based interventions to restore community or to modify people's behaviour. These viewpoints can be traced back to the classical sociology of Durkheim and Tönnies, and in the social democratic ideals of the post-war period. More recently, they have resurfaced, in a more highly-charged moralistic vein, in the ideas and values of 'communitarianism'.

The second section considers positions which see conflict in more positive terms – stressing its role in countering oppressive practices and positively transforming the existing social order. Here, conflict is viewed as desirable (even necessary) for democracy (and social wellbeing) to flourish whilst community provides a site for mobilising collective resistance against oppression. These perspectives – influenced by such thinkers as Weber, Marx, Gramsci, Habermas and Freire – emphasise the political dimensions of community and conflict, where communities represent potential sites for social action in pursuit of a more just society.

Focusing on community in these two ways offers important lessons for understanding the relevance of the concept for social policy developments. It allows us to unravel the utility of the notion for the state (its significance for the maintenance of social cohesion and the status quo) *and* for aiding the generation of collective social action (in pursuit of social justice). As such, 'the notion of community may be doing sociological and ideological work – work that ranges from simply reinforcing the status quo to challenging systems of oppression' (Creed 2006b: 4).

The regulation of conflict and community cohesion

Sociological positivist representations have invariably depicted 'community' in a normative and instrumental sense – that is, community is seen both as a source of a social problem ('dangerous' people in 'dangerous' places) and as part of the solution (a place of solidarity and cohesion, achievable through local people acting as an agent to change local circumstances – particularly with the support of outside intervention) (Taylor 2003). Community symbolises something both 'bad' ('deviance' and 'dysfunction') and 'good' (the kind of society we in industrial [and now post-industrial] times need to regain). In this latter respect, community invokes an image of togetherness, unity and consensus – the glue for maintaining social cohesion. Such references to community 'conjure to some degree qualities of harmony, homogeneity, autonomy, immediacy, locality, morality, solidarity, and identity' (Creed 2006b: 5). Moreover, in this sense, community 'carries with it assumptions about the way we should live' (Taylor 2003: 36). It becomes more than merely place or locality, but is 'used to refer to a set of relations that exist between individuals and govern their moral or social behaviour with one another' (Little 2002: 370). The utility of community here is as a moralising discourse which establishes the boundaries of acceptable behaviour within which individuals must conform. Such a community 'would demand stern obedience in exchange for the services it renders or promises to render' (Bauman 2001: 4). Used in this way, community is about setting boundaries in pursuit of compliance and domination.

Classical sociological thinking

For Emile Durkheim, social cohesion in modern society requires a sense of organic solidarity where people recognise their mutual interdependence. In *The Division of Labour in Society* (1933/1893), Durkheim maintained that organic solidarity in modern societies would emerge through individuals and groups acknowledging that their activities and interactions were complementary. The importance of social interaction for creating social solidarity was also highlighted in his later studies on *Suicide* (1952/1897) and *The Elementary Forms of the Religious Life* (1976/1915). In these works, Durkheim emphasised the significance of individuals interacting with each other (through religious or other cultural activities) for social bonding. He saw an important role for voluntary associations as a means of regulating social divisions and fostering cohesion. Durkheim shared Auguste Comte's belief in the value of rituals as a focus for community cohesion – for rituals offer sites for individuals to meet, learn together and unite around shared values (Pickering 1993, Pope 1998).

Durkheim also believed that the threat of moral sanctions – reflecting the common consciousness of the collective – was crucial for constraining an individual's behaviour and maintaining social cohesion. His analysis of suicide, for example, argued that social groups with lower rates of suicide belonged to more cohesive, moral communities – Catholics, for instance – compared to those with higher rates of suicide – such as Protestants. Durkheim suggested that such moral communities had been eroded with industrial capitalism. However, he also believed in the possibility of 'orderly social change and steady moral progress' within the context of 'Western capitalist democracy' (Parkin 1992: 86). Overseeing this change and progress is, for Durkheim, a benign state apparatus – 'a politically neutral force which acts impartially for the common good' (Parkin 1992: 74) – *and* civil society in the form of professional bodies and occupational guilds – 'moral communities in the most complete sense' (Parkin 1992: 77).

> Durkheim's enthusiasm for this form of social organization appears to have been fuelled by his understanding of the medieval guilds.... [He] was evidently impressed by the moral energy which the guilds displayed and by their highly developed sense of collective identity....The new guilds would [also] put an end to [industrial] strife by reining in their members' demands and inculcating the habit of self discipline. (Parkin 1992: 77)

The need to train the lower orders to restrain their aspirations (in the interest of social cohesion) was central to Durkheim's thoughts on one of the main purposes of education: to 'teach the child to rein in his desires, to set limits to his appetites of all kinds' (Durkheim 1925/1961, cited in Parkin 1992: 71). As we saw in the previous chapter, Methodism played an important role in shaping the consciousness of the English working classes and Methodist education stressed that working people should not expect their desires to be met in this world but 'in a future state' (cited in Thompson 1991/1963: 398).

The extent to which moral communities had been eroded by industrial capitalism, as gauged by Durkheim, is contestable. Raymond Williams, for instance, noted how, in the new industrial towns, the rituals, mutuality and shared moral values of the medieval guilds became important aspects of 'what is properly meant by "working-class culture"... [i.e.] the basic collective idea, and the institutions, manners, habits of thought, and intentions which proceed from this' (Williams, cited in Thompson 1991/1963: 462). As E.P. Thompson describes it in his history of the making of the English working class:

> In the simple cellular structure of the friendly society, with its workaday ethos of mutual aid, we can see many features which were reproduced in more sophisticated and complex forms in trade unions, cooperatives, Hampden Clubs, Political Unions, and Chartist lodges. At the same time, the societies can be seen as crystallizing an ethos of mutuality very much more widely diffused in the 'dense' and

'concrete' particulars of the personal relations of working people, at home and at work. Every kind of witness in the first half of the nineteenth century ... remarked upon the extent of mutual aid in the poorest districts. In times of emergency, unemployment, strikes, sickness, childbirth, then it was the poor who 'helped every one of his neighbour'. (Thompson 1991/1963: 462)

This culture of mutual aid amongst the poorest and the responsibilities they bear for the extreme wretchedness amongst their communities stands in stark contrast to the individualism of middle-class values. As Thompson observes:

[B]y the early years of the nineteenth century it is possible to say that collectivist values are dominant in many industrial communities; there is a definite moral code, with sanctions against the blackleg, the 'tools' of the employer or the unneighbourly, and with an intolerance towards the eccentric or individualist. Collectivist values are consciously held and are propagated in political theory, trade union ceremonial, moral rhetoric. (Thompson 1991/1963: 463)

Durkheim's concerns for the foundations of social order in modern society had been addressed earlier by Ferdinand Tönnies in his book *Community and Association*, first published in 1887. Tönnies contrasted *die gemeinschaft* ('community') with *die gesellschaft* ('association'). *Die gemeinschaft* characterises life in rural, agrarian society where individuals have similar occupational roles and hold shared values. In such a society, social solidarity is strong. *Die gesellschaft* describes life in modern, industrial society where traditional solidarities have been broken by the industrial division of labour and the movement of populations to new urban centres. In modern society, traditional social bonds have been replaced by associations, where individuals are linked by market relationships, contractual agreements and actions based on 'rational' choices (Tönnies 1955/1887). As Delanty explains, 'with modernity, society replaces community as the primary focus for social relations. Community is "living", while society is mechanical. The former is more rooted in locality and is "natural", while the latter is more a "rational", "mental" product and one that is sustained by relations of exchange' (Delanty 2005: 33).

Whilst Tönnies' distinction was not intended to describe 'realities' but ideal types (different ways of thinking) about how to live (interact) in modern society – that is, people may be motivated by a desire to build and maintain social bonds that benefit, on the one hand, the community or, on the other hand, the individual – with modernity came the privileging of 'relations of exchange' and the depletion of family, folklores and religion around which community (social bonding) could thrive. In these circumstances, there was greater potential for social conflict and disorder. As a consequence, following Tönnies, 'modern sociology became greatly preoccupied with the problem of the survival of community in modernity' (Delanty 2005: 34). This preoccupation has invariably associated community with romanticised notions of social cohesion in rural society – not necessarily intended as a defence of the countryside 'but rather an imagined ideal conjured to shape and improve urban life' (Creed 2006a: 26). In respect of this, however, 'the positive elements of community associated with the rural past were no more empirically valid than the negative ones, yet they remain elements of the community concept and project' (Creed 2006a: 27). Various studies have challenged the idealised view of rural life – exposing the conflicts and lack of cohesion in many rural places, as well as 'the dreadful constraints that rural communities imposed on their members in the past' (Creed 2006a: 32). Community can be oppressively stifling.

Social democratic perspectives

Social democratic perspectives on community are largely founded on T.H. Marshall's ideas on 'citizenship' and the need to maintain social cohesion. Marshall believed that community tensions could be minimised by allowing all to 'participate' in the essential elements of society. All citizens should be allowed equal rights to protection under the law, the ballot, and to the social necessities of life (principally education, health care, a minimum income and housing) – these being individual rights. Furthermore, citizenship should embrace the right to participate in politics and policy making, again either as an individual member of a political authority or as an individual involved in the election of such authority. These rights should be regardless of people's individual circumstances (Marshall 1950). Citizen participation is also functional for resolving conflict in society – again, important for the maintenance of social cohesion. Characterising societies in this Durkheimian sense – as solid and non-conflictual – serves an ideological purpose, idealising the existence of co-operative, stable communities, compliant with the dominant social order. Conflict and community are viewed as incompatible and, where conflict does arise, conflict resolution techniques – such as community development – offer the means to re-establish consensus (Creed 2006a). For social democrats, conflict causes inefficiencies and, therefore, needs to be managed through conciliation, mediation and arbitration – otherwise, more disruptive forms of protest might emerge. Conflict avoidance is, therefore, preferable – and this is more likely to be successful where state institutions appear more open and representative – that is, 'pluralistic'. Social democrats support the involvement of community groups in welfare organising because they can serve to manage any sudden and radical demands from their individual constituents. This 'politics of regulated conflict' helps to ensure evolutionary social change (reformism) rather than a radical break with the past (revolution). However, this support for community engagement is conditional upon such groups being regulated within an organised structure of bodies – effectively, a combination of elected representation and delegated authority overseen by the social democratic state (Cooper and Hawtin 1997).

The social democratic position also supports a notion of 'freedom' as the 'activity of self-development, requiring not only the absence of external constraint but also the availability of social and material conditions necessary for the achievement of purposes or plans' (Gould 1990: 32). This requires a model of social relations founded on equal rights of participation in the political, economic and social spheres – achieved largely through universal suffrage, a political accommodation with organised labour and state action to minimise social and economic hardship and enhance individual choice through education. This approach, applied during the Keynesian programme rolled out after the Second World War, reflects the Fabian tradition within social democracy – a position which does not extend to questioning the ability of capitalism to deliver 'equal rights'. This effectively denies the very existence of structured patterns of inequality within capitalist systems. Moreover, the basis of citizenship within social democratic thinking – its emphasis on rights possessed by individuals – is at the expense of collective rights and the potential of collective action in pursuit of positive social transformation. As we argued in the previous chapter, whilst sections of the working class made significant gains from policies implemented during the social democratic consensus of the post-war years – in particular, from the decommodification of housing and health provision – as Turner, for example, argues, 'the institutions of citizenship ... functioned to ameliorate the condition of the working class without transforming the entire property system' (Turner 1993, cited in Byrne 2006: 28). Effectively, social democracy in action served to enable the capitalist system, and its inherent tendency to exploit and alienate, to function more smoothly for a time, and to enable the capitalist class to maintain its privileges of property and wealth. In relation to this, the concept of citizenship has (like the concept of community) been strategically important for the maintenance of social cohesion and existing power relations in Britain.

Communitarianism and 'active citizenship'

As we saw in the previous chapter, the social democratic consensus broke with anti-Keynesian welfare state developments from the 1970s. Influenced by the political philosophy of Hayek, the administrations of Thatcher's New Right-influenced Conservatives sought to enhance the 'freedom' of the individual by removing state coercion. Hayek characterised the state interventions under social democracy as 'the road to serfdom' (Hayek 1944). The ideological underpinning of Thatcherism was a return to free-market individualism – a notion of freedom which had little meaning 'for the majority of the population who lived in poverty' (Turner 1993, cited in Byrne 2006: 28). Under New Right ideology, so long as the state set 'adequate' minimum standards in absolute terms for meeting the needs of disadvantaged communities, then the existence of inequalities in relative terms did not matter and there should be no need to impinge further on the freedom of individuals in pursuit of minimising this disparity. As we saw in the previous chapter, as social inequality widened from the 1980s onwards, the conceptualisation of poor communities took an increasingly punitive turn with the emergence of the 'underclass' thesis – a perspective of disadvantage which lays the blame on the 'moral and behavioural delinquency' (Levitas 2005: 7) of the disadvantaged them-selves. For Charles Murray, the underclass represented a contagious cultural 'disease' spread by 'people whose values are contaminating the life of entire neighbourhoods' (Murray 1990: 23). Such a position served to legitimise further harsh sanctions aimed at re-socialising these path-ologically dysfunctional communities – in particular, the tightening of the eligibility criteria for, and value of, welfare benefits. These measures only served to exacerbate the social divide which, in turn, presented a further threat to social cohesion. As Ralf Dahrendorf argued, besides being morally unacceptable, 'widening income differentials result in a serious disjuncture in the commitment of different groups to the values and institutions of society' (Dahrendorf 1995, cited in Levitas 2005: 45). The problem here is that widening income inequality threatens the possibility of social cohesion built upon shared values and commit-ments: too much inequality undermines the social order by generating too much fear.

Given the context of post (or late) modernity – the dissolution of traditional social bonds and the emergence of the 'risk society' – it is not surprising that notions of 'community' and 'citizenship' have been (re)evoked in mainstream social policy discourse. In contrast to those who have gained most from the neo-liberal 'revolution' – the affluent and privileged, who can be left to conduct their lives as freely as they choose – the losers require regulation through 'community involvement' – a process of 'sanitizing the potential "difficulty" [these] communities pose' (McGhee 2005: 182). Community becomes a site for managing social problems and 'unruly' behaviour – a means of containing the 'dangerous Other' through shaping their lifestyles. In this sense, community work takes on an ideological purpose, acting as 'a conduit for the transmission and affirmation of particular attitudes and values' (Shaw and Martin 2000: 402). This particular use of community is strongly associated with communitarianism – a philosophy that puts, as Thatcherism did, 'the family first and then the community as the site of moral norms and obligations, of responsibilities as well as rights' (Taylor 2003: 39).

In keeping with the concerns of Durkheim and Tönnies, communitarians dispute unfettered individualism because its fails to benefit the wider interests of the group or community. For communitarians, as with Durkheim, community is 'a life with meaning based on the mutual interdependence of individuals' (Ledwith 2005: 16). The communitarian preoccupation with community is therefore largely:

> driven by the desire to create 'a new moral, social and public order based on restored communities...' (Etzioni 1995, p. 2). Communitarians...hold two fundamental beliefs: i) that normal human relationships only thrive through trust, cooperation and mutuality, and ii) that this gives rise to increased social cohesion in which democracy flourishes, promoting a more egalitarian society. (Ledwith 2005: 22)

Etzioni's notion of communtarianism is based on a belief that individuals not only have rights but also responsibilities. He believes that there is a need to correct what he sees as a 'current imbalance between rights and responsibilities' (Etzioni 1993, cited in Lister 1997: 31) by encouraging people to engage more with the civic institutions of society – primarily, the family and a range of community organisations. For Etzioni, democracy and greater equality is achieved through individuals participating more in civil society as 'active citizens'.

As we shall see in the next chapter, Etzioni's concept of 'active citizenship' has been taken up by New Labour and applied to its modernisation agenda for public services. In particular, New Labour's reforms aimed to improve the standard of public services by making them more accountable to 'citizens' through 'expanding the reach of choice and voice' (Clarke 2005: 449). For Blair, choice was 'one important mechanism to ensure that citizens can indeed secure good schools and health services in their communities' (Blair 2004, cited in Clarke 2005: 449). However, not all communities appear to experience the same opportunities with regard to choice – see Beckmann and Cooper (2004, 2005b), for instance, in respect of the lack of real choice within the British education system. Similarly, government commitments to strengthen 'voice' through community involvement in social programmes have also been regarded with some scepticism. As Clarke observes, 'whose voices get to be recognized and heard, and what the consequences of being heard are, remain critical issues around participation. Empowerment is an ambiguous condition' (Clarke 2005: 450–451).

The attractiveness of the communitarian discourse on community and active citizenship for government, particularly with its notions of voluntarism and self-help, is clear given the emerging consensus in British social policy around neo-liberal orthodoxy and the decline in welfarist solutions to social problems. In this context, community acts as a form of governance. As Nikolas Rose observes, community (or civil society) provides a 'third space' between the state/market and individuals – acting as a new site of governance made necessary by the decline of the social state:

> As the state shirks social responsibilities, individuals, firms, and organisations...are made responsible for taking up the slack via notions of individual morality, organizational responsibility, and ethical community. [Rose] then suggests that this concept of community has been made technical through expert discourses and professional vocations evident in 'community development programs' run by 'community development officers', protected by 'community policing', and analyzed by sociologists pursuing 'community studies'. Rendered technical, community can become a means of governance (N. Rose 1999: 176–177). (Cited in Creed 2006a: 43)

The notion of 'ethical community' has clear benefits for maintaining social control in a withered welfare state. 'The attraction of community may be explained by its moral overtones, for the subject of community is one with civic obligations and moral commitments to society. This produces the political effect of disburdening the state of responsibility and diluting social citizenship' (Delanty 2005: 88). As we saw in the previous chapter, the post-war Keynesian welfare state consensus, which did much to smooth over the economic cycles of boom and bust whilst offering social protection against risk (Jordan 2006), came to an end by the late-1970s. Between 1979 and the election of New Labour in 1997, Britain became an increasingly divided society with deepening social conflict. By 1997 there was a growing consensus that free-market neo-liberalism alone would not heal these divides and tensions. Given this context, the appeal of communitarianism came to the fore in New Labour's policy agenda for it appeared to offer the ideal prescription for regenerating 'broken communities'. From the communitarian perspective, the community, along with 'the family' and the church, is an important part of the glue holding civil society together. However, as with the family and the church, it is also seen as something in decline and in need of restoration. As Blair put it:

> Britain, by 1997, had undergone rapid cultural and social change in recent decades. ... [S]ome social change had damaging and unforeseen consequences. Family ties were weakened. Communities were more fractured....Civil institutions such as the church declined in importance. At the start of the 20th century, communities shared a strong moral code. By the end of the century this was no longer as true. (Blair 2005: 30)

Community here is seen both as the problem (something broken) and, simultaneously, part of the solution (the antidote to social conflict and the breakdown of the moral order). The communitarian emphasis on responsibilities as well as rights – including the notion of the 'responsible community' (as well as 'responsible' individuals and families) as an important source of social cohesion and mutual support (Jordan 2006) – appeared to offer the formula for healing community breakdown and managing the damaging and wasteful conflicts wrought by too much individualism. As Clarke explains: 'The movement from expansive or welfarist liberalism to advanced or neo-liberalism is characterised by this shift towards the production of self-regulating subjects.... New Labour appear as exemplary practitioners of this form of governmentality – seeking to create subjects who understand themselves as responsible and independent agents' (Clarke 2005: 452).

The aim of social policy after 1997 largely builds on the foundations of change developed under the Conservative New Right – particularly in relation to discouraging 'welfare dependency'. As we will see in the next chapter, New Labour continued the task of activating previously 'passive recipients of state assistance into … self-sustaining individuals' (Clarke 2005: 448), particularly through welfare-to-work programmes such as the various New Deals. Effectively, the communitarian emphasis on duties and responsibilities appears to complement the New Right agenda neatly by offering a blueprint for making it work even better:

> Such responsibilities are substantial and wide-ranging. At their core is the responsibility to produce the conditions of one's own independence – ideally by becoming a 'hard working' individual or family. … Citizens must manage their lifestyles so as to promote their own health and well-being. Members of communities must eschew anti-social behaviour so as to promote harmony, inclusivity and civility. Parents must take responsibility for controlling and civilizing their children. (Clarke 2005: 451)

It is clear to see the utility of community-focused initiatives here for encouraging the self-help ethic at a time of growing concern over the cost of public spending and a breakdown in community cohesion.

> The idea of the 'enabling state' seems to be virtually embodied in professional community work with its traditional emphasis on 'encouraging the helpless to help themselves' – almost tailor-made, it seems, for the task of delivering the community to policy. Furthermore, the self-help ethic performs an ideological function by reinforcing the attack on the 'dependency culture' in ways which have actually facilitated the shifts in policy necessary to transmute 'public issues' into 'personal troubles'. In other words, community work can operate to remoralize communities into the new welfare culture. (Shaw and Martin 2000: 407)

The communitarian political project is about the (re)construction of communities of hard-working, law-abiding, responsibilised citizens who increasingly govern themselves through 'technologies of the self' (Foucault 1988). Those who fail to be activated or incentivised – the idle and feckless, the anti-social and irresponsible – will be targeted differently. These 'Others' 'become the objects of intensified surveillance, criminalization and incarceration in the drive to extend civility, reduce anti-socialness and enhance community safety' (Clarke 2005: 458). The influence of this project in New Labour thinking is evident in Blair's basic philosophical justification for his legislation on 'anti-social behaviour' (outlined in more detail in the next chapter):

It is not just about tough versus soft but about whose civil liberties come first. ... Social democratic thought was always the application of morality to political philosophy. One of the basic insights of the left, one of its distinguishing features, is to caution against too excessive an individualism. People must live together and one of the basic tasks of government is to facilitate this living together, to ensure that the many can live without fear of the few. That was why it was important that rights were coupled once again with responsibilities. (Blair 2005: 30)

Blair went on to cite R.H. Tawney, the Fabian economic historian, educator and activist, to support his argument: 'As Tawney once put it: "what we have been witnessing... is the breakdown of society on the basis of rights divorced from obligation"' (Blair 2005: 30). However, what Blair failed to mention was that Tawney's view of obligation emphasised the moral responsibility of social institutions (not just the state, but also the private institutions of industry and commerce) to their communities – which included social responsibilities as well as economic. Tawney, unlike Blair, was also a socialist who recognised that capitalism worked against the interest of equality, opportunity and social cohesion. He had faith in the potential of popular social movements to challenge the ruling orthodoxy – believing that the hold of dominant ideologies is never complete – and to bring about social change where human relationships could become more fulfilling. Tawney believed that the key to such a transformation was lifelong education. Again, 'education, education, education' was Blair's mantra on being elected in 1997 – the three most important themes for his government to address. But unlike Blair's vision of lifelong education, which was effectively about maximising work-related skills (Jordan 2006), Tawney advocated a style of lifelong education that was 'both liberal in its range and concerned with the fostering of a more just and enriching communal life' (Smith 2001: 1). Education for Tawney had an important political dimension as 'an engine of change in society – and an important means of attaining greater justice' (Smith 2001: 1). 'All serious educational movements have in England been also social movements. They have been the expression in one sphere – the training of mind and character – of some distinctive conception of the life proper to man and of the kind of society in which he can best live it' (Tawney 1966, cited in Smith 2001: 1).

Tawney's vision of education contrasts sharply with New Labour's narrow concern with 'educating' for labour market needs and social control (Beckmann and Cooper 2004, 2005b). In contrast to the ideas of Tawney, 'social democratic' philosophy under New Labour, as influenced by communitarianism, has increasingly focused on the enforcement of the responsibilities of individuals, families and communities – no matter how poor or disadvantaged they might be – to overcome their own difficult circumstances. Meanwhile, the responsibilities of the state, industry and commerce for fulfilling their contribution to achieving the social democratic aim of greater social justice, as imagined by Tawney, have been 'conveniently' brushed aside.

Blair's notion of social democracy – which he claimed stood for 'the rights of the many' (Blair 2005: 30) over the few – is one intolerant of difference and diversity; one that 'Others' the minority and favours the 'freedom … of harms from others' (Blair 2005: 30). It exemplifies Henry Thoreau's concern about the development of a powerless minority 'while it conforms to the majority' (Thoreau 1849: 1). Taylor notes that this style of communitarianism fails to acknowledge what Deborah Eade has described as community's 'dark side': 'Community has a dark side that can be both oppressive and exclusive. … [C]ommunity is defined as much by Them as Us. … Tester … goes so far as to say that: "it is precisely the identification of an abhorrent 'them' which makes 'us' possible"' (see Taylor 2003: 50–51).

Communities are, by definition, exclusionary. Defining who is 'included' also defines who is 'excluded' – the 'Other'. Moreover, socially constructing the 'Other' as 'dangerous' has been a consistent practice for systematically protecting the interests of the established order in capitalist societies. As we saw in the previous chapter, such constructions are evident in the social investigations and commentaries of the early nineteenth century which generated a growing apprehension amongst the new industrial middle class about the stunted moral development and disgusting behaviour of the labouring classes. We also saw in the previous chapter how these characterisations led to 'moral panics' and the legitimisation of punitive social policy responses that aimed to keep 'the Other' in check. At the same time, throughout history, those who could – the powerful and privileged – have always sought to escape community, particularly following the increased accessibility of transport in the late nineteenth century that facilitated suburbanisation and the widening social and geographical divide between the classes which has continued to this day.

> We could argue that it is the wealthiest people in the world who have lost community, insulated from the rest of the world, transferring from their gated mansion in their gated neighbourhood to their bullet-proofed car, their private plane, and to the five-star hotel in some other anonymous town, which is pretty much the same hotel in any other country. No one is prescribing them community. (Taylor 2003: 82)

Not only are the privileged prescribing something to the poor which they themselves have consistently sought to escape, they are doing it at a time when British society has become increasingly individualised and divided as a consequence of the neo-liberal reforms from the late-1970s to the present. As Taylor observes: 'It seems almost bizarre to expect communities excluded by the rest of society to be inclusive themselves, especially in a society which celebrates individualism so strongly' (Taylor 2003: 79). Because communities are not homogeneous, and because neighbourhoods are largely made up of people with different interests and perspectives, attention needs to be given to the more complex dynamics of community relations or, to be more precise, to power relations more generally in society. As Taylor has argued:

> Communities and networks are as likely to create exclusion as to resolve it; that too much trust can lead to corruption and abuse; that the moralities produced by communities can be oppressive; and that civil society is a place riven with conflicts and inequalities. The words that go missing from much of this discourse in popular use... are 'power' and 'conflict'. (Taylor 2003: 62–63)

Furthermore, there is no acknowledgement of the structural causes of social inequality and social injustice in the communitarian analysis. Responsibility for tackling the economic and social disintegration reaped by almost thirty years of neo-liberal social reform is placed squarely on the shoulders of some of the most vulnerable and disadvantaged people in society. Moreover, the 'symbolic construction' (Cohen 1985) of community in social policy serves to assign particular values such as cohesion, security, trust and consent 'whether or not these underpin or characterise the policy in practice' (Taylor 2003: 38), demonstrating the utility of the imagery of community-based social policy interventions for facilitating the improved regulation of existing social arrangements and the maintenance of the contemporary social order.

Rebuilding social capital

Communitarianism's concern for civic virtue and the desire for individuals to participate more in public life reflects to some degree a disquiet about contemporary social problems such as 'crime' and 'disorder' – problems whose causes are seen to lie in the decline of civic engagement and 'social capital'. Here, social capital stands for such values as trust, commitment and social solidarity – values which communitarians believe are essential for democracy to work but which they feel have been eroded in recent times. A key proponent of this perspective is Robert Putnam who in his book *Bowling Alone* discusses the loss of social capital in the US – evidenced by a decline in civic engagement and collective values (observed by people going to bowling alleys on their own), and an increase in individualism and consumerism to the detriment of democracy (Putnam 1999). In order to achieve greater democracy and equality, therefore, we need to encourage people to re-engage in the civic institutions of society – to participate 'in community'. The health of a community can be measured by the number of informal and formal civic associations available for individuals to engage in. In this sense, human wellbeing is seen to lie in the quality and quantity of our social connections, and the influence this provides in respect of access to decision-making processes and resource distribution. The need to rebuild social capital in deprived neighbourhoods has been a central strategy in the communitarian agenda for restoring community cohesion and safety (Woolcock 2003).

In Britain, the notion of social capital has been pushed by Demos, the think tank and research institute which has had a profound influence on New Labour's policies – in particular, through its support of Etzioni's style of communitarianism. This support has taken various forms, including advocating 'no rights without responsibilities', pushing the idea that 'tired old ideological conflicts' have been replaced by a 'new common sense', and arguing the need to 'bring back shame' (Cohen 1997: 1). In 2003, New Labour issued its guidance on promoting social capital in its Home Office report *Building Civil Renewal* – a process 'engaged with the formation and utilization of "social capital"' (Byrne 2006: 167). The Home Office define this as:

> '*a way to empower people in their communities to provide the answers to our contemporary social problems.*' Civic renewal depends on people

having the skills, confidence and opportunities to contribute actively in their communities, to engage with civil institutions and democratic processes, to be able to influence the policies and services that affect their lives, and to make the most of their communities' human, financial and physical assets. (Home Office 2003, cited in Byrne 2006: 167 – emphasis in original)

The Home Office go on to report the UK Government's formal adoption of the Organisation for Economic Co-operation and Development (OECD) definition of social capital as:

'networks together with shared norms, values and understandings that facilitate co-operation within or among groups.' It has also been defined as *'shared understandings, levels of trust, associational memberships and informal networks of human relationship that facilitate social exchange, social order and underpin social institutions'* .... In particular, it involves building 'bonds' and 'bridges' between people as a foundation for social support and community relationships. Effective community involvement, especially horizontal involvement and networking, are key elements in the building of social capital. (Home Office 2003, cited in Byrne 2006: 167 – emphasis in original)

Others have less faith in the ability of civic institutions and social networks to address *'our contemporary social problems'* – in particular, the lack of genuine democracy and social inequality. Ledwith, for example, argues: 'From a Gramscian perspective, civil society, far from being a collective spirited expression of citizenship as rights and responsibilities, is the site in which the dominant ideas of the ruling class infiltrate people's thinking by ideological persuasion – a more powerful force than state coercion' (Ledwith 2005: 22). This is perhaps why governments today hold such high expectations of civic institutions.

However, the communitarian belief in the ability of individuals to engage freely 'in community' and to influence decision making – implying, as Robson argues, that we are all repackaged as equal 'stakeholders' in a suddenly rediscovered 'civil society' (Robson 2000) – suggests a naïve concept of community as 'unity' and ignores the reality of intense competition and conflict within communities based on 'race', class, gender, age, sexualities and disability (Ledwith 2005). This lack of sophistication in communitarian thinking is perhaps due to the fact that traditionally, the concept of community formed part of the armoury and radical language of the critical left as a site of resistance. Now, the idea of community is 'incorporated into communtarianism and diluted' (Ledwith 2005: 23) in order to present a more moderate reformist agenda for change – as such, losing much of its lucidity. This is similar to Berner and Phillips' reflections on how the radical concept of 'participation' has also been 'co-opted into mainstream theory and diluted in potential' (see Ledwith 2005: 24). In particular, communitarianism's advocacy of participation as self-help 'obscures the social justice argument for redistribution of resources' (Ledwith 2005: 24). Moreover, it fails to recognise:

> that the poor cannot be self-sufficient in escaping poverty, that 'communities' are systems of conflict as well as co-operation, and that the social, political and economic macro-structure cannot be side-stepped. ... [N]aïve interpretations of *community* that assume unity and reciprocity are created by *outsiders* who 'see homogeneity and harmony where there is complexity and conflict' (Berner and Phillips 2005: 24). (See Ledwith 2005: 24 – emphasis in original.)

By creating the illusion that we are all united together and living in harmony, communitarianism obscures the reality of conflict within communities, thereby paving the way for potentially authoritarian state interventions against those who dissent. An example of this is the concern within communitarian thinking for the preservation of the dominant culture to which minority communities are expected to conform. This is a notion of community as 'sameness' and 'the absence of the Other' (Bauman 2001: 115) – the preservation of identity through assimilation and the minimisation of difference. 'The attraction of the community of communitarian dreams rests on the promise of simplification: brought to its logical limit, simplification means a lot of sameness and a bare minimum of variety' (Bauman 2001: 148). The danger here of course is that the policy prescriptions that emerge from communitarian thinking will exacerbate the social ailment – people's sense of alienation and anxiety in an unsafe world – it professes to remedy. As Little argues:

> the spirit of community will be invoked to superimpose consensus and inclusion where none may exist. Here lies the peril of regarding community as a definitive type of entity when diverse, contemporary societies contain many different forms of association that are worthy of recognition but may not fit fixed criteria for what a community

should look like. This danger is particularly pertinent for those minority communities which may coalesce precisely because of a perceived threat or lack of recognition from majority groups. Thus the invocation of community can be as much a way of excluding the other rather than embracing it, particularly if we erect strict criteria as to what is and isn't a community. (Little 2002: 370)

The power of the 'world community'

The discursive appeal of community for ideological purposes has also taken on a global dimension, particularly since Francis Fukuyama's famous pronouncement (following the collapse of the Soviet bloc) declaring the 'end of ideology':

> Modern history, we were assured, culminated in the 'unabashed victory of economic and political liberalism'. A public ideology indistinguishable from the United States – with liberal democracy, the cultural ethos of the pursuit of individual happiness, free-market capitalism and the rule of law – was the fate of the world: 'the universalization of Western liberal democracy as the final form of human government'. (Morrison 2006: 2)

There was no purpose in challenging the neo-liberal model of global capitalism anymore (TINA – 'there is no alternative') – the corollary being the abandonment of any utopian search for social justice (Morrison 2006). We had to be pragmatic and accept the right of international capitalist organisations – the International Monetary Fund (IMF), the World Bank (WB), the World Trade Organisation (WTO) and so forth – to set the rules. As Samuel Huntington makes clear in his 1993 essay 'The Clash of Civilisations?':

> The West is now at an extraordinary peak of power in relation to other civilisations. Its superpower opponent has disappeared from the map. ... It dominates international political and security institutions and with Japan international economic institutions. ... Decisions made at the UN Security Council or in the International Monetary Fund that reflect the interests of the West are presented to the world as reflecting the desires of the *world community*. The very phrase 'the world community' has become the euphemistic collective noun (replacing 'the Free World') to give global legitimacy to actions

reflecting the interests of the United States and other Western powers. (Cited in Morrison 2006: 327 – emphasis added)

As American journalist Robert Kaplan puts it: 'the "prize" for winning the Cold War' was that '"*We and nobody else will write the terms for international society*" .... The US is thus the only "credible force" that can stand for individual freedom, democracy and economic development' (see Morrison 2006: 5 – emphasis in original). The US has succeeded the British Empire as leader of the 'world community', and 11 September has required *that* community to demonstrate 'strength of common endeavour' – exemplified in Blair's speech to the Labour Party Conference in October 2001: 'Round the world, 11 September is bringing governments and people to reflect, consider and change.... There is a coming together. The power of community is asserting itself' (cited in Morrison 2006: 33).

However, beyond this notion of community asserting itself as a new technology of power and conflict management, there lies the counter idea of 'community empowerment'. As Stewart and others (some referred to above) have argued, the language and practice of community has been appropriated by the political right into a discourse of domination rather than empowerment – as 'a *means* of government.... [G]overning through community' (Rose 1996, 1999, emphasis in original, cited in Stewart 2001: 121). As we have seen, appealing to community seeks to reinforce notions of individual and family responsibilities, allegiances, moral duties, ties and loyalties within and to the 'community'. However, because community remains a contested concept this 'opens it up as a legitimate site of struggle' (Shaw and Martin 2000: 405) at both a local level and (thanks to advancements in new information and communications technology) globally. As Ledwith argues, 'civil society remains a site of both liberation and domination with a narrow divide between the two' (Ledwith 2005: 27). In the next section, we consider the emancipatory potential and transformative possibilities of community engagement in conflict.

Community, conflict and social transformation

The assertion in Durkheimian and communitarian thinking on the desirability of social harmony and community cohesion regulated via the sanctions of a benign state and its civic associations (representative of the common consciousness of the moral majority) is highly problematic. Importantly, it fails to acknowledge the crucial matter of power and legitimacy, and the capacity of the moral majority to influence the way we see the world. In the discussion that follows we focus on alternative understandings of community and conflict as positions from which to generate different insights into the nature of power relations that allow the disadvantaged to become more fully conscious of their social world on their own terms.

Classical sociological positions

As Weber's account of bureaucratic organisations demonstrates, society's rules are largely the outcome of power struggles between conflicting interests and do not necessarily reflect universal needs. And as structural Marxists argue, the state apparatus and civil society exist to represent the interests of the bourgeoisie (Parkin 1992). Both Weber and Marx – in contrast to Durkheim – also believed that the western capitalist system was incapable of being humanised or reformed. However, whereas Weber accepted the fate of industrial capitalism as inevitable, believing its overpowering drive towards bureaucratic rationalisation acted as an 'iron cage' of domination into which 'men will be forced to fit themselves helplessly' (Löwith 1982: 54), Marx believed that 'men' could transform their situation and 'regain control over the manner of their mutual relations' (Löwith 1982: 25). Gramsci's (1971) concept of 'hegemony', and his belief in the possibilities of generating a radical counter hegemony or common sense rooted in socialist ideals, is also enlightening here. Gramsci stressed the centrality of will and human agency, and the potential of educating the working class – through helping them to see the relevance of politics to their everyday experiences – to engage in class conflict (see Hoffman 2007).

Community conflict and radical democracy

The assumption within communitarian thinking that consensus and unity in communities is both desirable and feasible, particularly for ensuring a single, coherent 'voice' in social policy deliberations, not only fails to acknowledge difference and diversity within communities but also closes off prospects for open critical dialogue. As Little argues, in communitarian philosophy: 'the public sphere is emasculated. Despite the rhetoric of a renewed polity and forms of governance that could regenerate community, the denial of the complexity of communities serves to de-politicize the real differences and conflicts that exist...' (Little 2002: 374).

Communities are not simply homogeneous formations built on shared values, but more often than not represent a local site where competing values and aspirations are contested. It is important to recognise that 'conflict is part of community' (Creed 2006a: 39) and that rather than seek to oppress conflict it needs to be seen as essential to struggles for social justice. As Lister argues:

> It is the local rather than the national which provides the arena for
> many citizenship struggles…. As a process, community action can
> both strengthen deprived communities and, through collective
> action, promote the citizenship of individuals within those commu-
> nities. Such action can boost individual and collective self-confidence,
> as individuals and groups come together to see themselves as political
> actors and effective citizens. This is especially true for women for
> whom involvement in community organizations can be more per-
> sonally fruitful than engagement in formal politics which are often
> experienced as more alienating than empowering. (Lister 1997: 33)

Little draws on radical democracy theory and Chantal Mouffe's critique
of New Labour's third way conviction on the need to manufacture
political consensus. For Mouffe, this is simply an attempt to close off
avenues for the expression of political dissent, and to distract attention
away from inequalities of power (Little 2002). Moreover, there will
invariably be situations where irreconcilable differences emerge within
communities – due to 'value pluralism' (where several conflictual values
exist, all equally valid) – and, therefore, conflict becomes an inherent
part of social life and, consequently, democracy:

> In this sense democracy is envisaged not as the mechanism for solv-
> ing disagreements but rather as a means of enabling their expression.
> Thus radical democracy provides a counterpoint to the perfectionism
> of theories that see consensus as a healthy state of affairs by recognis-
> ing the untidy contingency which emanates from incommensurable
> value pluralism. (Little 2002: 378)

Radical democracy requires the establishment of political arrangements
which provide the means for individuals and communities to express
their interests freely and to be heard. This will necessitate opening up
more public spaces (in a wide range of locations) to political debate so as
to enable the participation of a broad range of interest communities. It
requires an acceptance that it is never possible to create a fully-inclusive,
consensual community (i.e. a politics without conflict) and that the task
is to establish a political system that accommodates difference and
diversity – 'politics *with* conflict' (Hoffman 2004: 37 – emphasis added),
with never the possibility of final reconciliation. It requires arrangements
that allow differences and dissent to be freely expressed in a public space.
Consequently, for Mouffe, any notion of community that seeks to operate

as a unifying mechanism is essentialist and would deny free expression to diverse voices. In contrast, Mouffe's interest lies in the construction of a political project that 'allows us to grasp the diversity of ways in which relations of power are constructed, and helps us to reveal the forms of exclusion present in all pretensions to universalism and in claims to have found the true essence of rationality' (cited in Little 2002: 377).

Mouffe's project is close to Habermas' interest in constructing the 'ideal speech situation' where generalisable interests can be represented and discussed effectively and rationally, through open, non-coerced debate. For Habermas, the ideal democratic communication procedure would allow for open-ended possibilities – that is, it cannot be dominated by pre-determined expectations and, through communication, a range of political outcomes become possible. So long as parties engaged in such communications are knowledgeable about the issues under discussion and are open to the line of reasoning of others, Habermas believes that rational and optimal solutions to social problems, based on the broadest consensus, are possible (Habermas 1981). Although, as Doyal and Gough point out, some critics argue that 'such a view of rational debate is hope-lessly idealistic, since all known speech situations are dominated by the contingencies of power and resource constraint' (Doyal and Gough 1991: 123), Habermas was describing an 'ideal' – a political goal.

> Habermas is acutely aware of the difficulties of reconciling his vision of human liberation with existing social realities. He argues that the life world where the everyday dramas of action and interaction occur has been 'colonised' – dehumanised and compartmentalised – by the organisational and instrumental rationality of capitalist enterprise and the state. The task of liberational struggle is to peel away the false ideological beliefs about what it is impossible for individuals and collectives to try to achieve, beliefs which lead people to define the frag-mentation of everyday life within capitalism as natural and to equate capitalism itself with social progress. (Doyal and Gough 1991: 124)

If the notion of freely-expressed and plural forms of communicative exchange is unrealistic and utopian, due to the ideological control of communication mediums in capitalist society, then it is clear that any transformative struggle needs to be constructed from within the capitalist system. As Hardt and Negri argue:

> Habermas's conception of ethical communication in a democratic public sphere appears completely utopian and unrealizable ... because it is impossible to isolate ourselves, our relationships, and our

communication outside the instrumentality of capital and the mass media. We are all already inside, contaminated. If there is going to be any ethical redemption it will have to be constructed inside the system. (Hardt and Negri 2005: 261)

If this is indeed the case, that is, that any transformation of the social order – be it regaining control over our situation (as Marx suggested); developing a 'counter hegemony' to the prevailing order (in the Gramscian sense); or establishing the 'ideal speech situation' free from the stranglehold of false ideological beliefs (as envisioned by Habermas) – must be constructed from within the existing social system, then a set of tools for realising this are provided in the critical pedagogy of Paulo Freire and his radical approach to community development.

Critical pedagogy and radical community development

Freire's pedagogy offers a mechanism for working with oppressed communities in ways that will potentially enable them to identify, understand and counter the instrumental hold capitalist ideology has over their (and all of our) lives. Central to Freire's philosophy is the belief that people have an ontological vocation to become more 'fully human'. Moreover, 'humans are aware, both of themselves as conscious beings, and of their existence in space and time. Human awareness allows for ... the capacity for creative thinking and, hence, potentially at least, the capacity to transform rather than merely adapt to reality' (Blackburn 2000: 5).

This comes close to Burkett's argument that 'it is imagination, creativity and uncertainty rather than reason, evidence and certainty which lie at the heart of the possibility for postmodern community development' (Burkett 2001: 243). However, whilst people clearly have the potential to improve their situation in creative and positive ways, 'society appears to exclude some from realizing that freedom' (Blackburn 2000: 5). Freire's principle of community development seeks to enable disadvantaged people to overcome barriers to freedom by allowing them to develop a new awareness about themselves, including an understanding of how opportunity has been (and is being) denied them, and to explore the possibilities for surmounting oppressive practices and engaging in action for social change. Freire believed that:

[H]umans exist within a certain historical context, with its economic, social, political, and cultural norms, structures and institutions. History for Freire is a human creation ... 'reflecting the way that those humans possessing the power to do so have imposed their intentions upon the social world, and created the structured conditions under which people live.' (Lankshear, 1993, p. 97). Like Marx, Freire believes that the structures of capitalist societies are founded on relations of exploitation of certain groups or individuals by others. Prevailing historical conditions in capitalist societies make it difficult, therefore, for exploited individuals and groups...to pursue their ontological vocation. (Blackburn 2000: 5)

For Freire, dominance over oppressed people is maintained through a 'culture of silence' where resistance is submerged through the denial of critical consciousness by the social institutions of society – particularly the formal education system. He therefore sought to establish the principles for a rehumanised education system – one that could act as a subversive force for change and offer new possibilities for achieving greater social wellbeing. As Richard Shaull explains in his foreword to Freire's *Pedagogy of the Oppressed*:

> every human being, no matter how 'ignorant' or submerged in the 'culture of silence' he or she may be, is capable of looking critically at the world in a dialogical encounter with others. Provided with the proper tools for such encounter, the individual can gradually perceive personal and social reality as well as the contradictions in it, become conscious of his or her own perception of that reality, and deal critically with it. In this process, the old, paternalistic teacher-student relationship is overcome. ... 'People educate each other through the mediation of the world'. (Shaull, foreword in Freire 1996: 14)

Through transforming education from a system of conformity to a practice of freedom, participants can learn to appreciate community conflict as an expression of human agency essential for challenging oppression. 'To surmount the situation of oppression, people must first critically recognize its causes, so that through transforming action they can create a new situation, one which makes possible the pursuit of a fuller humanity' (Freire 1996: 29). One of the foremost barriers to freedom of oppression is the way the disadvantaged have 'adapted to the structure of domination in which they are immersed, and have become resigned to it, are inhibited from waging the struggle for freedom so long as they feel incapable of running the risks it requires' (Freire 1996: 29). This is the dual bind the oppressed experience: 'without freedom they cannot exist authentically. Yet, although they desire authentic existence, they fear it. They are at one and the same time themselves and the oppressor whose consciousness they have internalized' (Freire 1996: 30). This clearly raises a crucial question: 'How can the oppressed, as divided, unauthentic beings, participate in developing the pedagogy of their liberation?' (Freire 1996: 30).

Freire describes the need for a liberating education – a 'pedagogy of the oppressed' – with two distinct stages:

> In the first, the oppressed unveil the world of oppression and through the praxis commit themselves to its transformation. In the second, in which the reality of oppression has already been transformed, this pedagogy ceases to belong to the oppressed and becomes a pedagogy of all people in the process of permanent liberation. In both stages, it is always through action in depth that the culture of domination is culturally confronted. In the first stage this confrontation occurs through the change in the way the oppressed perceive the world of oppression; in the second stage, through the expulsion of the myths created and developed in the old order, which like spectres haunt the new structure emerging from the revolutionary transformation. (Freire 1996: 36–37)

The first stage of Freire's educational philosophy emerges through a process whereby oppressed people generate a critical consciousness about their situation followed by engagement in collective action to transform their world. This process is aided by a critical pedagogy – 'a democratic process of education that takes place in community groups and forms the basis of transformation. It is founded on *conscientisation*, the process of becoming critically aware of the structural forces of power that shape our lives, and leads to action for change' (Ledwith 2005: 95 – emphasis in original). This way, disadvantaged communities can begin to understand the mechanisms of social injustice and to formulate their own agenda for change. Critical pedagogy works through facilitating dialogue: '*Dialogue* focuses on the stories of the people, and in *problematising* personal/local issues, exposes socially constructed identities that have been silenced' (Ledwith 2005: 95 – emphasis in original). Freire's aim was to enable people to critically discover the true causes of their oppression and to develop strategies to transform their situation. This allows them to avoid accepting the harshness of their lives fatalistically – to not blame themselves for their poverty and disadvantage (e.g. because they are not clever enough or they should have worked harder at school). It allows them to develop critical consciousness – 'the stage at which connections are made with the way in which structures of society discriminate, reaching into people's being, shaping their lives in prejudiced ways' (Ledwith 2005: 97) – effectively, an insight into the connection between individual problems and their structural underpinnings. Critical consciousness is therefore the antithesis to false consciousness generated through hegemony – the way political, social, economic and cultural domination lead people to accept social injustice unquestioningly (Ledwith 2005). It offers the means by which people can learn to understand the way the dominant ideology is infused throughout all areas of society and to develop counter strategies to resist this process. As Ledwith, drawing on the ideas of Herbert Marcuse, explains:

> Critical thought is discouraged in a world that is founded on capitalism; one in which the interests of the powerful are served by the subservience of the many. Herbert Marcuse...identified structures of domination and social control that produce an advanced state of conformity.... Marcuse talks about false consciousness being the conceptual repression of understanding life experience: 'a restriction of meaning' (Marcuse, 1991, p. 208). (Ledwith 2005: 71)

However, whilst recognising that capitalist societies are capable of retaining domination through restricting meaning, Marcuse also acknowledged that, at the same time, 'forces and tendencies exist which may break this containment and explode the society.... Both tendencies are there side by side – and even the one in the other' (Marcuse 1991: xiv). Through facilitating the development of critical reason, Freirean pedagogy offers possibilities for easing the release of these forces and breaking down structures of domination. Building critical consciousness and expanding meaning are key functions of the educational aims of radical community development – in contrast to the educational aims of mainstream schooling which serve to produce 'docile bodies' (Foucault 1976). 'For Freire, education can never be neutral: its political function is to liberate or domesticate. In other words, the process of education either creates critical, autonomous thinkers or it renders people passive and unquestioning' (Ledwith 2005: 53). As Bourdieu concludes: 'A large part of social suffering stems from the poverty of people's relationship to the educational system, which not only shapes social identities but also the image they have of their destiny (which undoubtedly helps to explain what is called the passivity of the dominated ...)' (Bourdieu 2004: 43).

In contrast, critical pedagogy provides an opportunity not only for people to identify – in a dialectical way – the contradictions in society that affect their life chances, but also for facilitating collective transformative action. Critical pedagogy is therefore not merely a theoretical process but a dynamic, dialectical process involving action and reflection (what Freire called 'praxis'). 'Praxis, which can also be understood as the fusion of theory and action, lies at the root of Freire's pedagogy, and flies in the face of the hierarchical and oppressive tendencies inherent in what Freire called banking education' (Blackburn 2000: 7).

Banking education is used by Freire to characterise the formal education system – a system where teachers deposit 'superior' information into their pupils/students who, in turn, merely memorise and repeat that information. In contrast, Freire proposed an education process that would allow the oppressed (as participants) to take control of their own learning and development rather than passively accept the specifications of the state-sponsored system. Freire believed, as did Marcuse, that the role of the educator (or intellectual) is fundamental to preparing the ground for liberating the oppressed – requiring a fundamental 'revolution in thinking': 'the educator must shed ingrained attitudes of "anti-dialogue" which may have become automatic. Not only must the educator be prepared to respect the participants' knowledge as valuable as his own, he must also be prepared to enter into the reality of the participants' lives' (Blackburn 2000: 8).

The role of the educator, therefore, is to facilitate a process whereby the oppressed educate themselves within the context of their own reality. This will require the educator engaging in preparatory work with the participants – conducting interviews, focus groups and participant observation exercises over a period of time – from which he/she will be able to extract a number of themes which are central to their life experience. Subsequent group meetings will involve discussions based on these themes. 'This preliminary phase of investigation by the participants into their reality is the first stage of conscientization, as the participants will become gradually (and in some cases dramatically) aware that the problems of their lives have causes which can be addressed, and transformed through action' (Blackburn 2000: 8).

Such an approach to working with disadvantaged communities forms the basis of radical community development. Through radical community development, it is possible to channel the collective anger people may feel when faced with the realisation that their suffering is due to gross inequalities in society attributable to the political choices of governments rather than their own failings and weaknesses.

'Anger … generates an energy that can be redirected into positive action. Working with Freirean pedagogy, we know that *relevance* is the key to unlocking the energy to act, and relevance is located in people's every day reality' (Ledwith 2005: 53 – emphasis in original).

Community, therefore, offers a site where individuals can critically engage with their world and reflect – through dialogue with others – on the way opportunities and life-chances are shaped in the context of dominant social, political, economic and cultural arrangements, and to connect with others in social relations of trust, mutuality and respect in order to challenge and transform situations of oppression and injustice. As Glass explains:

> The oppressed are challenged to see beyond individualistic experiences and particular situations to discern the force of systems and ideologies that permeate their daily lives, structure oppression (dehumanization), and bind people together in larger, and sometimes global, contexts. The connections between everyday experience and these larger forces highlight the features of problematic 'limit-situations' that must be changed by collective 'limit-acts' that both contest those systems and ideologies and aim at 'untested feasibilities' or possible futures with more space for self-determination. (Glass 2001: 18)

Once stage one of Freire's liberating education model is complete and the reality of oppression has been transformed, critical pedagogy then becomes the property of all people as a process of permanent liberation within the new social order. Community must continue to offer a space where political dissent can thrive – the oppressed must not become the new oppressor:

> The correct method for a revolutionary leadership to employ in the task of liberation … lies in dialogue. … Propaganda, management, manipulation – all arms of domination – cannot be the instruments of their rehumanisation. The only effective instrument is a humanizing pedagogy in which the revolutionary leadership establishes a permanent relationship of dialogue …. (Freire 1996: 49–50)

Freedom is not fixed in the here and now, so liberation requires continual critical reflection and constant struggle towards a vision of a more just, democratic society that sustains diverse communities. Here, Freire differs from Marx in that he does not envisage ever arriving at a 'just' egalitarian society at some future time. Instead,

> Human liberation, or what Freire calls humanization, is a goal that for Freire can never be fully achieved because it requires an ongoing encounter with reality, which is itself permanently changing. Life and history are thus dynamic processes, of which man is both fully a part, and yet unable ever fully to control. (Blackburn 2000: 5)

As Glass suggests:

> Freire understood how fragile and contingent this struggle had to be, and accepted that no guarantees could warrant the humanistic reinvention of citizenship. Conscientization is thus a mode of life always in the process of becoming, one that enacts ongoing cultural action for liberation that accepts an ethic of the 'fineness of the striving' as 'a job to do in history' (Freire, 1994b, p. 50). This ethic indicates precisely the importance of education as a practice of freedom for a successful revolution because it enables the ongoing reinvention and recreation of democratic culture. (Glass 2001: 19)

Liberation education is therefore central to the practice of freedom and democracy.

> Without this kind of praxis, human beings cease to be the 'makers of their way' and they become simply what history makes of them. For Freire, to be human means to make and remake one's self through making history and culture, to struggle against the limiting conditions that prevent such creative action, and to dream into existence a world where every person has this opportunity and responsibility. (Glass 2001: 19)

Sustained conflict against oppression, therefore, is essential for freedom and democracy to thrive. As McGhee suggests, referring to the work of John Solomos, 'antagonism, disagreement and conflict are essential to the democratic process' (McGhee 2005: 183) and, particularly with the aid of critical pedagogy, offer a means whereby the structural underpinnings of discrimination and disadvantage which deny opportunity can be identified, challenged and transformed. However, it is because of this potential for social transformation through critical pedagogy that there has been, as Bauman observes, concerted efforts in mainstream community development programmes to direct dissent towards attaining the government's agenda ('community safety', for example) – effectively, 'the channelling of public concerns away from the primary sources of contemporary anxiety' (Bauman 2001: 148–149).

> In the course of this kind of articulation of the purpose and function of community, the other aspects of community missing from contemporary life (the ones directly relevant to the sources of present troubles) tend to be left unthematized and off the agenda. The two tasks which should be invoked by community to counter head-on the pathologies of the atomized society of today on a battleground that truly counts are equality of the resources necessary to recast the fate of individuals *de jure* into the capacities of individuals *de facto*, and collective insurance against individual incapacities and misfortunes. (Bauman 2001: 149)

Consistent with a Freirean perspective, Bauman supports the notion of redefining community as a site for mobilising individuals collectively in a struggle to seize control over the conditions that shape life chances.

Criticisms of Freire

In a similar vein to criticisms levelled against Habermas' concept of the 'ideal speech situation' (i.e. that this is utopian and non-realisable given the dominance of capitalist hegemony), Freire has been criticised for being overly idealistic about the possibility of realising a pedagogy free from ideological or cultural invasion. Blackburn, for example, citing Rahnema, argues that the main difficulty with dialogical education is that 'external activists who adopt Freire's ideas suffer from an "inherent tendency to…manoeuvre and manipulate [the oppressed] and impose on them their own ideological frameworks and definitions of the aims of the struggle"' (Blackburn 2000: 11). However, whilst this may be a genuine criticism of state-led community development, it does not mean community educators cannot work in ways envisaged by Freire. Indeed, Blackburn tends to contradict himself by suggesting that 'any pre-determined vision of liberation introduced from the outside is ultimately paternalistic, since it presupposes that the oppressed are incapable of determining their own endogenously produced vision of liberation' (Blackburn 2000: 12). It is clearly paternalistic to presuppose that the oppressed are incapable of appreciating when they are being stage-managed and controlled.

A further criticism aimed at Freire is his apparent failure to deal adequately with the contestable nature of knowledge – a criticism that could also be directed at Habermas. Glass, for instance, argues that Freire's claim that the oppressed need to develop an authentic, knowledge-based grounding from which to understand and ultimately challenge the nature of their oppression does not acknowledge the possibility that the explanations they arrive at may be false. As Glass puts it, 'knowledge of the self and the social world and their causal relations is significantly less certain and has far less reliable mechanisms for testing than knowledge claims about the natural world, which are themselves notoriously unwarranted' (Glass 2001: 21). However, as Glass also acknowledges, Freire did stress the importance of 'an ongoing critical questioning that refuses to be seduced into certainties that eliminate all traces of doubt' (Glass 2001: 21).

> As Freire always maintained, the cultural and historical praxis that is at the heart of being human is unending. We cannot transcend our existence as 'unconcluded, limited, conditioned, historical beings' and this limit actually provides the 'opportunity of setting ourselves free' insofar as we join the 'political struggle for transformation of the world' (Freire, 1994 ...). (Glass 2001: 22)

As Blackburn suggests, for Freire to be truly understood requires 'an acceptance that nothing can truly ever be understood ... and that there are no immediate or exact answers to any particular situation or problem. Even the word "conclusion" is anathema to Freire given that he saw human life as an "unfinished project" that could never be "concluded"' (Blackburn 2000: 13).

Finally, Freire's theory seems ambivalent in respect of violent struggle. Whilst Freire 'personally abhorred violence ... [h]e readily asserted that revolution might entail violent means' particularly given 'the unrelenting violence of the oppressor' (Glass 2001: 22). This leads us to ask the question, is violent conflict in struggles for social justice ever legitimate?

Is violent conflict legitimate?

John Grayson argues that power will never be given up by the powerful and therefore it can only be taken, and that this relies on the effective organisation, tactics and strategies of political campaigns. Sometimes, this may require violence (acknowledging that 'violence' is a contested concept). In his archaeology of the history of working-class social movements, Grayson identifies violence as essential to the success of a number of campaigns (Grayson 1977). This theme is developed further by Crouch in his discussion on the evolution of the post-war welfare state – a development he explains in terms of a compromise forced upon the capitalist class by a complicated set of factors which included economic instability, struggles with trade unions, a deteriorating social infrastructure and the growing appeal of social democracy (Crouch 2004). In relation to this, Crouch asks:

> How essential were the reality and fears of chaos and disruption within that complex general equation? It is impossible to pretend that they played no part. Both the social compromise of the mid-twentieth century and the associated interlude of relatively maximal democracy...were forged in a crucible that included turmoil. It is necessary to remember this, as we condemn sections among the no-global demonstrators for their violence.... We must ask ourselves: without a massive escalation of truly disruptive actions of the kind that those demonstrators advocate, will anything reverse the profit calculations of global capital enough to bring its representatives to the bargaining table, to force an end to child slavery and other forms of labour degradation, to the production of levels of pollution that are now visibly destroying our atmosphere, to the wasteful use of non-renewable resources, to growing extremes of wealth and poverty both within and between nations? (Crouch 2004: 123)

Inevitably, community action as violent conflict is condemned by mainstream politicians, policy makers and academics alike as 'irrational' 'criminal' acts. This mainstream perspective has, however, been challenged by radical theorists. For example, Black nationalists invariably depict such activities as 'rebellions' or 'insurrections' – thereby ascribing these events with political rather than criminal descriptions. This position is characterised in some of the punk and reggae music released immediately prior to the disturbances of the early 1980s (described in the previous chapter) – for example, Steel Pulse's *Handsworth Revolution* (1978), the Ruts' *Babylon's Burning* and *Jah War* (1979), and Linton Kwesi Johnson's *Independent Intravenshan* and *Fite Dem Back* (1979). Conflict here is synonymous with legitimate political protest by 'communities of resistance' defending themselves 'against an oppressive and all-too-frequent, repressive, system' (Hasan 2000: 181) – exemplifying the importance of community as a site for resistance. As Gilroy observes, 'localised struggles over education, racist violence and police practices continually reveal how black people have made use of notions of community to provide the axis along which to organise themselves' (Gilroy, cited in Hasan 2000: 181).

Marxists have understood violent urban conflict as a 'form of class struggle outside the workplace' (Hasan 2000: 191). Gary Younge, for example, argues that urban rioting is a class-based act and a rational response to the lack of opportunity to voice an alternative democratic position. He argues that a riot:

> is often the last and most desperate weapon available to those with the least power. Rioting is a class act. Wealthy people don't do it because either they have the levers of democracy at their disposal, or they can rely on the state or private security firms to do their violent work for them. (Younge 2005: 31)

Rioting can be the only available option in the face of oppression or the only means of achieving progressive social reform. As African-American abolitionist Frederick Douglass explains:

> If there is no struggle, there is no progress…. Those who profess to favour freedom and yet depreciate agitation are men who want crops without ploughing up the ground; they want rain without thunder and lightening. They want the ocean without the awful roar of its many waters…. Power concedes nothing without a demand. It never did and it never will. (Cited in Younge 2005: 31)

Younge suggests that Douglass' thesis offers a more plausible explanation of urban unrest than those which conceptualise rioters as mere 'scum'. Discussing the French riots of November 2005, Younge remarks:

> Those who wondered what French youth had to gain by taking to the streets should ask what they had to lose. Unemployed, socially excluded, harassed by the police and condemned to poor housing, they live on estates that are essentially open prisons. Statistically invisible (it is against the law and republican principle to collect data based on race or ethnicity) and politically unrepresented (mainland France does not have a single non-white MP), their aim has been simply to get their plight acknowledged. (Younge 2005: 31)

Younge also believes the riots were, in a sense, successful, leading to offers by the state of 'greater social justice' (Younge 2005: 31) – though this was largely in the form of work incentive schemes and investment in education rather than significant redistribution (i.e. in terms of power and wealth). The main principle that remains, however, is:

> in certain conditions rioting is not just justified but may also be necessary, and effective.... From the poll tax demonstrations to Soweto, history is littered with such cases.... When all non-violent, democratic means of achieving a just end are unavailable, redundant or exhausted, rioting is justifiable. When state agencies charged with protecting communities fail to do so or actually attack them, it may be necessary in self-defence. (Younge 2005: 31)

Bourdieu has also argued that violent conflict may be a necessary strategy to counter the injustices of global institutions and super-powers – an understandable reaction to what he sees as the existence of: 'Western arrogance, which leads people to act as if they had the monopoly of reason and could set themselves up as world policemen, in other words as self-appointed holders of the monopoly of legitimate violence, capable of applying the force of arms in the service of universal justice' (Bourdieu 2004: 19–20).

Like Freire, Bourdieu refers reservations about the use of violence by the powerless to the issue of the remorseless violence of the powerful:

> Terrorist violence, through the irrationalism of the despair which is almost always at its root, refers back to the inert violence of the powers which invoke reason. Economic coercion is often dressed up in juridical reasons. Imperialism drapes itself in the legitimacy of international bodies. And, through the very hypocrisy of the rationalizations intended to mask its double standards, it tends to provoke or justify, among the Arab, South American or African peoples, a very profound revolt against the reason which cannot be separated from the abuses of power which are armed or justified by reason (economic, scientific or any other). (Bourdieu 2004: 20)

Legitimated in the name of the 'international community', Blair's 'Britain' engaged (and continues to engage under Gordon Brown) in US-led violent assaults on a sovereign nation state, Iraq – engagements George Monbiot characterises as 'illegal acts of aggression' (Monbiot 2005b: 31). Monbiot describes the 'liberation' of Falluja in November 2004 when US marines repeatedly used warheads containing around 35 per cent thermobaric novel explosive and 65 per cent standard high explosive. An article published in the *Marine Corps Gazette* in 2000 described the use of thermobaric weapons by the Russians in Grozny. They form a cloud of volatile gases or finely powdered explosives:

> This cloud is then ignited and the subsequent fireball sears the surrounding area while consuming the oxygen in this area. The lack of oxygen creates an enormous overpressure.... Personnel under the cloud are literally crushed to death. Outside the cloud area, the blast wave travels at some 3,000 metres per second... [having] the effect of a tactical nuclear weapon without residual radiation.... Those personnel caught directly under the aerosol cloud will die from the flame or overpressure. For those on the periphery of the strike, the injuries can be severe. Burns, broken bones, contusions from flying debris and blindness may result. Further, the crushing injuries from the overpressure can create air embolism within blood vessels, concussions, multiple internal haemorrhages in the liver and spleen, collapsed lungs, rupture of the eardrums and displacement of the eyes from their sockets. (Cited in Monbiot 2005b: 31)

At Falluja, the US inflicted their assault on a city harbouring between 30,000 and 50,000 civilians – leading Monbiot to ask 'is there any crime the coalition forces have not committed in Iraq?' (Monbiot 2005b: 31). At the same time, no person has been held to account for these massacres.

The inability to hold the powerful to account for their human rights' violations globally has been mirrored domestically – particularly since 11 September – by the erosion of democracy, persistent poverty and widening inequality, and the wearing away of civil liberties. This inability to access political representation and to address poverty and injustice at home is partly a consequence of the present engagement of Britain in permanent global warfare.

> Not only does the permanent state of war suspend democracy indefinitely; the existence of new pressure and possibilities of democracy are answered by the sovereign powers with war. War acts as a mechanism of containment. ... War tends to become a form of rule. This shift is reflected ... in the mechanisms of the legitimation of violence employed by the sovereign powers. (Hardt and Negri 2005: 341)

It is within this context of legitimised violence at both the global and local level that the emerging forces of democracy now find themselves.

Because of this, strategies of resistance to oppression need to move beyond the mere local level and engage in struggles for wider structural change at the global level – struggles that challenge the crimes and abuses of the powerful.

Whether such struggles can avoid violence is open to deliberation. Hardt and Negri argue the need for the democratic use of force and violence in such struggles, although their definition of such a form of violence is rather imprecise – other than it being: (a) only pursued for political ends 'at the service of the political decisions of the community' (Hardt and Negri 2005: 342); (b) only pursued in defence (as an act of resistance); (c) organised democratically (rather than imposed by an undemocratic authority); and (d) based on a careful reflection of what weapons would be the most effective to use. In the case of this latter point, Hardt and Negri refer to the possibility of inventing new weapons – for example, the use of 'shock tactics' such as the 'kiss-ins' conducted by Queer Nation, or the various forms of carnival organised at anti-globalisation protests. This comes closer to what Glass (2001) describes as the use of 'militant non-violence' in struggles for freedom – similar to the non-violent civil disobedience advocated by Mahatma Gandhi and practised by Martin Luther King Jnr. Other forms of militant non-violence might include abstaining from voting in general elections – advocated by the A World to Win (2005) campaign. Abstention on a significant scale would amount to an unprecedented rejection of the existing political system and what passes for democracy:

> The current political system is blatantly undemocratic. For example, only one in four of all voters endorsed New Labour in 2001 yet they won a huge majority. The House of Commons is a farce and has no independent power. It endorsed the Iraq war and backed authoritarian measures against civil liberties…. (A World to Win 2005: 1)

Whilst A World to Win acknowledges that the right to vote was won through class struggle over hundreds of years, they argue the need to take action to ensure that the right to vote means something again. This includes proposals for extending democracy and creating a political system that people can influence directly. This would involve 'bringing democracy to the workplace, giving those who create and consume goods and services shared ownership and control;…putting people in charge of their own lives at local as well as national level, through Assemblies representing different community interests' (A World to Win 2005: 1).

George Monbiot's solution to the same impasse also advocates non-violence – that is, non-violent protest via direct action: 'The formula for making things happen is simple and has never changed. If you wish to alter a policy or depose a prime minister between elections, you must take to the streets' (Monbiot 2004: 23). In the light of British and US aggression in Iraq, John Pilger also supports the case for non-violent direct action in the form of civil disobedience: 'There is only one form of opposition now: it is civil disobedience leading to what the police call civil unrest. The latter is feared by undemocratic governments of all stripes' (Pilger 2004a: 27). Inspiration for non-violent direct action can be found in the words of activist and humanist Rachel Corrie. Corrie was killed by an Israeli bulldozer in the Gaza strip on 16 March 2003 whilst working in Rafah for a non-violent resistance organisation – the International Solidarity Movement – striving to stop the demolition of Palestinian homes. The month before she was killed she wrote the following email to her parents:

> I look forward to seeing more and more people willing to resist the direction the world is moving in, a direction where our personal experiences are irrelevant, that we are defective, that our communities are not important, that we are powerless, that our future is determined, and that the highest level of humanity is expressed through what we choose to buy at the mall. (Cited in Corrie and Corrie 2005: 28)

Glass identifies in such examples of militant non-violence a number of important lessons that can be used to reformulate Freirean theory:

> Freire noted that the 'ethical and political awareness of the fighters is of paramount importance' for the success of liberation struggles even when they are military ones…. Nonetheless, Freire clearly failed to see the possibility that the theory and strategy of militant nonviolence offered a way to construct an integrated historicist theory of liberation education that combined consistent ontological, epistemological, ethical, and political positions. (Glass 2001: 22–23)

The problem with trying to condone or legitimate the use of violence in liberation struggles is that it is likely to raise strong moral objections that are exceptionally difficult to counter. In contrast,

> Cultural action for liberation wedded to militant nonviolence furnishes an ethical and political framework consistent with a

historicized and always partially opaque ontology and a historicized, perspectival epistemology…. This is a method of radical action unconstrained by meanings and knowledge claims that are historically situated and culturally constructed, and that is suited to a polyvocal discourse giving expression to identities marked by contradictory, multiple, and shifting boundaries. It gives shape and transformative force to struggles within intensively contested contexts without reinscribing violence or reinstantiating discourses and relations of domination. Such an interpretation of cultural action for liberation fortifies the basic principles of a pluralistic democracy, and is also capable of combating armed force, defending territory, and facing up to the real politics of an armed and aggressive world. (Glass 2001: 23)

In other words, it is argued that militant non-violence can be more easily authenticated as a strategy and, as a consequence, it is therefore more likely to attract and sustain the backing of a wider constituency of support. Glass sees in this reformulation of Freire's theory a consistency with his notion of dialogue and the importance of ideological struggle in overcoming oppression. Moreover, it 'provides a political strategy that makes more credible the demand for a permanent struggle for liberation since it preserves to all equally the power to seek self-determined hopes and dreams' (Glass 2001: 23).

Conclusions

The fact that community and conflict have remained durable concepts in sociological discourse throughout modernity provides evidence of the value of these notions for academics, policy makers and social activists alike. Whilst community and conflict remain inexact and contestable concepts, what is important is the meaning of these terms as they are utilised and experienced. As the above discussion has demonstrated, the way community and conflict have been utilised has differed substantially. More specifically, notions of community and conflict have been embraced and utilised by the powerful in order to generate or maintain social cohesion and reinforce existing power relationships in society. At the same time, community and conflict have been something experienced – something shared by people – which distinguishes their interests from others and provides a potential site, context and incentive for mobilising social action against oppression and in pursuit of social justice. Focusing on community and conflict as it is used in these ways allows the utility of these concepts for both state action (through social policy interventions aimed at managing conflict in communities in order to maintain the status quo) and for social activism (where the oppressed collectively engage in conflict in pursuit of social change) to be recognised and understood.

The analytical framework established in this chapter will be used to examine New Labour's community-focused policies in the chapter that follows. We focus on two priority policy areas New Labour inherited in 1997 – that is, community safety and urban regeneration – and one which became a priority area after 'rioting' in the summer of 2001 – community cohesion. As we have already explained, thinking within the Labour Party leadership had become profoundly influenced by communitarian ideology by the time of the 1997 election – an ideology based, as we have argued, on highly dubious and problematic assumptions about the nature of community. In particular, the communitarian emphasis on the need to responsibilise individuals to generate the conditions of their own wellbeing (through hard work, thrift and engagement with likeminded others 'in community') relieves the state (the collective) of its responsibility to attend to the wider structural threats to social wellbeing founded on unequal and exploitative power relations. Consequently, our assessment raises concerns with regard to whose interests are being served by New Labour's strategies on community safety, community cohesion and urban regeneration, and about who is benefiting and who is losing out.

3

New Labour, Community Safety, Cohesion and Wellbeing

Introduction

This chapter presents an assessment of New Labour's policy discourse on community safety, cohesion and wellbeing, and how this discourse translated into social policy measures and practices rolled out over the ten years following Blair's election victory in 1997. More specifically, the chapter will deal in turn with three key priority areas of New Labour's social policy agenda – community safety, urban regeneration and community cohesion. It will briefly describe the background issues to each of these policy areas followed by a critique of the policies themselves.

As we saw in Chapter 1, throughout the two decades prior to New Labour's election Britain became an increasingly divided society – a situation largely caused by economic restructuring and neo-liberal social policy reforms. Amongst the hardest hit by these changes were sections of the working classes and ethnic minority groups – Britain's increasingly marginalised populations abandoned by the political system. Inevitably, social tensions intensified – a corollary of which was an escalation in the public's fear of crime and disorder. Consequently, restoring community safety and repairing 'broken' neighbourhoods had become key priorities for government by 1997. Later, following civil disturbances in three areas with significant Asian settlement in 2001, community cohesion was added to these priority areas.

As discussed in the previous chapter, New Labour's approach to the themes of community safety, cohesion and urban regeneration has been firmly rooted in the communitarian tradition – a discourse that emphasises the need for the state to generate social interaction between individuals 'in community' in order to strengthen civic society and, thereby, enhance community safety, cohesion and social wellbeing. However, as we also saw in the previous chapter, the communitarian notion of community is in itself problematic – based, as it is, on an assumption that community is synonymous with groupings of individuals holding shared values and where there is an absence of conflict. As we have seen throughout history, this is rarely the case. At the same time, the existence of power differentials within communities invariably means that any invitation to engage local constituencies in state-sponsored social regeneration programmes will inevitably lead to the more powerful participants dominating the agenda – with significant implications for the outcomes of these initiatives.

New Labour and 'community safety'

By the time Labour returned to government in 1997, the problem of 'crime and disorder' in Britain had risen up the social policy agenda and had become a more pressing priority for government than other areas of social welfare (particularly housing and social protection). An additional feature of this concern was a growing consensus within the media and mainstream politics that something needed to be done about the perceived rise in 'incivility' and 'anti-social behaviour' in British society. In attempting to succeed the Conservative New Right's stranglehold over the law and order debate, Labour repositioned itself in the 1990s as *the* political party that would be toughest on crime and disorder. New Labour politicians (particularly Blair, Straw and Blunkett) increasingly engaged in a political rhetoric around 'no more excuses' for crime and the need to make people feel morally responsible for their 'anti-social behaviour'. Fuel for such rhetoric was provided by Left Realists within academia – in particular, the work of Jock Young. Young played down claims by radical criminologists (particularly those that argued that 'deviance' and 'crime' are largely socially constructed by the powerful) and maintained instead that anti-social behaviour and crime were serious problems that particularly harmed disadvantaged communities. As a consequence, he saw the need for a more pragmatic approach to dealing with crime – for example, through improved street lighting and the regeneration of housing estates to design out crime, or through more effective (democratic) models of community policing – rather than dwelling on structural issues (Reiner 2007, Rock 2007). In a way, this built upon the shift in ways of conceiving and responding to the threat of crime that had been emerging since the 1980s, with an increasing focus on crime prevention and the involvement of communities.

From crime prevention to community safety

In 1983, the government established the Crime Prevention Unit within the Home Office – reflecting a shift in emphasis in criminal justice policy from detection to prevention. In the following year, it issued Interdepartmental Circular 8/84 which set out details of a multi-agency approach to crime prevention – declaring that 'preventing crime is a task for the whole community' (cited in Crawford 2007: 889). A key vehicle for rolling out crime prevention partnerships was announced in 1988 with the Safer Cities Programme. This would provide limited short-term funding for local crime prevention initiatives involving a range of organisations representing businesses, the voluntary sector, and the public sector. These partnerships were dominated by the police and tended to adopt police-led strategies (Crawford 2007).

In 1989, the Grade Report on the Fear of Crime acknowledged that the fear of crime (as much as the reality) was a major public (and therefore policy) concern. This was followed in 1990 with Interdepartmental Circular 44/90 which set out terms of reference for the Morgan Committee (alluded to in Chapter 1) to conduct a review of progress on crime prevention since Circular 8/84. The Morgan Report, published in 1991:

> fostered a significant shift in the emerging discourse. It advanced a series of significant recommendations…. The two most important were conceptual and institutional. Conceptually, it suggested that the term 'community safety' be preferred to 'crime prevention'. The latter was seen to be too narrow and too closely associated with police-related responsibilities. Community safety, by contrast, was perceived to be open to wider interpretation which could encourage 'greater participation from all sections of the community in the fight against crime'…. It was also seen as an umbrella term under which situational and social approaches could be combined rather than juxtaposed. Institutionally, the Morgan Report recommended that local authorities should be given 'statutory responsibility', working with the police, for the development and promotion of community safety. (Crawford 2007: 892)

The Conservative government rejected the central recommendations of the Morgan Report – reflecting their ideological hostility to munici-pal socialism (discussed in Chapter 1) – and focused instead on 'promoting active citizenship through the special constabulary and Neighbourhood Watch and sponsoring the expansion of CCTV' (Crawford 2007: 892). It was therefore left to New Labour to take up the mantle of community safety and, under the 1998 Crime and Disorder Act, they set out the institutional framework for implementing community safety partnerships.

Community safety partnerships

The 1998 Act set out to establish a comprehensive and targeted approach to crime control involving multi-agency partnerships in consultation with all sections of the local community. It diverged from the Morgan recommendations by placing a joint statutory duty on local authorities and the police to develop and implement crime and disorder strategies. A total of 376 partnerships were established in every local authority in England and Wales – called Crime and Disorder Reduction Partnerships (CDRPs) in England, Community Safety Partnerships (CSPs) in Wales – and each is required to conduct a triennial crime and disorder audit within its area and to deliver a strategic response. Section 17 of the 1998 Act also requires local authorities, 'in exercising their various functions, to consider the crime and disorder implications and the need to do all they reasonably can to prevent crime and disorder' (Crawford 2007: 894). The aim of this duty was to: 'give the vital work of preventing crime a new focus across a very wide range of services...putting crime and disorder considerations at the very heart of decision making, where they have always belonged' (Home Office 1997, cited in Crawford 2007: 894). The anticipation of crime is now expected to be part of the everyday activities of local government – an expectation that might have direct implications for planning decisions.

On the surface, New Labour's community safety agenda appeared to offer genuine possibilities to address the broader concerns of local communities – not just in respect of conventional crime and disorder issues, but also in relation to other social harms caused, for instance, by environmental pollution and social deprivation. Indeed, the government's guidance on statutory crime and disorder partnerships invited local partners 'to think laterally about the preparation of strategies, and even to approach their new duties in ways other than those explicitly suggested in the guidance' (see Whyte 2004: 54). As the guidance stated, 'Crucially the [Crime and Disorder] Act does not prescribe in any detail what the agenda for the local partnership should be, nor what structures will be needed to deliver the agenda' (Home Office 1998, cited in Whyte 2004: 54). Moreover, the guidance appeared to offer prospects for genuine community involvement in determining local community safety strategies. As Whyte suggests, in developing such strategies, 'the tone of the guidance does suggest that community groups with a broad interest in "community safety" should be considered for inclusion' (Whyte 2004: 55).

Evaluating community safety policies

Despite the initial promise, the implementation of community safety partnerships has not lived up to the rhetoric which accompanied their launch. In particular, building genuine partnerships between different agencies has been problematic – largely due to a general unwillingness to share information or resources, conflicting interests and priorities, and lack of inter-organisational trust. One major reason for this is that:

> the managerialist emphasis on target-setting and performance measurement has fostered an *intra*-organizational focus on meeting narrow goals that pays little attention to the task of managing inter-organizational relations and networks.... The myopic implications of performance measurement afford scant regard to the complex process of negotiating shared purposes.... In such a wider policy climate, it is difficult to encourage partners for whom crime is genuinely a peripheral concern to participate actively in community safety endeavours whilst they are being assessed for their performance in others fields. (Crawford 2007: 898 – emphasis in original)

A corollary of this has been that prospects for genuine community influence in determining the nature of local community safety strategies has not materialised. This is largely because the focus of partnerships has, despite the rhetoric of localism, been compliance with centrally-defined priorities and performance indicators – narrowly focused on crime reduction and measured against police-recorded crime figures (Crawford 2007) – rather than more holistic notions of community wellbeing (Cooper 2006, Squires 2006a). The concerns of the least powerful and socially disadvantaged have seldom been addressed – leading to what Squires terms 'the social divisions of safety' (Squires 2006a: 4).

In summarising research findings on community safety strategies to date, Squires highlights:

- a general focus on crime and disorder management rather than community wellbeing issues;
- strategies that work to a 'community agenda' dominated by older white-male representatives with a disproportionate focus on the misdemeanours of young people; and

- strategies that work to a 'partnership agenda' dominated by commercial interests, and which prioritise economic regeneration and town centre surveillance. (Squires 2006a)

As Gilling confirms, 'community consultation (and participation) has been one of the least well developed features of CDRP work in most places' (Gilling 2005: 749). This suggests that the use of 'community' in respect of crime and disorder is little more than a rhetorical device to generate an impression of general consent whilst simultaneously reinforcing the notion that it is now the collective responsibility of the community to assist in the war on crime. The government's lack of commitment to genuine local control is evident in their unwillingness to allow even the elected representatives of communities – local councillors – to take a lead role in running CDRPs. The government preferred instead to see local authorities take executive administrative control (rather than political control) over local crime prevention strategies through the Chief Executive officer – arguably to avoid antagonising other partners (particularly the police) (Hughes and Edwards 2005). In practice, therefore:

> it was a governmental agenda that drove partnerships, rather than any genuine commitment to the rhetoric of *local solutions for local problems*; and this was manifested particularly in suggestions that local strategies reflected not the results of the local audit or local consultation, but rather the crime reduction priorities of central government, which local partnerships were urged not to forget. (Gilling 2005: 741 – emphasis in original)

In order to ensure that the government agenda was prioritised, therefore, 'there has been an emphasis on the administrative and managerial rather than the political nature of crime prevention and community safety activity' (Hughes and Edwards 2005: 19). The pressure to deliver 'what works' and minimise costs means that less priority can be given to more imaginative solutions aimed at tackling the underlying structural causes (or context) of social problems faced by disadvantaged communities. The 'top-down' centrally-imposed performance agenda prioritises the core business of agencies, making it 'harder for accountability mechanisms to be exercised, meaningfully, from below, thus establishing a structural disregard for genuine community governance' (Gilling 2005: 749).

At the heart of the government's 'safety' agenda has been a meaning of safety restricted to 'sources of danger occasioned by human agents acting criminally or in disorderly ways' (Hughes and Edwards 2005: 20) – sources of danger occasioned by the most disadvantaged and vulnerable. This limited conceptualisation of safety is found in further legislation subsequent to the 1998 Act – for example, the 2002 Police Reform Act (which introduced new powers in relation to drug offences); the 2003 Anti-social Behaviour Act (which extended the responsibilities of CDRPs towards 'anti-social behaviour'); and the introduction of national targets for crime reduction with regard to vehicle crime, domestic burglary and robbery. 'Local partnerships continue to be seen as being at the forefront of work associated with the central government's stated commitment to delivering a reduction in crime, the fear of crime, anti-social behaviour and in reducing the harm that drugs cause to communities, individuals and their families' (Hughes and Edwards 2005: 21).

A particularly controversial aspect of New Labour's community safety strategy is its use of Anti-Social Behaviour Orders (asbos). Despite the many reservations about asbos – in particular, the degree to which they depart from due legal process – the number of orders issued has been increasing significantly. Between April 1999 and December 2004, 4649 asbos were issued in England and Wales. By the end of December 2005, that number had increased by 100 per cent to 9853 (Home Office 2007). Asbos have been particularly targeted against vulnerable young people (Foot 2005). For example, a 15-year-old boy with Asperger's syndrome was given an asbo declaring that he was not to stare over his neighbour's fence; an asbo was also served on another 15-year-old boy with Tourette syndrome (which may involve an inability to stop shouting out profanities) banning him from swearing in public – 'something made impossible by the gravity of his disorder' (Bright 2005a: 7). These cases reflect a growing intolerance in British society not only to children and young people generally, but also to young people experiencing behavioural difficulties. As Matt Foot argues:

> Asbos are primarily being used against the mentally ill, the elderly, the very young, drug and alcohol addicts, sex workers and beggars ... vulnerable people with complex problems. The order does nothing for such problems .... It is a national scandal that as a result of Asbos 10 young people a week are being jailed, and that beggars and prostitutes are being imprisoned even though begging and prostitution are non-imprisonable offences. (Foot 2005: 20)

Asbos represent an attack on civil liberties, reflecting a growing preoccupation within government for authoritarian forms of 'risk management' and crime prevention. As Bill Durodié, director of the international centre for security analysis at King's College London, explains:

> 'Insecurity is the key driving concept of our times…. Politicians have packaged themselves as risk managers. There is also a demand from below for protection'. The real reason for this insecurity…is the decay of the 20th century's political belief systems and social structures: people have been left 'disconnected' and 'fearful'. (Cited in Beckett 2004: 4)

Furthermore, because the government expects CDRPs in planning their local strategies to adopt a co-ordinated approach to data collection and analysis that links to the National Intelligence Model (NIM)[1] – an actuarial technique that seeks to target resources more effectively – this process invariably leads to the disproportionate targeting and further marginalisation of specific disadvantaged social categories. This is because actuarial techniques use statistical calculations to differentiate between those most likely to commit a criminal act and those not, and to use this information to assess the risk of future offending and to determine the most appropriate interventions to prevent this. Because these techniques are inclined to focus on specific populations (Logan 2005), there is a tendency for these same populations to be identified as 'most at risk' of offending. As a consequence, these groups will be disproportionately targeted by these surveillance and control procedures. 'Familiar examples of specific groups include rough sleepers, beggars, travellers and refugee/ asylum seekers; broader categories include black and minority ethnic groups, and arguably, in the present climate, young people as a whole' (Prior 2005: 360). Meanwhile, community safety strategies appear to contain blind spots in relation to more serious threats to local communities (such as environmental pollution – see Whyte 2004).

The 'Respect' agenda

Building on its crime and disorder agenda, in January 2006 the government announced further measures aimed at promoting 'acceptable behaviour', setting out a 'framework of powers and

---

[1] The NIM is a business-planning model for policing that aims to make available intelligence that will assist senior managers in strategic decision-making, in prioritising resources and in managing risk. It is a model adopted by all police forces, and seeks to ensure a more targeted and consistent approach to policing across the UK.

approaches to promote respect positively' (Respect Task Force 2006: 1) – the Respect Action Plan. Respect is defined in the Action Plan as:

> something people intuitively understand. ... The conditions for respect in society are not difficult to define. They depend ultimately on a shared commitment to a common set of values, expressed through behaviour that is considerate of others. Almost everyone of any age and from any community understands what it is and thinks it is right. (Respect Task Force 2006: 5)

Hazel Blears, the minister responsible for overseeing the delivery of the Action Plan, conceptualised the Respect agenda in terms of 'the politics of decency':

> One basic value that is part of the armoury of a civilised society is decency. We need to rebuild this basic value in our society.... Decency ... is the shorthand way to describe the established norms of behaviour in a cohesive society. In previous periods, the Left has struggled successfully to reclaim ideas like 'family values', 'law and order' and even 'freedom' from their appropriators on the political right. Today, Labour must reclaim decency as a left-wing value. (Blears 2005: 13)

The Respect agenda seeks to complement the legal remedies designed to deal with 'anti-social behaviour' contained in the Crime and Disorder Act 1998, the Police Reform Act 2002 and the Anti-social Behaviour Act 2003. The Respect Action Plan sets out the governments intentions to:

- increase access to constructive activities for young people;
- ensure parents take responsibility for their child's behaviour in school and when excluded from school, and to target persistent truants;
- tackle irresponsible parents and improve parenting skills;
- establish a national network of intensive family support schemes – including sanctions for those who refuse to take up offers of help (e.g. loss of housing benefit);
- ensure that public-service providers demonstrate accountability to their local communities for tackling anti-social behaviour;
- strengthen summary powers to ensure swifter responses to anti-social behaviour – e.g. new fixed penalty notices for disorder, conditional cautioning, new powers of eviction and night-time curfews. (Respect Task Force 2006)

Under the Action Plan, the police would also be expected to hold briefing sessions with the local community who, in turn, would be given the power to trigger police action against 'anti-social behaviour'. Schools would also be allowed to seek parenting orders for families of pupils who misbehave in school. As with its community safety agenda, New Labour will seek to promote respect by enabling communities 'to be more able to act together to make their neighbourhoods safer and better' (Respect Task Force 2006: 5). All these measures were needed, according to Tony Blair, because the present criminal justice system was 'utterly useless' in protecting the public from low-level disorder such as 'the person who spits at an old lady on her way to the shops' (Blair, cited in Travis 2006: 6).

As Rafael Behr argues, far from being 'something people intuitively understand', 'respect' is a contestable concept:

> The word was once defined from the top down, by the deference-demanding classes for whom respectfulness was important for its surface manifestations of reverence, courtesy and good manners. It was something that was bred into people. But in its new guise 'respect' fought its way up from the bottom. It is earned and fought over. For black culture in particular it has profound connotations, reaching back to the civil rights movement in Sixties America.
>
> The respect that Martin Luther King demanded, the one that Otis Redding and Aretha Franklin sang about, was not the mannered cap-doffing of social protocol. It was an inalienable right. All people born equal are entitled to it, but a minority were denied their share. So they marched to get it back. Thus was the word 'respect' reborn as a totem of empowerment, of assertiveness against oppression. From then on it belonged to the people, passed around in the knuckle-to-knuckle salute that became an alternative handshake. It was a powerful and important call to arms. (Behr 2005: 16)

Given the contestability of the notion of respect, to moralise on it is naïve and problematic. Respect is a complex concept that has attracted substantial philosophical attention. In particular, a fundamental distinction has been observed between the idea of *respect for persons* and *self-respect* – a distinction that raises important lessons for building a 'safer, more just and tolerant society'. Immanuel Kant was one of the first western philosophers to place respect at the heart of moral theory. Writing in the eighteenth century, Kant (1785/1964) argued that people, as ends in themselves, had an absolute dignity that was worthy of respect. As Dillon argues, this notion of *respect for persons* 'commonly means a kind of respect that all people are owed morally just because they are persons, regardless of social position, individual characteristics or achievements, or moral merit' (Dillon 2007: 7) – a position shared, as we saw above, by the American civil rights movement. This stance does not mean that people's qualities cannot be assessed and differentiated in other ways – they can be, of course – but these judgements should not be made in a way that denies people their due respect.

Kant's notion of due respect was, argues Dillon, a strictly negative one – 'consisting in not engaging in certain conduct or having certain attitudes' (Dillon 2007: 10) that might impinge on the wellbeing of others. In contrast, 'many philosophers have argued that respecting others involves positive actions and attitudes as well.... We... respect them (positively) by protecting them from threats to their autonomy... and by promoting autonomy and the conditions for it' (Dillon 2007: 10). This touches on the notion of *self-respect* – something 'regarded both as morally required and as essential to the ability to live a satisfying, meaningful, flourishing life – a life worth living – and just as vital to the quality of our lives together' (Dillon 2007: 14). If people have no sense of self-respect, how can they be expected to have respect for others? This leads to a consideration of 'what aspects of the social context... support or undermine self-respect?' (Dillon 2007: 14). Addressing this, Dillon draws on the work of John Rawls (1971) and his notion of self-respect as 'an entitlement that social institutions are required by justice to support and not undermine' (Dillon 2007: 17). It is a:

> 'primary good'... vital to the experienced quality of individual lives and to the ability to carry out or achieve whatever projects or aims an individual might have. It is, moreover, a social good, one that individuals are able to acquire only under certain social and political conditions.... [I]ndividuals' access to self-respect is to a large degree a function of how the basic institutional structure of a society defines and distributes the social bases of self respect, which include... the distribution of fundamental political rights and civil liberties, access to the resources individuals need to pursue their plans of life, the availability of diverse associations and communities within which individuals can seek affirmation of their worth and their plans of life from others.... (Dillon 2007: 14)

As we saw in Chapter 1, societal support for self-respect has been eroded in Britain since the late-1970s – reflected in widening inequality, and the marginalisation and stigmatisation of disadvantaged and vulnerable groups. A recent analysis of community wellbeing by Richard Wilkinson explored the effects of this widening divide on social interaction. His findings suggest that it is the degree of inequality in a society that most affects the quality of social relations between people (rather than the degree of overall affluence):

> [T]he quality of social relations is better in more equal societies where income differences between rich and poor are smaller. ... [I]n these more equal societies, people are much more likely to trust each other, measures of social capital and social cohesion show that community life is stronger, and homicide rates and levels of violence are consistently lower. (Wilkinson 2005: 33)

According to Wilkinson, and as we have already argued, it is the structural context in which social relationships are played out that is crucial. Societies with greater degrees of inequality will be more prone to disrespectful behaviour – due largely to the breakdown in trust and social cohesion generated in these societies. New Labour's Respect agenda, however, fails to acknowledge the importance of social context, representing instead a highly-charged authoritarian agenda – enforced, as we have seen, on some of the least powerful. Blears understanding of this agenda is little short of legitimised vigilantism – where 'a successful community [makes it known] where the boundaries lie [and enforces the rules] *without the need for intervention by external authorities*' (Blears 2005: 15 – emphasis added) – an approach Blears claims is based on 'solidarity and mutual interdependence' (Blears 2005: 20)!

New Labour's approach to community safety is far from solidaristic. For one, in relation to asbo procedures, there is evidence of a:

> mismatch between what the British Crime Survey (BCS) 'perceptions of ASB' survey reveals to be the chief concerns of its respondents and the actual patterns of enforcement being adopted. Aside from additional measures such as curfews and dispersal orders specifically designed for youth, something like three-quarters of ASBOs are imposed upon young people.... Yet 'teenagers hanging around' only emerged as the sixth priority for BCS respondents, behind speeding traffic, inconsiderate parking, rubbish or litter, fireworks, and vandalism and graffiti. (Squires and Stephen 2005: 519)

This focus on the 'problem of youth' for adults perhaps reflects the finding that community safety liaison groups established around

England are dominated by residents in their fifties and sixties (Squires and Stephen 2005) – hardly a representation of 'solidarity and mutual interdependence' within communities, but the demonisation and (ultimately) criminalisation of one section of the community (the young) by another (the middle-aged), a situation that serves to selectively reinforce 'local intolerance, divisions and social conflicts' (Squires and Stephen 2005: 519). In the process of enforcing 'decency' in society, for example, 'local authorities distribute leaflets depicting the photographs of young people to whom ASBOs have been issued, along with the conditions imposed by the court, soliciting the assistance of residents in monitoring the compliance of the young people concerned' (Squires and Stephen 2005: 523). Guildford set up a public 'wall of shame' on to which photographs and details of asbo recipients are projected (Squires and Stephen 2005), whilst local and tabloid newspapers are increasingly displaying similar photographs and details on their front pages. 'Britain's "naming and shaming" is supposedly based upon the practice of reintegrative shaming and underpinned by a broader philosophy of restorative justice …, except in Britain's case the shaming appears to isolate the already excluded whilst offering little in the way of opportunities for reintegration' (Squires and Stephen 2005: 523).

It is not intended here to downplay the impact of disruptive behaviour on community life. However, given their divisiveness and lack of due legal process, it can be argued that asbos are highly questionable in terms of effectiveness, proportionality and social justice. Bob Reitemeier, Chief Executive of the Children's Society, has warned that the effects of New Labour's existing powers – asbos, dispersal powers and curfews – have made many young people feel 'demonised, disrespected and alienated within their communities' (see Curtis and Cowan 2006: 7). Moreover, responding to the announcement that £80million of Home Office funding would be made available over two years to fund the Respect programme, Andrew Webb, co-chair of the Association of Directors of Social Services' Children and Families Committee, placed this into context by highlighting the existing underfunding of family support services provided by social services – a shortfall of around £600million in 2006/2007 (Travis 2006: 6). At the same time, as Foord and Young observe, parenting policy has been pushed to centre stage of the crime and disorder agenda – an agenda 'increasingly driven by a moralising turn to regulate and control the behaviour of marginalised families' (Foord and Young 2006: 180) – a throwback to the punitive and moralising approach pioneered by the Charity Organisation Society in the nineteenth century. As a consequence, it is an agenda fraught with intrinsic contradictions and pitfalls. In particular, such policies fail to acknowledge the structural context – the poverty and disadvantage which make coping profoundly difficult and often beyond the capacity of families to deal with. In this context, Bauman seems right when he argues that:

> the poor cease to be an ethical problem – they are exempt from our moral responsibility. There is no more a moral question of defending the poor against the cruelty of their fate; instead there is the ethical question of defending the right and proper lives of decent people against assaults likely to be plotted in mean streets, ghettos and no go areas. (Bauman 1998, cited in Pemberton 2004: 81)

This describes the punitive turn in social policy in Britain which started, as we saw in Chapter 1, at the end of the 1970s and which has accelerated since 1997. Tackling 'anti-social behaviour' rather than poverty and inequality is now at the heart of the Labour Party's social policy agenda. Moreover, as Rodger argues, the government is increasingly looking to welfare sanctions as part of its armoury targeted at incivility: '[T]he future role of the welfare state is, perhaps, imperceptibly changing as part of a broader movement in what has been described as the "criminalisation of social policy" … or the "criminalisation of incivility" … as the boundaries between social policy and criminal justice blur' (Rodger 2006: 123).

According to Rodger, New Labour's policy agenda on tackling social problems is increasingly being reframed in terms of the management of problem populations and the imposition of social control. Whilst acknowledging that the welfare state has always been preoccupied with social control, Rodger's identifies a particular focus in New Labour's welfare reforms on changing people's social values and inculcating in people, particularly young people, certain standards of behaviour and 'respect' for others. Changing value orientations has involved a refocus in the government's approach to community development – consistent with neo-liberal and communitarian notions. Under New Labour:

> [C]ommunity development has been displaced by community safety as the most pressing issue in post-employment neighbourhoods. It is taking this form because the problem has been understood in terms requiring punitive behaviour modification in the short to medium term of those identified as being deviant. … The decline in welfarism

in the field of criminal justice has been accompanied by the rise in crime prevention partnerships that have encouraged public participation in the formulation of policies to tackle antisocial behaviour and, simultaneously, increased sensitivity to the incidence of incivility in the local neighbourhood. The politics of enforcement is now concerned with releasing the power of the community to deal with its own deviants. (Rodger 2006: 137–138)

New Labour and urban regeneration

New Labour's return to government coincided with extreme social inequality and urban decay. By the 1990s, Britain had become a more unequal society than at any time since the establishment of the post-war welfare state (Hills 1998), and Labour's 1997 election manifesto contained a commitment to 'tackle the division and inequality in our society'. Since their election, a number of initiatives have been rolled out to address multiple deprivation in urban areas, and to promote the regeneration of run-down neighbourhoods and communities. These included the establishment of the Social Exclusion Unit whose report *Bringing Britain Together* (1998) identified 3,000 neighbourhoods with high concentrations of poverty and disadvantage (defined in terms of unemployment, poorer quality schools and health provision, fewer shops and other services, and higher levels of litter, vandalism and crime).

New Labour's approach to tackling urban deprivation (now conceptualised as 'social exclusion') is primarily based around a three-pronged strategy – getting people to work better (through engaging in education, employment or training, and not engaging in risky or 'anti-social behaviour'); getting places to work better (through area-based policies targeting health, education, crime and 'anti-social behaviour', and improving neighbourhood management by *inter alia* involving 'the community'); and getting service providers to perform better (through 'joined-up' thinking, and improving the co-ordination and integration of service provision). For Levitas, it is an approach that combines elements of a moral underclass discourse (where the prime concern is the flawed behaviour of the poor and their 'dependency culture') and a social integrationist discourse (where the prime concern is inclusion through paid work) (Levitas 2005).

Imrie and Raco (2003) describe the vast range of policy programme initiatives under New Labour that have direct relevance for urban regeneration. These are organised under ten themes: business and investment;

community; crime and community safety; education and training; environment; health and wellbeing; homes and housing; land and planning; leisure and sport; and transport and traffic. Responsibility for implementing these initiatives has not been given to local government but 'partnerships' working with local communities – including Neighbourhood Renewal Teams, Local Strategic Partnerships and Regional Development Agencies, all operating under central government control. This partnership approach was intended to redress criticisms levelled at the previous Conservative government's urban regeneration practices which had largely disregarded the interests of inner-city working-class communities (Byrne 2006). However, as with the establishment of 12 Urban Regeneration Companies, New Labour's strategy remained 'indicative of a quango-led approach to regeneration, not unlike that pursued by Thatcher in the 1980s' (Imrie and Raco 2003: 17), aimed largely at meeting the interests of development finance. Consequently, the benefits flowing down to working-class communities have been minimal (Byrne 2006).

A national strategy for renewing deprived neighbourhoods

In 2000, the government launched its National Strategy for Neighbourhood Renewal – an area-based approach to regeneration. This strategy was to be largely co-ordinated through the Neighbourhood Renewal Unit, established in 2001 as part of the government's 'new commitment to neighbourhood renewal' set out in its National Strategy Action Plan (SEU 2001). In seeking consistency in approach between the different neighbourhood renewal strategies, the government has established Public Service Agreement (PSA) targets for deprived areas covering goals for increasing employment rates; generating sustainable enterprise; reducing burglary; raising educational attainment; closing the health divide; and improving social housing, air quality and the recycling of waste (Imrie and Raco 2003).

New Labour continued to seek to tackle urban deprivation and poverty at the neighbourhood level. Their first term in office saw a proliferation of area-based schemes including Single Regeneration Budget and Neighbourhood Renewal Fund projects, Education Action Zones, Health Action Zones, New Deal for Communities (NDC), Sure Start, Excellence in Cities and Employment Action Zones. From these there has emerged 'a plethora of initiatives...aimed at reducing worklessness and crime, improving skills, health, housing and environments, and lessening social divisions' (Ledwith 2005: 18–19).

The NDC was launched in 1998 with the stated aim of reversing the poverty gap in England's 39 most deprived neighbourhoods over ten years. Each of the 39 areas was allocated around £50million. 'The programme aimed to offer a holistic socio-economic approach to regeneration, recognising that the causes of entrenched neighbourhood disadvantage were due not only to economic decline over decades...but an erosion of social networks in communities and deteriorating public services' (Salman 2007: 1). Central to New Labour's renewal strategy was the notion that communities need to be 'fully engaged in shaping and delivering regeneration' (SEU 2000: 5). For example, while previous regeneration initiatives had been criticised for failing to involve local communities effectively, 'a key strand of the New Deal for Communities was that residents should be at the heart of the decision-making' (Salman 2007: 1). Moreover, the Urban White Paper *Our towns and cities – the future: delivering an urban renaissance* (2000) stated that 'we intend to build the capacity of communities to help themselves and bring about social cohesion right across the country' (cited in Imrie and Raco 2003: 21). This became the remit of the Active Community Unit, established within the Home Office in 1998 to support community organisations through the provision of small grants and advice. The government also set up a Community Empowerment Fund to provide residents with training and consultation support, Community Chests to support community groups and a Voluntary Sector Investment Fund to enhance the capacity of communities to assist in the delivery of welfare services (Imrie and Raco 2003).

Evaluating neighbourhood renewal

Despite the government's stated commitments to community involvement in the delivery of its urban policies, evidence would suggest that significant obstacles remain to effective participation – due largely to a rift between the rhetoric and reality:

> Evidence points to the fact that community involvement is not working in practice; that 'public involvement in neighbourhood regeneration work has yet to live up to its own ambitions' (Burton 2003, p. 29)....[C]ommunity involvement strategies are 'poorly conceived, inadequately resourced and developed far too late in the cycle to be very effective' (Burton 2003, p. 28). (Cited in Ledwith 2005: 19)

In a similar vein to the previous discussion on community safety, community involvement strategies in urban regeneration schemes continue to lack any sincere commitment to 'bottom-up' approaches – which also acts as a disincentive to people to engage with service providers (Foley and Martin 2000). In truth, communities lack real power and influence in initiatives which continue to be led by centrally-defined performance criteria and timescales which run counter to meaningful local involvement (Foley and Martin 2000). This view is shared by Byrne who argues that whilst communities are encouraged to participate in NDC partnerships, evidence suggests that they have 'no strategic role in relation to the determination of overall regeneration objectives' (Byrne 2006: 163). As an example, and speaking in respect of the West Gate NDC partnership in Newcastle, Councillor John O'Shea of the city council is cited as claiming community involvement was a 'window dressing to get the money' (cited in Byrne 2006: 163). The subsequent regeneration programme implemented has been described as 'ethnic cleansing…. [T]he largest programme of actual gentrifying displacement of poor working-class people attempted in the UK since before the First World War!' (Byrne 2006: 164). In addition, there is no evidence that any of the NDC partnerships established have attempted to address the structural causes of deprived neighbourhoods (Byrne 2006). As Shaw and Martin's analysis of the utility of community in social welfare discourse suggests, the structuralist critique of social policy in Britain remains as convincing as ever – as does 'the warning of the medicinal properties of the rhetoric of [community] participation … in the absence of greater economic and social equality' (Shaw and Martin 2000: 405).

A study by Rowe and Devanney on urban regeneration identified a number of tensions between the partners involved (similar to those discussed above in relation to community safety partnerships) which invariably ran counter to successful partnership working. As in the case of CDRPs, partnership members often held different priorities and targets, making it difficult to integrate these diverse interests around a common agenda. Moreover, genuine partnership working is rarely possible due to the unequal resources held by the groups involved, with public sector officials, regeneration professionals and others with substantial resources tending to dominate proceedings. Those with least resources in the community had little or no influence. Lastly, as with the CDRPs, mutual distrust tended to permeate relationships between participating sectors – with residents suspicious of service providers, and service providers suspicious of businesses (Rowe and Devanney 2003).

Another problem identified with partnership working is the 'commonsense assumption' held – one consistent with communitarian thinking – that for democracy to flourish in partnerships it is desirable that the partnership works cohesively in a climate without conflict. In reality, such desire for cohesion can serve to work against democratic decision making by silencing the voices of minority group interests. In his discussion on partnership working, for example, Gilling warns of the danger from too much belief in unity and consensus:

> [T]he danger of this ideology is that it can lead to strategies of conflict avoidance, where power differentials between agencies, and their different...programmes, are left unchallenged. Conflict avoidance may be motivated by the need to preserve the impression of unity, but also by the felt need to preserve good relations at an interpersonal level: the ideology makes it important that individuals, as well as organizations, are seen to 'get on'. (Gilling 2005: 748)

A consequence of this is that the priorities of minority communities are unlikely to be met. 'One manifestation of conflict avoidance may be to privilege the programmes of specific agencies, such as the police, because, in the absence of the kind of debate that is a healthy part of the checks and balances of government..., the police's programme is facilitated' (Gilling 2005: 748). The police agenda and the government's desire to be seen 'tough' on 'crime and disorder' clearly shaped strategies adopted by the CDRPs in England. Additionally, with the advancement of new technologies from the 1980s – in particular, CCTV – urban regeneration initiatives in England have increasingly been directed at the 'situational prevention' of crime and anti-social behaviour involving 'the management, design, or manipulation of the immediate physical environment to reduce the opportunities for specific crimes' (Crawford 2007: 872). Concern has been expressed about the impact of situational crime prevention strategies for the urban environment – in particular, the implications of generating 'gated communities' and 'gated public spaces' for social cohesion (Crawford 2007). These developments continue to privilege the interests of the commercial sector and the more affluent communities whilst exacerbating the exclusion of the least powerful. The government's failure to permit meaningful widespread community dialogue in its regeneration strategy contradicts its own Policy Action Team 17's verdict – set out in *Joining It up Locally* – that urban regeneration initiatives since the 1960s had failed because they did not adequately involve or empower communities in the process (see Hughes 2007).

A further contradiction in New Labour's regeneration strategy is its persistence with *area-based* approaches. This not only disregards the experience of past area-based programmes (which failed to address externalities crucial to a neighbourhood's wellbeing) but also the findings of its own advisor – the Social Exclusion Unit – which questioned the effectiveness of area initiatives in its own consultation on a National Strategy for Neighbourhood Renewal (SEU 2000). As Atkinson and Moon argue, given the influence of broader social, political and economic forces on the wellbeing of neighbourhoods:

> In such a context the area approach was rendered largely redundant as both an explanatory variable and as a viable strategy to revive economic fortunes. The forces which determined an area's decline were now recognised as originating outside it and to have nothing to do with a local population's behavioural characteristics. (Atkinson and Moon 1994: 50)

The underlying causes of urban deprivation – such as unequal power relations and wealth distribution, or the investment decisions of financial markets and government departments – are not taken in hand through area-based initiatives.

Meeting the interests of finance capital

As we saw in Chapter 1, since the late-1970s governments in Britain have abandoned efforts to manage capitalism in a way that would allow dependable economic growth, or to pursue social policies that would reduce social inequalities. Now, '[f]inance is the dominant interest and decision-maker, at home and abroad' (Jordan 2006: 54). Instead of Keynes' vision of a politically accountable global economy, what has emerged in Britain over the past 30 years is an economic system where major investment decisions are increasingly taken by the financial sector (banks, pension funds, insurance companies and investment funds) – largely unaccountable authorities whose interests are represented in the 'new model of the world economy' (Jordan 2006: 66) through the International Monetary Fund (IMF) and the World Bank (WB). It is the financial sector which takes the major decisions in respect of credit worthiness, which development projects will be approved for funding, and which individuals or households will be offered personal loans to consume. Neo-liberal regimes, therefore, rely on the financial markets not only for capital funding for new development (which sustains economic growth and employment opportunities) but also for personal credit (so that individuals and households can consume goods and services). A consequence of this reliance is that the scope

for redistribution is limited. As Jordan argues, 'The US and UK governments are...very cautious about adopting policies which might be
perceived as challenging the strategies of financial institutions....
Instead, these governments adopt social policies at home which favour
the financial sector and enable its expansion' (Jordan 2006: 71).

New Labour's urban regeneration policies, whilst appearing to be
concerned about poverty and social exclusion, have largely been consistent with Jordan's observations. In particular, there has been a sharp
focus on meeting the interests of the financial and commercial sectors
by incentivising more people to engage in low-paid work as part of the
new flexible labour market. As Jordan explains:

> The new model of the world economy redirected government's atten-
> tion from 'aggregate demand' to the 'supply side'.... In labour markets,
> this meant that the education, training and adaptability of the work-
> force were more important targets of social policy than their wages,
> which should be allowed to find their own levels through competi-
> tion.... In the USA and the UK, the 'human capital' of the workforce
> became the focus of flagship government programmes under the
> Third Way administrations of Bill Clinton and Tony Blair.... Policy
> aimed to improve skills, incentives, the work ethic and enterprise, see-
> ing the workforce as the key to national prosperity.... Starting from
> high rates [of unemployment] following restructuring of labour mar-
> kets under Reagan and Thatcher in the 1980s, the USA and the UK
> adopted active measures to reintegrate unemployed people into for-
> mal work in the 1990s. The Clinton and Blair governments justified
> 'welfare-to-work' programmes of training and counselling, combined
> with threats to curtail benefits for failure to take available opportuni-
> ties. (Jordan 2006: 66)

At the heart of New Labour's urban regeneration strategy has been
efforts to (re)engage unemployed people with paid work 'and thus bring
themselves – and their communities – out of poverty' (Imrie and Raco
2003: 24). New Deal programmes since 1997 have offered the long-term
unemployed work experience or training, with the Jobcentre Plus initiative (established in 2002) offering a 'one-stop' jobs and benefits
advice service with personal advisers. However, this over-reliance on a
supply-sided economic strategy cannot ensure that paid work will be
created. At the same time, many of the jobs that do exist do not guarantee an income that assures social inclusion. Moreover, placing a moral
duty on people to accept whatever paid work comes available may
impact on the 'work-life balance'. It also discounts the value of engaging

in 'non-paid' activities such as caring for others or community action. The government's strategy also ignores structural inequalities within the world of paid work based on class, 'race' and gender differences. There has also been little attempt to improve benefit levels for the unemployed (other than a few targeted increases for pensioners, severely disabled people and children under-11 years old) and there has been a continued reliance on means-testing (a disincentive to claim).

All in all, New Labour's approach is consistent with previous government policies, seen throughout modernity, which have pathologised the urban poor and sought to modify their behaviour. This focus on making people more responsible – particularly in respect of their duty to engage in paid work (a duty that extends to lone parents and disabled people) – continues to place the spotlight for the cause of concentrated poverty on 'residents' behaviour' (Pierson and Worley 2005: 220) rather than the wider structural causes of poverty. Instead of addressing these structural factors, policies and practices continue to place the blame on the 'flawed behaviour' of residents living in 'dysfunctional' places. As Pierson and Worley observe: '[D]isadvantaged social housing estates and areas of low demand and housing abandonment are viewed by government as spaces where anti-social behaviour, parenting deficits, education deficits among children, and workless households have become the chief elements of urban disadvantage' (Pierson and Worley 2005: 218).

Therefore, 'Tackling anti-social behaviour, tightening parental control over children's behaviour, raising educational attainment, reducing the fear of crime, and getting people "job ready" all became recurrent features of regeneration packages' (Pierson and Worley 2005: 219).

By pursuing regeneration strategies that facilitate the interests of financial markets – that is, by making urban areas more attractive for investors – New Labour have continued to engage in strategies directed at the 'purification' of places (Hughes 2007).

> Urban regeneration programmes in the UK over the past twenty years have increasingly focused on attracting investors, middle-class shoppers and visitors by transforming places and creating new consumption spaces. Ensuring that places are safe and are seen to be safe has taken on greater salience as these flows of income are easily disrupted by changing perceptions of fear and the threat of crime. (Raco 2003, cited in Hughes 2007: 173)

Urban regeneration in Britain has increasingly been about achieving a more effective socio-spatial ordering of place, largely achieved through cleansing the streets of visibly 'dangerous people' and 'flawed consumers' – for example, the homeless, beggars, certain youth cultures and the unemployed. A range of techniques have been deployed in pursuit of this purification process – for example, CCTV technology, zero-tolerance policing, gated shopping malls, community wardens, curfews, dispersal orders and asbos. As such, urban governance in the first decade of the twenty-first century can be characterised in terms of 'militarized control, targeted containment, [and] privatized consumption ... aided and abetted by a morally stifling and authoritarian neo-conservative communitarianism' (Hughes 2007: 190).

A stark example of this purification process and practices in targeted containment is the way cities have been prepared to host the Olympic games. The legacy of hosting the Olympics is said to be beneficial for cities – 'they are meant to produce resounding economic benefits and help the poor' (Monbiot 2007: 31) whilst the urban infrastructure (such as public transport systems) is expected to be vastly improved (BBC Radio 4, 2007). However, in reality the distribution of benefit is highly differentiated with the 'transfer of wealth from the poor to the rich' (Monbiot 2007: 31). Additionally, a study published by the Centre on Housing Rights and Evictions showed that in every city it examined (i.e. all those hosting the games since 1988) the Olympics became a catalyst for mass purification programmes:

> Since the 1988 Olympics in Seoul, more than 2 million people have been driven from their homes to make way for the Olympics. ... The 1988 games ... were used ... as an opportunity to turn Seoul from a vernacular city owned by many people into a corporate city owned by the elite – 720,000 people were thrown out of their homes; people who tried to resist were beaten by thugs and imprisoned; tenants were evicted without notice...; street vendors were banned; homeless people, those with mental health problems, alcoholics and beggars were rounded up and put into a prison camp. (Monbiot 2007: 31)

In Barcelona in 1992, Roma communities were evicted and dispersed, and the municipality designed a plan to 'clean the streets of beggars, prostitutes, street sellers and swindlers [and] annoying passers-by' (cited in Monbiot 2007: 31). In the six years leading up to the Olympics house prices rose in the Olympic district by 240 per cent whilst the public housing stock fell by 76 per cent (Monbiot 2007). The 1996 games in Atlanta, already a highly segregated city, generated a new ethnic cleansing programme involving the demolition of large public housing projects occupied primarily by African-Americans – 'about 30,000 families were evicted' (Monbiot 2007: 31) and their properties replaced with middle-class homes. In the year prior to the games 9,000 homeless people were arrested with many 'locked up without trial until the games were over' (Monbiot 2007: 31). Before Sydney in 2002 there were mass evictions from boarding houses and rented housing, and before Athens in 2006 2,700 Roma were evicted. In Beijing, 1.25million people have been displaced and another quarter of a million are due to be evicted. Already in London – many years before the games are due – Gypsies and Travellers are being evicted from Clays Lane in Newham and Waterden Crescent in Hackney; 430 people are being evicted from Clays Lane housing co-op; and a 100-year old allotment is being taken over for a concrete path that will be used for the four weeks of the games. A total of 9,000 new homes are being built, but 'far more will be lost to the poor through booming house prices....The International Olympic Committee raises no objection to any of this. It lays down rigid criteria for cities hosting the games, but these do not include housing rights' (Monbiot 2007: 31). In the interest of regenerating cities for the wellbeing of the powerful and privileged, democratic processes can be conveniently sidestepped whilst the unproductive, 'dangerous Other' – those who might 'offend' middle-class sensibilities or deter would-be investors – must be cleared out of sight. 'There can be no debate, no exceptions, no modifications. Everything must go' (Monbiot 2007: 31).

New Labour and 'community cohesion'

Community cohesion emerged as a central theme in New Labour's policy discourse following the 2001 civil disturbances in Burnley, Oldham and Bradford. 2001 was described as a 'momentous year for race relations in the UK' (Race in Britain Special Edition 2001: 1). Following the unrest in the June of that year, the British National Party (BNP) secured its best ever result in a General Election – gaining more than 11,000 votes in Oldham. Two months later, Firsat Dag, a 22-year-old Kurdish asylum seeker, was killed in Sighthill, Glasgow (Race in Britain Special Edition 2001). In relation to the experience of Pakistani people in Oldham: 'To the youth, pessimism and aggression seem all too natural responses to their surroundings. Oldham suffers some of the worst social conditions in the country. And the wards where most of the Asian Muslim communities live...are among the town's worst' (Wazir 2001: 4).

Given the disproportionate deprivation experienced by Asian Muslims in Britain, it is not surprising to discover that young Asian men are increasingly dissatisfied with British notions of social justice. Moreover, it also comes as no surprise to hear that 'young Asian Men...nearly all believe in the theory of a Western conspiracy to denigrate Islam' (Wazir 2001: 4). The wars against Afghanistan and Iraq abroad, and the political and media onslaught against Muslims at home, will have some influence on shaping these beliefs – as they have shaped the views of many people.

The blueprint for community cohesion

The government responded to the disturbances of 2001 by setting up a Ministerial Group on Public Order and Community Cohesion, chaired by John Denham, with the remit to 'examine and consider how national policies might be used to promote better community cohesion, based upon shared values and a celebration of diversity' (Home Office 2001a, foreword). The concerns raised by this group are summed up by Imrie and Raco as: the lack of shared social values between diverse communities; a territorial mentality among young people; an inability to broker relations between key interests; and an erosion of trust in civic institutions (Imrie and Raco 2003). The group recommended that a local community cohesion plan should be set up to promote 'cross-cultural contact between black and ethnic minority and white communities to foster understanding and respect and break down barriers' (Kearns 2003: 49). The group referred to the relevance of Putnam's notion of social capital for restoring community cohesion – highlighting its importance for allowing people 'to resolve collective problems more easily' and to 'facilitate the achievement of common goals' (cited in Kearns 2003: 50).

At the same time, the government established an 'independent' review team (chaired by Ted Cantle) to consult with residents and community leaders in the affected areas and other parts of the country, and to report on what they perceived to be the causes of the disturbances and to make recommendations on how to prevent similar circumstances recurring. A key perspective emerging from the Cantle review was that the troubles were largely due to the lack of interaction between people of different cultural, religious and racial backgrounds: 'Separate educational arrangements, community and voluntary bodies, employment, places of worship, language, social and cultural networks, means that many communities operate on the basis of a series of parallel lives. These lives often do not seem to touch at any point, let alone overlap and promote any meaningful interchanges' (Home Office 2001b: 9).

The review team went on to suggest that this separation was largely due to a lack of commitment by some agencies to work together and a 'reluctance to confront the issues and to find solutions' (Home Office 2001b: 9). The solution proposed, therefore, was:

> to promote community cohesion, based upon a greater knowledge of, contact between, and respect for, the various cultures that now make Great Britain such a rich and diverse nation. It is also essential to establish a greater sense of citizenship, based on (a few) common principles which are shared and observed by all sections of the community. (Home Office 2001b: 10)

This reflects a clear desire to generate a sense of commonality and consensus about 'Britishness' as a concept around which difference and diversity ('multiculturalism') can be more easily managed. Amongst the common principles suggested in the report were: an agreed notion of 'nationhood'; an acceptance of 'principal national institutions'; and the idea of a 'statement of allegiance' to the British state. To foster mutual understanding between ethnic groups in the troubled areas, the report advocated cross-cultural contact through, for instance, holding inter-faith dialogue or twinning schools (Home Office 2001b).

These reports provided the blueprint for the government's community cohesion agenda. Following their publication, a new Community Cohesion Task Force was established under David Blunkett who simultaneously initiated a national debate suggesting immigrants take an 'oath of allegiance' to the British state, adopt British norms and speak English in their homes.

At the local level, responsibility for promoting cross-cultural contact would rest with local authorities who would be required to prepare local community cohesion plans. These plans would be expected to achieve central government targets – set out in Public Service Agreement 9 – and 'bring about a measurable improvement in race and community cohesion' (cited in Worley 2005: 487) – although it is by no means clear what 'measurable' means in this context. In paragraph 3.2 of their report, the review team attempt to characterise community cohesion according to five domains identified by Forrest and Kearns. These are:

1. Common values and a civic culture (described as common aims and objectives; common moral principles and codes of behaviour; support for political institutions and participation in politics).

2. Social order and social control (described as the absence of general conflict and threats to the existing order; absence of incivility; effective informal social control; tolerance, respect for differences and inter-group co-operation).

3. Social solidarity and reductions in wealth disparities (described as harmonious economic and social development and common standards; redistribution of public finances and of opportunities; equal access to services and welfare benefits; ready acknowledgement of social obligations and willingness to assist others).

4. Social networks and social capital (described as a high degree of social interaction within communities and families; civic engagement and associational activity; easy resolution of collective action problems).

5. Place, attachment and identity (described as a strong attachment to place; inter-twining of personal and place identity). (Forrest and Kearns 2000, cited in Home Office 2001b)

Forrest and Kearns suggest that the simplest observable measure of community cohesion 'would be of groups who live in a local area getting together to promote or defend some common local interest' (Forrest and Kearns 2000, cited in Home Office 2001b: para. 3.2). A year following the review team report, the Guidance on Community Cohesion Report (2002), produced for local authorities by the Local Government Association (LGA), offered four domains to define a cohesive society. These were where:

1. There is a common vision and a sense of belonging for all communities;

2. The diversity of people's different backgrounds and circumstances is appreciated and positively valued;

3. Those from different backgrounds have similar life opportunities; and

4. Strong and positive relationships are being developed between people from different backgrounds in the workplace, in schools and within neighbourhoods. (LGA 2002, cited in McGhee 2005: 47)

The LGA suggest that this programme of work could include the following objectives:

1. The development of conflict resolution strategies;

2. The development of a programme of 'myth-busting' to counter traditional stereotypes;

3. An ongoing series of events and programmes to foster openness and cross-cultural contact;
4. Developing festivals and celebrations that involve all communities. (LGA 2002, cited in McGhee 2005: 52)

In achieving these objectives, the LGA expect to see the emergence of a 'culture of "diversity appreciation"' (McGhee 2005: 52) in local areas, measured in terms of the following outcomes:

1. An improvement in community cohesion for the local area;
2. A reduction in inter-racial tension and conflict;
3. A reduction in perceived or actual inequalities for all sections of the local community;
4. Creating value from the diversity of the local community;
5. Adding to the quality of life and sense of well-being; and
6. Greater participation and involvement in civic life from all sectors of the community. (LGA 2002, cited in McGhee 2005: 52)

Facilitating dialogue between communities and implementing a strategic vision of community cohesion will require, the LGA argue, a leading role for the Neighbourhood Renewal Unit (i.e. central government) working with the regional government offices through to the local authorities who, in turn, would provide community facilitators in local areas (LGA 2002, cited in McGhee 2005: 54). The Ministerial Group on Public Order and Community Cohesion had previously stated that it expected the Neighbourhood Renewal Unit to make 'community cohesion a central objective of all its programmes' (cited in Kearns 2003: 51). This is a clear example of central government adopting the concept of 'community' to impose its agenda on 'undesirable' forms of association at the local level – to get them to 'alter their ways of thinking about, doing and being communities' (McGhee 2005: 54).

Both the review team reports and the LGA share the same understanding of the 2001 conflicts 'as being the result of failed integration, where migrant communities become established in areas yet are not integrated with the "host" community' (McGhee 2005: 48). Such an understanding leads on to the simple conclusion that, by opening up channels of communication between the migrant and host communities and generating a commonality around shared core values, these conflicts will get resolved. By generating an open discussion involving the whole community, a basis of a shared vision is possible. Once this vision has been found, 'the newly de-polarized and "other-aware" communities [can] proceed to collectively design a programme of work that will outline what needs to be done to make the shared vision...a reality' (McGhee 2005: 52).

Community cohesion and a 'crisis of multiculturalism'

In his assessment of the community cohesion debate, McGhee raises serious concerns about the way the government's discourse portrayed 'Asian – particularly Pakistani-Muslim – "culture" and community formations as being emblematic of failed integration at the heart of British immigration policy' (McGhee 2005: 42). By focusing on these cultural aspects, cultural difference and the lack of community interaction are situated at the heart of the problem – not the structural context in which community relations are played out. Responsibility for the 2001 tensions is clearly placed on those Pakistani-Muslim communities who are either unable or unwilling to integrate into the 'British way of life'. Consequently, responsibility for resolving these tensions and re-establishing social cohesion lies with these communities – in particular, they must learn to blend in with New Labour's notion of 'Britishness' – however vague and contestable that may be. Arun Kundnani, of the Institute of Race Relations, described the Cantle Report as effectively:

the government's race manifesto. It provides a new formula, in which the separate cultural development that had been encouraged for decades is to be subsumed to the demands of 'community cohesion'. A set of core values is to put limits on multiculturalism and black people are required to develop 'a greater acceptance of the principal national institutions'. (Kundnani 2002: 3)

The 2001 'riots' in northern England and the attacks on the US that followed on 11 September led to what Modood describes as a 'turning point for the idea of multiculturalism in Britain' (Modood 2007: 10). Several commentators from the so-called 'centre-left' came to attack multiculturalism, including Kenan Malik, who argued that it had 'helped to segregate communities far more than racism', and Hugo Young, who wrote that it provided 'a useful bible for any Muslim who insists that his religio-cultural priorities, including the defence of jihad against America, override his civic duties of loyalty, tolerance, justice and respect for democracy' (cited in Modood 2007: 11). Trevor Philips, then Chair of the Commission for Racial Equality, 'declared that multiculturalism...made a fetish of difference instead of encouraging minorities to be truly British' (Modood 2007: 11). The anti-multiculturalism discourse reached a new height in Britain after the London bombings of 7 July in 2005. The fact that individuals involved in the bombings were born and/or brought up in Britain led many to conclude that multiculturalism had failed (Modood 2007).

The government's current discourse on multiculturalism re-engages with the assimilation agenda of the 1960s and 1970s (Worley 2005). For example, the Home Office briefing paper, *Improving Opportunity, Strengthening Society*, states: 'For those settling in Britain, the government has a clear expectation that they will integrate into our society and economy.... [W]e consider that it is important for all citizens to have a sense of inclusive British identity' (Home Office 2005, cited in Worley 2005: 489). This expectation of anglo-conformity was also stressed by Tony Blair on 8 December 2006 when he warned immigrants that they must accept Britain's 'core values of democracy, tolerance and respect for the law. ... Our tolerance is part of what makes Britain, Britain. Conform to it; or don't come here' (Blair, cited in Woodward 2006: 1). Blair went on to state:

> For the first time in a generation there is an unease, an anxiety, even at points a resentment that our very openness, our willingness to welcome difference, our pride in being home to many cultures, is being used against us; abused, indeed, in order to harm us. ... When it comes to our essential values – belief in democracy, the rule of law, tolerance, equal treatment for all, respect for this country and its shared heritage – then that is where we come together, it is what we hold in common. It is what gives us the right to call ourselves British. At that point no distinctive culture or religion supersedes our duty to be part of an integrated United Kingdom. (Blair, cited in Woodward 2006: 2)

As Appleton observes, what the government is effectively expecting of agencies working with immigrants is the abandonment of policies based on multiculturalism and the assimilation of immigrants into a (however vague) notion of 'Britishness' (homogenised and Anglo-Saxon) (Appleton 2002). The government's vision of community cohesion is based on enforced dialogue and assimilation. As McGhee argues, New Labour has pursued a 'politics of assimilation where...migrants are Anglicized...through the mobilization of pedago-gies of "allegiance" and "attitude" re-orientation' (McGhee 2005: 180). It is effectively a project of social engineering, concerned with managing 'problematic communities' – in particular, managing 'the overly bonded, self-segregating Pakistani community ... [which is] seen as an undesirable form of social association (in terms of its potential inhibition of participation with mainstream society and neighbouring 'cultural groups')' (McGhee 2005: 174). McGhee shares Furedi's (2004, cited in McGhee 2005) concern that working with communities in this way represents:

> the emergence of regimes of therapeutic education ... wedded to forms of behaviour modification that not only target conduct, but also attempt to alter feelings and emotions. In the UK, the best example of these types of intervention can be found among the various community and educational initiatives that have sprung up in Oldham to tackle 'segregation'. (McGhee 2005: 177)

McGhee refers to the Inter-Community Peer Support Project which is dedicated to changing the mindsets of racist young people by challenging their prejudices and racial stereotypes. The project brings together both White and Asian young people to encourage cross-cultural contact. Whilst McGhee finds it hard to be too critical of such initiatives, he alludes to one important concern raised by Furedi in respect that:

> [T]he current problematization of so-called negative emotions and prejudices distracts attention from the fact that perhaps it is the conditions (the social and economic context) that give rise to them that also needs to be addressed (Furedi 2004). Thus, the emphasis in all of these programmes ... is on cleansing or sanitizing 'polluting persons' .... Once again the cultural takes precedence over the material in the solutions to counter-modern social risks .... (McGhee 2005: 179)

Similar initiatives have been mooted more recently to address what some politicians have described as the 'culture of violence' amongst inner-city black youth. Jack Straw, the new justice secretary under Brown, has backed plans to support the social development of disaffected black youth by 'providing them with successful black mentors, including army officers' (White 2007: 12). What these projects fail to address is the way black people in Britain have been systematically discriminated against – structurally, institutionally and subjectively (Appleton 2002, Braham et al. 1992, Williams 1996). These issues have been brushed aside in New Labour's community cohesion discourse. 'Instead of asking how society excludes Muslims/migrants ... the questions asked are about Muslims refusing to integrate ... Muslims having to become more British. It is thus their "alien" values that are the problem rather than our racist values' (Kundnani 2005, cited in Worley 2005: 490).

What this suggests is that a more nuanced structural perspective on 'community cohesion', and the relevance of this for social relations in a multicultural society, is needed.

A structural perspective on 'community cohesion' and its implications for social relations in a multicultural society

The emphasis of New Labour's community cohesion initiative is consistent with Foord and Young's observations on New Labour's approach to community safety, referred to earlier, and its drive to remoralise and change the behaviour of dysfunctional people and their flawed cultural values. Meanwhile, the structural causes of the troubles, be they the 'riots' in Burnley, Oldham and Bradford or Cardiff, Oxford and Tyneside – that is, socio-economic inequalities, poverty, racism and discrimination – are de-emphasised:

> The de-emphasis of these factors associated with the injustices of redistribution are [sic] similar to Levitas's (2005) observations concerning the 'discursive containment' in New Labour social exclusion discourse, where conflict is constructed as a problem of the pathologized few, which diverts attention away from the essentially class-divided character of society and allows a view of society as basically benign to co-exist with the visible reality of poverty. Fairclough (2000) takes Levitas's observations further, by suggesting that by focusing on those who are excluded from society and coming up with ways of including them, the government's 'social inclusion strategies' shift away from inequalities and conflicts of interest among those who are included, and presupposes that there is nothing inherently wrong with contemporary society as long as it is made more 'inclusive' through government policies. (McGhee 2005: 57)

Addressing the underlying causes of civil disturbances requires, in other words, a robust understanding of the context within which inter-community conflicts arise and are played out. The then Home Secretary Blunkett described the 'rioters' in Bradford as 'maniacs' and those who questioned Judge Gullick's sentencing – which was harsher than for those sentenced in Oldham and Burnley – as 'bleeding heart liberals' (cited in McGhee 2005: 59). As was the case in the 1980s and 1990s, the urban unrest of 2001 was reduced by the media, political establishment and criminal justice system to irrational criminality – 'deviant and anti-social behaviour rather than legitimate protest' (McGhee 2005: 60). Yet many involved in the troubles were simply 'people who had had enough, who could not depend on the police or the government to do anything about their situation' (McGhee 2005: 62). Perhaps it is too much to expect that the establishment could have accepted that the troubles actually epitomised Forrest and Kearns' simplest observable indicator of community cohesion defined above – that is, a group of people who live in a local area getting together to defend some common local interest. By failing to recognise this, the possibilities of more imaginative social policies on race relations and community wellbeing were denied.

In contrast to New Labour's discourse – which has served to foster the notion that multiculturalism has fragmented society by cultivating the 'cultural separatism and self-imposed segregation of Muslim migrants' (Modood 2007: 11) – Lord Professor Bhikhu Parekh, chair of the 2000 report of the Commission for Multi-Ethnic Britain (CMEB), *The Future of Multi-Ethnic Britain*, presents a more nuanced understanding. In an interview with Cindi John of the BBC, Parekh argues:

> Multiculturalism is sometimes taken to mean that different cultural communities should live their own ways of life in a self-contained manner. This is not its only meaning and in fact it has long been obsolete. Multiculturalism basically means that no culture is perfect or represents the best life and that it can therefore benefit from a critical dialogue with other cultures. In this sense multiculturalism requires that all cultures should be open, self-critical, and interactive in their relations with each other. (Parekh, cited in BBC News 2004: 2)

It also requires a sustained public examination about what it means to be British in the twenty-first century. For Modood, an important aspect of the CMEB's notion of multiculturalism was that:

> the story a country tells about itself to itself, the discourses, symbols and images in which national identity resides and through which people acquire and renew their sense of national belonging, had to be revisited and recast through public debate in order to reflect the current and future, and not just the past, ethnic composition of a country. (Modood 2007: 18)

Karen Chouhan, Chief Executive of the 1990 Trust, a black-led human rights organisation, adds that becoming a society of open cultures also requires us to 'move forward with a serious debate about how far we have to go in tackling race discrimination in every corner of society, not move it back by forcing everyone to be more (white) British' (Chouhan, cited in BBC News 2004: 2).

Recognising multiculturalism in these ways paves the way for advancing a more meaningful public debate on community cohesion – one that allows the kind of plural styles of political engagement imagined by Habermas and Freire (discussed in the previous chapter). It offers possibilities for creating other visions of British citizenship that are not confined to any homogenised state version but which are 'dispersed across society; compatible with the multiple forms of contemporary groupness; and sustained through dialogue, plural forms of representation that do not take one group as the model to whom all others have to conform, and through new, reformed national identities' (Modood 2007: 20)

It is highly unlikely, of course, that the British state will acknowledge multiculturalism in this way because such a notion will be perceived as a threat to its power base. As Terry Eagleton argues:

> It is culture, in the sense of the everyday habits and beliefs of a people, which beds power down, makes it appear natural and inevitable, turns it into spontaneous reflex and response. ... It is easy to see why a diversity of cultures should confront power with a problem. If culture is about plurality, power is about unit. How can it sell itself simultaneously to a whole range of life forms without being fatally diluted? (Eagleton 2007: 32)

Multiculturalism is a danger because it threatens the creation of the kind of 'tight cultural consensus' (Eagleton 2007: 32) that the British state needs to pursue its divisive policy agenda (both at home and abroad).

> This is why the Blair government pursued an agenda aimed at fostering a shared notion of historical origin, language, kinship and identity. As long as these things are fairly uniform, political power can afford to leave them alone. It is when they become too diverse to scoop into one rigid set of categories that the state risks being undermined, and thus seeks to override them. Culture then becomes part of the problem rather than the solution. It ceases to be a spiritual

solvent of material conflicts ... and becomes instead the very terms in which those conflicts are articulated. (Eagleton 2007: 32)

For government, multiculturalism represents a political threat, a politics of identity around which the claims of 'the Other' might be collectively organised. As McGhee observes:

> In multicultural societies, community, culture, tradition and identity were assumed to define one's politics; they gave minority groups their position from which to act politically, to stake their claim, demand recognition, resources, equality of opportunities .... In the new Britain, community, culture and identity will no longer be seen as key political resources, and sites of action, as they were .... (McGhee 2005: 168)

Instead, Britain's moral guardians continue to demand the obedience of immigrants to 'our culture', 'our way of life'. From 1 November 2005, new migrants applying for a British passport were expected to prove that they had 'a sense of inclusive British identity' by answering 24 questions in a citizenship test – questions British-based citizenship and English for speakers of other languages (Esol) teachers found too hard to answer. The immigration and citizenship minister responsible for the test, Tony McNulty, argued that 'An understanding of the British language and *our way of life* is vital' (McNulty, cited in Travis 2005b: 3 – emphasis added). In June 2007, the government introduced further plans to incentivise migrants to integrate. Under these plans, local government are given the role of issuing a 'life in Britain good neighbour contract' to all migrants. Ruth Kelly and Liam Byrne, the government ministers behind the proposals, warned that there is:

> a critical risk that after 40 years in which diversity has grown, Britain's communities stop looking outwards, celebrating what they have in common and instead begin looking inward, stressing their differences and divisions. ... We risk seeing a more divided society, more suspicious of each other and a society less capable of coming together around shared goals. Surely our task as a society is not to plan for separation. We need a stronger sense of why we live in a common place and have a shared future. (Cited in Wintour and Travis 2007: 1)

Byrne added that new migrants needed to do more to 'understand British values and its way of life' (cited in Wintour and Travis 2007: 1).

Leaving aside the vagueness of such notions as Britain's 'values' and 'way of life', the expectations of the government continue to ignore the reality of people's lived experiences and sense of identity within communities. As Worley argues, it is a position that:

> ignores how identities can be and are transnational, or forged across and through other aspects of identity such as gender or religion. 'Our' identities may already be shared with 'theirs'. It reinforces a place-bound notion of belonging... and returns us to dichotomous constructions of identity, rather than seeing identities as multiple, and valuing them as such. (Worley 2005: 489)

The government's ambition to enforce a commitment to shared common values is a reflection of New Labour's communitarian emphasis in its social policy agenda. It is a strategy close to Giddens' 'third way' view of community cohesion and the need for greater understanding between different cultures, achieved through dialogue between civic associations. However, it is a strategy that remains deeply problematic for it neglects the urgent need to address specific structural barriers to community cohesion – particularly inequality, poverty, racism and discrimination. As McGhee argues, New Labour has been 'too focused on transforming minority groups (especially ethnic minority, migrant and established migrant groups) and not focused enough on transforming the hostile defence of monolithic White, "indigenous", "host" identities and communities' (McGhee 2005: 164). It is arguably the (re)emergence of the deep-rooted hostility to multiculturalism in Britain that represents the greatest threat to community cohesion. Nowhere is this hostility more evident than in the hardening of attitudes to asylum seekers and immigrants under New Labour.

Community cohesion, asylum and immigration

A survey of social attitudes by the National Centre for Social Research (NCSR) found that those wanting the number of immigrants to Britain to be curbed increased from two-thirds in 1995 to three-quarters in 2003. The NCSR report suggested that increasingly hard-line statements on asylum from Home Office ministers were fuelling hostility against immigrants. Lauren McLaren (University of Nottingham) and Mark Johnson (co-director of the NCSR attitudes survey) argued that:

> The traditional acceptance of multicultural practices in Britain seemed to come under sustained direct attack from the Labour

government, aided and abetted by the Conservative opposition. This, along with the announcement of the creation of new detention centres, sending asylum seekers back to their home countries en masse, and even tipping off television crews as to times and locations of deportations, may have contributed to the overall impression of the citizenry that immigration needed to be stopped. (Cited in Carvel 2004: 6)

A report to the UN Human Rights Committee (submitted by 11 British organizations) blamed British politicians for 'encouraging racist hostility in their public attitudes towards asylum seekers' (Sales 2002: 458).

Despite counter arguments recognising the economic and cultural benefits that immigration brings (Craig et al. 2004), New Labour's keenness to deter immigrants and asylum seekers is evident in its Immigration and Asylum Act 1999. This Act replaced cash benefits for asylum seekers with a voucher system (equivalent to 70 per cent of the income support rate) and introduced a national dispersal housing scheme. 'The voucher system is an explicit institutionalization of a culture of suspicion in UK immigration and asylum policy, in that it is an anti-fraud measure, which by default labels all asylum seekers as potential benefit fraudsters' (McGhee 2005: 68). On 11 August 2001, the UN condemned Britain's 'shameful' approach to asylum for treating applicants like criminals – over 1,000 asylum seekers at the time were being held in prisons alongside convicted criminals (Pyke and Dillon 2001). An assessment of ten years of New Labour's asylum policy by a Joint Committee on Human Rights concluded that the UK system was 'degrading and inhumane' (cited in Verkaik 2007: 26). Concerns were expressed in the assessment about the use of detention against vulnerable people including children, pregnant women and people with health problems. Robina Qureshi, director of Positive Action in Housing (a group which supports asylum seekers in Glasgow), agreed with the Joint Committee's assessment that British asylum policy was a breach of human rights:

The treatment these people receive amounts to them being tortured in a country which they have come to because they are fleeing persecution from their own. The system works on the basis that all applications are bogus and as a result is ruthless in its treatment of the most vulnerable people in society and inevitably leads to the decline in their physical and mental health. In the end, the weak ones are sent home and the strong simply join the underclass of

Britain's underclass, where they have to work in the underground economy. Many of these people end up sleeping in phone boxes, night buses and car parks. (Cited in Verkaik 2007: 26)

Kate Allen, director of Amnesty International, argues that the British government deliberately uses destitution as a deterrent against asylum seekers:

Forcing people into destitution as an attempt to drive them out of the country is backfiring badly and vulnerable people are suffering. Refused asylum seekers are being reduced to penniless poverty – forced to sleep in parks, public toilets and phone boxes, to go without vital medicines even after suffering torture, and to relying on the charity of friends or drop-in shelters to survive. (Cited in Taylor 2006: 8)

In 2001, the Refugee Council published a report arguing that the policy of enforced dispersal was adding to the mental health problems of asylum seekers – particularly due to the 'acute sense of isolation' it was generating (Benjamin 2001: 48).

New Labour has sought to legitimise its anti-asylum stance by generating a moral panic around the 'inability' of migrants to integrate and how this threatens stability within British society. The 2002 White Paper *Secure Borders, Safe Havens: Integration with Diversity in Modern Britain* refers back to the government's perspective on the cause of the previous year's disturbances in Oldham, Burnley and Bradford – painting 'a vivid picture of fractured and divided communities, lacking a sense of common values or shared civil identity to unite around' (Home Office 2002, cited in McGhee 2005: 71). The paper set out the government's intention 'to transform the process of "becoming British", of gaining British citizenship, from a bureaucratic process into "an act of commitment to Britain and an important step in the process of achieving integration into our society" (Home Office 2002)' (cited in McGhee 2005: 73). It outlined proposals for a series of induction, re-orientation and education programmes without which the 'migrant communities will not be civilized, loyal or committed enough to be part of Britain, and that what they lack (Britishness) could be the source of future social risk' (McGhee 2005: 74). As McGhee argues, this represents the fundamental assumption underpinning New Labour's discourse on asylum and immigration – that 'difference, especially racial difference, = lack = risk of future violence' (McGhee 2005: 74). Unless the government ensures the successful assimilation of migrants into the 'British way of life' there will be trouble ahead. 'This is evident in the Home Office's (2002) suggestion that "failing to ensure the successful integration of those settling in the UK today will store up problems for future generations"' (cited in McGhee 2005: 74). Moreover, consistent with New Labour's discourse on community cohesion, the '"social problem" of integration in the 2002 White Paper is similarly reduced to "cultural difficulty" portrayed as cultural lack in relation to the capacity for integration…. "[T]he cultural" is once again prioritized over "the material"' (McGhee 2005: 74).

The perceived link between asylum, immigration and future violence was reinforced by the events of 11 September in the US and 7 July in London. These assaults 'upset Western notions of personal and collective security and identity' (Morrison 2006: 3) because they were attacks that suddenly appeared on our own doorstep for a change (rather than somewhere else): 'A changed geography of security had an existential effect not only in New York but also throughout America and the West…. Terrorism had moved from being something that happened somewhere else – and that somewhere else a safe distance over the horizon' (Morrison 2006: 28).

The existential effects of 11 September and 7 July have resulted in there being little public outcry against the raft of anti-terrorism legislation hurriedly passed by both the US and British governments. A consequence of this in Britain is that the 'state now has the power to arbitrarily arrest and hold anyone on suspicion of terrorist activity (irrespective of whether it has been carried out) and to deport them from the country' (McGhee 2005: 98). The majority of suspects interned under anti-terror legislation in Britain have been asylum seekers – many fearful of torture if returned to their country of origin. In addition, as Sales observes, 'The conflation of "terrorism" and "asylum seeker" in much of the policy discourse has grave implications for the safety of asylum seekers, as the spate of racial attacks following 11 September demonstrated' (Sales 2002: 473). Following the London bombings, the Institute of Race Relations (IRR) recorded 20 separate incidents of racially motivated attacks between the 7th and 13th July 2005 that appeared to be linked to the bombings, including graffiti, arson and petrol-bomb attacks, and assaults on individuals (IRR 2005).

The 'war on terror' and the assaults on Muslims

In 2000, an estimated 2,000 Muslims were stopped and searched under anti-terrorism legislation in Britain; in 2003, this had risen to

35,000 Muslims, with less than 50 charged. According to a report published by the Commission on British Muslims and Islamophobia, a think-tank established by the Runnymede Trust, Islamophobia in Britain is becoming increasingly institutionalised – creating a climate of fear among Muslims. If this is 'not addressed, then more and more Muslims will feel excluded from British society and simmering tensions, especially in northern English towns, are in danger of boiling over' (McGhee 2005: 99).

Brushed aside in the community cohesion debate has been the harmful impact of Blair's foreign policy on community relations and cohesion. A paper commissioned by the home and foreign secretaries for the government in 2004, *Young Muslims and Extremism*, drew a direct link between Blair's foreign policy and disillusionment among young Muslims (a disillusionment, it goes without saying, shared by thousands of non-Muslims). The paper referred to 'a perceived "double standard" in the foreign policy of western governments … in particular Britain and the US' (cited in Norton-Taylor et al. 2005: 8). The paper identified:

> perceived western bias in Israel's favour…. The perception is that passive 'oppression', as demonstrated by British foreign policy, e.g. non-action on Kashmir and Chechnya, has given way to 'active oppression'. The war on terror, Iraq and Afghanistan were all seen by a section of British Muslims as being acts against Islam. (Norton-Taylor et al. 2005: 8)

On 2 April 2006, *The Observer* reported that a government enquiry had acknowledged that the war on Iraq had motivated the four alleged bombers involved in the 7 July attacks in London. The report suggested that, alongside disaffection caused by economic deprivation and social exclusion, the war in Iraq had contributed to the radicalisation of the four. One, Mohammed Sidique Khan, was captured on video tape accusing ' "Western citizens" of electing governments that committed crimes against humanity' (cited in Townsend 2006: 2). Osama bin Laden's deputy, Ayman al-Zawahiri, also appeared on the tape claiming Blair's decision to go to war in Iraq was responsible for the bombings. Blair himself insisted that the decision to go to war against Iraq would 'make Britain safer' (cited in Townsend 2006: 1). He claimed that the invasion had nothing to do with generating terrorism: 'We must reject the thought that somehow we are the authors of our own distress' (Blair, cited in Branigan 2006: 11). Blair described the war in Iraq as 'a clash about civilisation. It is the age-old battle between progress and reaction'

(Blair, cited in Branigan 2006: 11). It was part of 'our' defence against an 'extremist view of Islam' that is 'not just theologically backward but completely contrary to the spirit and teaching of the Qu'ran' (Blair, cited in Branigan 2006: 11) and a threat to 'our way of life' (cited at Democracy Now! 2005: 1). 'Our way of life' is classified as the way of life of the 'We' – ' "We" are those who believe in religious tolerance, openness to others, to democracy, liberty and human rights administered by secular courts' (Blair, cited in Branigan 2006: 11).

Meanwhile, Blair exploited the fear of terrorism to push through illiberal social reforms at home that negated human rights – although, most particularly, the human rights of British Muslims. In December 2004, the House of Lords ruled that New Labour's Anti-Terrorism, Crime and Security Act 2001 – which allowed foreign terror suspects to be imprisoned without charge or trial – was 'the real threat to the life of the nation' (cited in Verkaik and Grice 2004: 1) and a breach of human rights.[2] A report by the Commons home affairs select committee, published on 6 April 2005, argued that 'community relations have deteriorated' as a consequence of the 'war on terror', partly caused by a widespread perception that Muslim communities 'were being stigmatised' (Travis 2005a: 12). Hazel Blears, as minister responsible for New Labour's counter-terrorism strategy, stated that Muslims had to accept the 'reality' that they will be stopped and searched by the police more because the terrorist threat came from people 'falsely hiding behind Islam' (cited in Dodd and Travis 2005a: 1). Massoud Shadjareh, chair of the Islamic Human Rights Commission, accused Blears of 'demonising and alienating our community. It is a legitimation for a backlash and for racists to have an onslaught on our community' (cited in Dodd and Travis 2005: 1). Inayat Bunglawala, spokesperson for the Muslim Council of Britain, added that he feared Blears' comments legitimised anti-Muslim sentiment: 'It is wholly unacceptable if a government minister is using her office to scaremonger at the expense of our community to ease the passage of legislation designed to curb our civil liberties' (Inayat Bunglawala, cited in Dodd and Travis 2005: 1). The corrosive effect of the political and media assault on British Muslims is clearly described by Daud Abdullah, deputy secretary general of the Muslim Council of Britain:

What is claimed to be an assertion of free speech and democratic rights is rapidly becoming the demonisation of a community. Once

---

[2] On June 12th 2008, the House of Commons voted in favour of a Counter Terrorism Bill extending the time terror suspects can be detained without charge or trial from 28 days to 42 days.

they are dehumanised, who cares for their democratic, civil or human rights? Since John Reid demanded that Muslim 'bullies' must be faced down and Jack Straw declared the veil a 'statement of separation', ministers have fallen over themselves to make increasingly unbridled attacks on Muslims. The shadow home secretary, David Davis, has accused our communities of creating a 'voluntary apartheid' and colleges have taken action against veiled teachers and students. The tabloid press has declared open season on Muslims with one hostile front-page story after another. (Abdullah 2006: 32)

The lessons are not learned. Enmity against Muslims from the media and politicians continues to fuel wider public hostility. Following Jack Straw declaring his discomfort about Muslim women wearing the veil, verbal and physical attacks on Muslims rose: 'Women have had their scarves ripped off. Mosques and Islamic centres in Preston and Falkirk have been attacked by mobs and firebombed' (Abdullah 2006: 32). Rather than admit to its own disastrous foreign policy in Iraq and the divisive effect this has had on community cohesion – a foreign policy that was opposed by many communities in Britain, not just Muslim – New Labour politicians have sought to defame the Muslim community 'virtually alone' (Freedland 2006: 31) – the *new* enemy within. As Arun Kundnani argues, 'The greatest threat to integration in Britain today is the government's sustained assault on the civil rights of Muslims in the so-called war on terror. It is primarily in the universalism of human rights principles that we can all unite as citizens' (cited in Muir 2005: 7).

The erosion of human rights and civil liberties

Between 1997 and 2006 there were 16 acts of Parliament attacking human rights and civil liberties in Britain including: the 1997 Protection from Harassment Act (criminalising 'unruly conduct' such as protesting against scientists and governments); the 2000 Regulation of Investigatory Powers Act and subsequent 2002 order (removing the freedom to communicate privately without surveillance); the 2000 Terrorism Act (removing the right to protest in certain circumstances, the right to go about one's business without fear of police harassment, the right to freedom of association and the presumption of innocence); the 2001 Anti-Terrorism, Crime and Security Act (allowing the detention without trial of suspected terrorists); the 2005 Serious Organised Crime and Police Act (removing the freedom to demonstrate outside parliament); the 2003 Criminal Justice Act (removing the right to a trial in certain cases, the right of silence and the rule of double jeopardy); the 2005 Prevention of Terrorism Act (which removed the right not to be punished unless a court decides there has been a breach of law); and the 2004 Civil Contingencies Act (which allows ministers who believe that an emergency is about to occur to grant themselves powers to introduce special legislation in a seven-day period which permits the forced evacuation of people, the seizing of property without compensation, the banning of any assembly and the conferring of jurisdiction on any new court or tribunal they so wish) (see McGhee 2005, Porter 2006).

Under Part One of the 2006 Terrorism Act it becomes a criminal offence for a person to intentionally or 'recklessly' publish a statement which is likely to be understood 'as a direct or indirect encouragement or other inducement' to commit a terrorist act. The offence carries a sentence of imprisonment of up to seven years on conviction. Statements likely to be understood as encouraging terrorism include those that 'glorify' terrorist acts – when members of the public hearing the statement would understand 'what is being glorified as conduct that should be emulated by them' (HRW 2005). At the time of the drafting of this legislation, Human Rights Watch (HRW) argued that the scope of the Bill was:

> both ill-defined, particularly in relation to 'glorification', and overly broad – it uses a definition of terrorism that extends well beyond the conventional understanding of the term. As a result, it is likely to prove inconsistent with international standards guaranteeing free expression. Despite assurances from the government, it also remains unclear whether people who are unaware that their words are likely to incite violence can be held criminally liable. The new offence is likely to have a chilling effect on free expression in the classroom, the newsroom, and the mosque. (HRW 2005: 1)[3]

Given the context of such assaults on human rights, it is unsurprising that some people seek to restore a semblance of security in their lives by retreating to community as their primary defence against perceived injustice and oppression (again, epitomising Forrest and Kearns' simplest observable measure of 'community cohesion'). However, New Labour sees such forms of attachment as inhibiting the development of

---

[3] A recent example of the repression of such free expression is the arrest and detention without charge for six days of Rizwaan Sabir, a politics postgraduate research student at the University of Nottingham. Sabir was held under anti-terror legislation on suspicion of possessing extremist literature – an edited version of an al-Qaeda training manual that was freely available on the internet. His PhD topic was radical Islamic groups (Newman 2008).

a shared commitment to 'British values' – one around which community and national cohesion can be forged. They represent an undesirable form of community – the 'wrong' type of community – 'deficient in some critical respect or "dangerously disengaged"...[comprising] the over-active citizen who stretches the limits of social democracy too far' (Shaw and Martin 2000: 408).

Conclusions

New Labour's community policies continue to reflect concerns raised in classical sociology and, more recently, in communitarian discourse (discussed in the previous chapter) – threats from 'dangerous Others'. Dealing with these threats in the context of neo-liberalism – the ideology which has become the 'non-negotiable' political philosophy at the heart of British government – means that the kind of collectivist solutions envisaged under Keynesian welfarism are no longer (seen to be) at the disposal of government. There is now an unmistakeable focus on the need to restore social cohesion within communities – built upon shared common values based largely on notions of 'respect', 'decency' and 'Britishness' – and to reinstate the moral authority of the 'responsible community' (Jordan 2006: 128). This includes intolerance of attitudes and behaviour that might be perceived as a threat to 'community wellbeing' – in particular, work-shyness (generated by welfare dependency), minor incivility (generated by a breakdown in moral values) and non-patriotic sentiment (generated by multiculturalism). As Jordan suggests, this approach seeks to counter threats posed by 'dangerous Others' by encouraging, in Foucault's term, 'technologies of the self' whereby individuals develop different attitudes about their responsibilities and use these technologies 'to effect by their own means or with the help of others a certain number of operations on their own bodies and souls, thoughts, conduct and way of being' (Foucault 1988, cited in Jordan 2006: 130). Following interventions by state agencies, individuals will be expected to adapt and be more responsible – 'cured' of their 'anti-social' tendencies or 'alien' cultural values. They will become active citizens – generating the social capital necessary to deal with whatever social problems their communities might face (without the need for state interference). Those who fail to adapt will be criminalised, stripped of welfare entitlements or refused citizenship. This approach to social policy redefines the role of the state and individuals (in communities) by emphasising responsibilities over rights.

These policies will not succeed in generating social cohesion and community wellbeing for the many. This is because they are based on flawed communitarian notions of 'community' that continue to ignore power differentials and structured inequalities in society, and focus instead on the 'flawed cultures' of 'failed communities' – be they the feckless, workshy 'underclass' and their feral offspring, or the recalcitrant zealots amongst second generation Pakistani Muslims. The emphasis also remains managerialist and focused on meeting predetermined performance targets (centrally-defined) rather than allowing genuine dialogue in 'ideal speech situations'. At the same time, however, the appeal of 'community' in these policy areas serves as a useful rhetorical device for governance – generating an impression of 'empowerment' and the collective's involvement, consent and stake in the delivery of public services and social programmes, as well as a sense of solidarity and cohesion. As Byrne says, 'this is a vocabulary of a process in which there are no conflicts, no disputes of interest, merely a collective and unproblematic interest in the maintenance of a communally generated and mutually accepted social order' (Byrne 2006: 167). It is also a language that helps Labour distinguish itself from neo-liberal Conservatism – which cares little about social solidarity. It is, as Byrne puts it, 'neo-liberalism with a smiley face' (Byrne 2006: 151).

Community safety, urban regeneration and community cohesion policies are ultimately geared towards achieving the same objective: the purification of urban spaces for the benefit of the privileged. The most vulnerable are amongst the biggest losers – working-class young men, black and minority ethnic groups, asylum seekers, disabled people, the poor and homeless, and travelling communities. Commercial interests, financial corporations, senior executives and affluent consumers have most to gain. At the same time, because the vulnerable have become the main target of these measures, more serious threats to community wellbeing – those wrought by the activities of the powerful (in particular, the threats presented by the 'anti-social' policies of the British state at home and abroad, or the activities of powerful corporations) – remain intact.

In the chapter that follows we revisit the core concepts of community safety, cohesion and wellbeing in order to expose significant contradictions evident in the contemporary mainstream political discourse that is shaping New Labour's policy agenda. In doing so, we present a different reading of these ideas and themes, based upon a more nuanced understanding of threats to safety and wellbeing.

4
Rethinking Community Safety, Cohesion and Wellbeing

'Die Kleinen Dieb man henken thut – vorn grossen zeucht man ab den hut' –
'The little thief we hang – in front of the big ones, we doff our hat'.

(Austrian folk saying, anon)

Introduction

As we have argued, dominant notions of community safety, cohesion and wellbeing established in mainstream political and social policy discourse have largely served to socially construct a disproportionate understanding of major threats to human wellbeing in contemporary British society. In particular, by directing public attention on to risks posed by the relatively vulnerable sections of society, interest has been distracted from attending to more serious social harms resulting from the activities of the powerful. This chapter seeks to redress this diversion by refocusing the debate on community safety, cohesion and wellbeing in a way that offers greater recognition of social harms that are symptomatic of a dysfunctional political and economic system. In particular, the chapter will examine the destructive effects of 'anti-social' policies and practices of government and private corporations on community wellbeing. It will argue that the process of building safer communities will require greater attention to these issues, and the planning and mobilisation of a different democratic accord prepared and able to call the powerful to account. Once this process begins to happen then genuine possibilities may emerge for refocusing the social policy agenda towards generating a vision of a universalised approach to supporting human wellbeing.

A central concern of this chapter is the way dominant accounts of community safety in British social policy have focused attention on to the relatively minor misdemeanours of the least powerful (defined as 'crimes' or 'anti-social' acts) rather than the more serious threats to human wellbeing caused by the activities of the powerful. As Hillyard and Tombs have argued with reference to the criminal justice system:

> [A]mong those events that get defined as crime through the law, there are processes of selectivity in terms of which crimes are selected for control by criminal justice agencies. ... [As Reiman argues] 'the definitions of crime in the criminal law do not reflect the only or the most dangerous of antisocial behaviours'; ... There is little doubt, then, that the undue attention given to events, which are defined as crimes, distracts attention from more serious harm. (Hillyard and Tombs 2004: 12–13)

The notion of community safety driving New Labour's crime and disorder agenda is one that overwhelmingly concentrates on 'the *activities of* (rather than the harmful *experiences suffered by*) the marginalised 30 per cent of the population' (Tombs and Hillyard 2004: 31 – emphasis in original). This focus on the digressions of marginalised individuals means that 'the structural determinants which lead to harmful events – such as poverty, social deprivation and the growing inequalities between rich and poor – can be ignored' (Hillyard and Tombs 2004: 18).

Economic restructuring and social policy choices in Britain since the late-1970s, activities overseen by the powerful, have taken back many of the benefits produced by the Keynesian welfare state and widened the social divide – with profound consequences for society. As Wilkinson argues, 'Inequality promotes strategies that are more self-interested, less affiliative, often highly antisocial, more stressful, and likely to give rise to higher levels of violence, poorer community relations, and worse health' (Wilkinson 2005: 23). The state's retreat from Keynesian welfarism since the 1980s has affected the ability of many to satisfy their basic needs and interests in relation to accessing meaningful employment, an adequate income, a healthy diet, decent living conditions, a safe neighbourhood environment, a worthwhile educational experience, comprehensive health care, opportunities to socialise, self-esteem, emotional wellbeing and basic human rights. As Bauman argues:

> Communally endorsed insurance policies against individual misfortune, which in the course of the last century came to be known

collectively under the name of the 'social' ('welfare') state, are now being phased out, reduced below the level needed to validate and sustain confidence in security, or are no longer hoped, let alone trusted, to survive the next round of cuts. (Bauman 2006: 134)

Satisfaction of human needs requires certain societal preconditions to be set in place – including opportunities for individuals to engage in meaningful participation in decision making in respect of what these preconditions might be (Doyal and Gough 1991). Neo-liberal governments, however, have thwarted opportunities for meaningful involvement. As Neal Lawson points out in his diagnosis of Thomas Frank's work on the rise of 'market populism', 'with the market now viewed as the ultimate tool of democracy... [e]verywhere the collective voice... is replaced by atomised and competitive individualised choices' (cited in Bauman 2006: 134). This coincides with Marx's (1976) notion, set out in *Capital*, of how the masses accept gross inequality in capitalist societies rather than challenge the social order – it is because they remain 'alienated from any meaningful control over the material conditions of everyday life' (Myers 2004: 80). Neo-liberal market capitalism has become increasingly freed from democratic control – with devastating implications for human wellbeing. 'As the political tools once used to rein-in market forces have been steadily dismantled and disorganized, capitalism once again comes to resemble a ship on the high seas whose captain has gone mad' (Myers 2004: 81–82). These unfettered market forces are a major source of social harm: 'the neo-liberal economic paradigm is fundamentally harmful – it wrecks lives and creates harm on a wide scale – and these features are not some aberration, but integral and necessary aspects of this form of economic and political organisation' (Tombs and Hillyard 2004: 32).

Yet neo-liberalism has become a form of economic and political organisation that is presented to us as an 'inescapable reality' (Rustin and Chamberlayne 2002: 10) – a scientific fact. There is no alternative. As a consequence, we have to accept reductions in social assistance and employment rights, and the increasing commodification of public services. What were once defined as public issues – inadequate social protection (Bauman 1998), a divisive education system (Tomlinson 2001) and growing health inequalities (Acheson 1998) – have become individualised personal problems. While New Labour has attempted to promote 'opportunity' – particularly through New Deal and the Social Exclusion Unit – its emphasis has been on opportunity through 'employability', presented as 'something individuals must actively achieve.... Inclusion becomes a duty rather than a right' (Levitas 2005: 128). Such a strategy, however, is fundamentally flawed in today's flexible labour market where it is becoming increasingly difficult to obtain an adequate, regular income from paid work (Burden et al. 2000).

In parallel with the continuing narrowing of the scope of public welfare provision in Britain has been the opening up of public services to private gain. One example of this has been the concerted efforts of governments since the 1990s to withdraw welfare support to disabled people that have included the use of incentives to commercial interests. This is a particularly callous example which will be explored in some detail in the following sub-section. Subsequent sub-sections illustrate examples of the harmful effects of neo-liberal social reforms on social wellbeing in the areas of youth policy, education, housing and health. We also consider threats to community safety and wellbeing from the activities of powerful corporations and the rise of 'consumer society'. In addition, we examine implications for community cohesion and safety domestically from New Labour's collusion in the 'war-on-terror'. Finally, we consider the effects on social wellbeing of what some commentators have described as a rise in moral indifference to the suffering of others – where people increasingly 'turn a blind eye' to the uneasy reality of other people's misery and distress.

Given that these are substantial areas to cover, the explorations that follow will be indicative rather than definitive. What these examinations will offer is an indication of how dominant assumptions on community wellbeing within mainstream discourse have served to socially construct a disproportionate understanding with regard to the major risks faced by society whilst simultaneously mask the more serious social harms wrought by the anti-social policies and practices of governments and private corporations.

Incentivising welfare cut-backs to disabled people

Since the 1990s in particular, the British government has sought to reduce the benefit entitlement of disabled people. The 1994 Social Security (Incapacity for Work) Act introduced Incapacity Benefit (IB) alongside a range of key reforms aimed at reducing the number of new claimants. Peter Lilley, then Secretary of State for Social Security under a Conservative government, commissioned John LoCascio, second vice president of Unum, the leading US disability insurance company, to advise on more stringent medical tests for IB claimants. In 1997, a new All Work Test was introduced which assessed the general capacity of IB applicants to work rather than whether they were able to do their specific job. In addition, these assessments would be carried out by non-medical administrators. These changes brought a halt to the rise in IB claimants. At the same time as the All Work Test was introduced, Unum launched an expensive advertising campaign promoting its private disability insurance – raising ethical concerns in relation to their role in instituting benefit cuts (Rutherford 2007a).

Since their election, New Labour has continued to pursue measures aimed at withdrawing welfare support for disabled people. Because the All Work Test had failed to reduce the number of claimants with mental health problems, the 1999 Welfare Reform Act required all new claimants to attend a compulsory interview. The All Work Test was also replaced with the Personal Capacity Assessment (PCA) where the 'emphasis would no longer be on benefit entitlement but on what a person was able to do and the action needed to support them at work' (Rutherford 2007a: 44). In 2003, the government piloted its *Pathways to Work* projects where:

> all new 'customers' to IB undertake a work-focused interview (WFI) with an IB Personal Adviser (IBPA).…The role of the IBPAs is to actively encourage customers to consider a return to work, as well as discussing work-focused activity. Customers are offered a 'Choices' package of interventions to support a return to work. For claimants suffering mental illness, a Condition Management Programme is available, developed jointly between Jobcentre Plus and the NHS. (Rutherford 2007a: 45)

At the heart of these policy developments was UnumProvident (Unum and Provident merged in 1999).

> UnumProvident was building its influence. In 2001 it had launched New Beginnings, a public private partnership that acted as a pressure group…enabling the extension of the company's influence in shaping the policy making environment, particularly in relation to *Pathways to Work*.…Then in July 2004, it opened its £1.6m UnumProvident Centre for Psychosocial and Disability Research at Cardiff University. (Rutherford 2007a: 46)

UnumProvident now had both academic credentials as well as close connections with government ministers. 'Malcolm Wicks, Minister of State in the DWP, gave a speech praising the partnership between industry and the university' (Rutherford 2007a: 46). This partnership – a brainchild of neo-liberal thinking – provided the theoretical framework for New Labour's 2006 Welfare Reform Bill. This presents a largely bio-psychosocial critique of the 'old' biomedical model of illness:

'The old biomedical model of illness, which has dominated health care for the past century, cannot fully explain many forms of illness.' This old model assumes a causal relation between disease and illness, and fails to take into account how cultural attitudes and psychological and social factors shape illness behaviour. In other words it allows someone to report symptoms of illness, and for society to accept him or her as sick, without their having a pathology. ... Illness is a behaviour .... The degree of illness behaviour is dependent not upon an underlying pathology but on 'individual attitudes and beliefs', as well as 'the social context and culture in which it occurs'. Halligan and Wade are more explicit: 'Personal choice plays an important part in the genesis or maintenance of illness'. (See Rutherford 2007a: 47)

The IB trends, therefore, are seen as a social and cultural phenomenon rather than a welfare or health issue. Consequently, the solution is not to provide welfare and health care but to transform the social and cultural context. According to the UnumProvident industrial/academic partnership, the best way of doing this is through work incentivisation: 'work itself is therapeutic, aids recovery and is the best form of rehabilitation' (cited in Rutherford 2007a: 48). Unemployment is viewed as a serious risk to social wellbeing – a view that idealises work and ignores the alienation and ennui many experience from paid employment. There is no acknowledgement of structural causes of ill health such as low wages 'despite the argument that healthy living requires a healthy income' (Klein 2005: 65). The risks to health from social inequalities, identified in the Black Report and various subsequent studies (Townsend et al. 1992), are ignored. Instead, the UnumProvident industrial/academic partnership's position adopts a particularly authoritarian moral stance – that is, ill health and disability is largely the consequence of dysfunctional beliefs and attitudes held by individuals living in an imperfect social context. 'As Halligan and Wade argue: "Our model suggests that illness is a dysfunction of the person in his (or her) physical and social environment"' (cited in Rutherford 2007a: 48–49).

New Labour's 2006 Welfare Reform Bill, enacted in May 2007, aims to roll out *Pathways to Work* across the country, targeting unemployed single parents, older people and all the 2.6million people currently claiming IB (Wintour 2008b: 15). To achieve its target of reducing the number of IB claimants, the state will assist employers to be more effective in the management of sickness. Benefits will only be paid on the basis of an assessment of a person's capacity to work (not their disability or illness). The new legislation also paves the way for incentives for GPs and primary care workers to get individuals back into paid work:

> 'Employment advisers' will be attached to surgeries to help in 'bringing about a cultural change in the way work is viewed by families and individuals'. The PCA will be redesigned by two technical working groups, one for mental health and one for physical disability. Both groups involve representatives from UnumProvident and Atos Origin [a US corporation with responsibility for administering the PCA]. (Rutherford 2007a: 51)

This represents increasing corporate administrative interference into the judgements of medical professionals. Moreover,

> In 2008, IB will be replaced by a two-tier Employment and Support Allowance. Minister of State for Employment and Welfare Reform Jim Murphy...emphasised that the new allowance will 'focus on how we can help people into work and will not automatically assume that because a person has a specific health condition or disability they are incapable of work'. Apart from those with the most severe disabilities...'customers' who fail to participate in work-focused interviews or to engage in work related activity will be subjected to a 'motivational tool' [i.e. benefit cuts]. (Rutherford 2007a: 51)

As Rutherford understates, it is highly unlikely that threatening people who are ill or disabled with impoverishment will aid their long-term employment prospects and wellbeing. However, the lack of care for disabled people in Britain is systematic. A recent enquiry by the Healthcare Commission reported that threats and abuses against disabled people have been institutionalised within the NHS for some time. In Cornwall, for example:

> Vulnerable people suffering from such conditions as autism and cerebral palsy endured years of bullying, harassment and physical ill-treatment at the hands of NHS staff.... One severely disabled man was tied to his bed or wheelchair for 16 hours a day. Others were given cold showers, had food withheld and spent hours locked in their rooms. (Laurance 2006: 1–2)

A curious aside about UnumProvident's involvement in New Labour's welfare reforms is that, in 2003, an investigation by the Insurance Commissioner of the State of California alleged that they had conducted their affairs fraudulently. For example, it was alleged that they invariably compelled claimants to accept less than the amount due under the terms of their policies (if they refused, they would have to resort to litigation which would be problematic for families with a disabled or sick head of household on low incomes – presumably, something UnumProvident understood). Moreover, 'The following year a multi-state review identified four areas of concern: an excessive reliance on in-house professionals; unfair construction of doctor's [sic] ... reports; a failure to properly evaluate the totality of the claimants' medical condition; and an inappropriate burden on the claimant to justify eligibility for benefit' (Rutherford 2007a: 49).

In the view of Commissioner John Garamendi, UnumProvident is 'an outlaw company.... It is a company that for years has operated in an illegal fashion' (cited in Rutherford 2007a: 49). Yet it is a company New Labour is more than willing to work with in order to apply its own brand of private sector insurance practice to a radically reformed welfare regime. Similar contracts can be expected in the future as the appeal of private sector assistance in welfare retrenchment programmes grows within both major political parties – evident in both the Freud Review on welfare reform for New Labour, *Reducing dependency, Increasing opportunity: options for the future of welfare to work* (2007), and Shadow Chancellor George Osborne's response to this review – that is, he claimed that it did not go far enough because it failed to see the potential for paying private companies to get people off benefits on a ' "no-win, no fee" approach ... by results' (Rutherford 2007a: 49). However, not to be outwitted, Secretary of State for Health Alan Johnson, in an attack on what he calls the 'sick-note culture', subsequently announced his support for private employers 'to run health clinics in a bid to cut the estimated 175million working days lost to sickness each year' (BBC News 2008: 1).

The demonisation and marginalisation of 'problem youth'

Since the beginning of the twenty-first century there has been continuing high-profile media, political and academic interest in the 'problem of youth'. This 'problem' has largely been interpreted in terms of either youth as a threat ('feral yobs' in need of surveillance and control, and to being incentivised to work, train or volunteer) or as victims in need of protection – in either case, a 'deficit model'. The nature of the problem initially had a class/gendered dimension – with the focus of attention clearly 'dangerous' young working-class men. It is also a problem that has been with us throughout modernity, although the way the problem has been interpreted and responded to has changed over time. The post-war Keynesian welfare state appeared to have moved us a long way from the harsh realities of Victorian workhouses, penal institutions, reformatories and Methodist schooling regimes – offering working class children and young people greater opportunity through improvements in social protection, health care, housing conditions and education. At the same time, young people benefited from access to informal education based in professional youth work settings. However, support for this was short lived and, by the late 1970s, youth work was in decline as neo-liberalism began to bloom. Since the 1980s, social policies have been increasingly shaped within a neo-liberal political orthodoxy involving the abandonment of support for full-employment policies and comprehensive social welfare, and the 'modernisation' (reorientation) of welfare provision to the needs of a post-industrial economy. Implementing this modernisation agenda has been enforced through the imposition of the new managerialism throughout all areas of welfare organising (Burden et al. 2000).

Young working-class people have been harshly affected by these changes. Deindustrialisation and the loss of manufacturing jobs particularly affected working-class 'youth' in northern urban areas. Moreover, changes to the occupational structure of the workforce has left a greater divide between the well-paid, secure professional or management jobs and the poorly-paid, insecure service-sector jobs working-class youth are reliant on. This divide has been exacerbated by a decline in trade union recognition and collective bargaining powers which has impacted on job security and wages (Allen and Massey 1992). These changes have also had significant implications for gender, including what has been described as a 'crisis of masculinity' for traditional working-class males (Campbell 1993) – a situation whereby these males cannot live up to the requirements of hegemonic masculinity (Goffman 1963). By the 1990s, argues Messerschmidt, hegemonic masculinity in contemporary western society was defined through: 'work in the paid-labor market, the subordination of women, heterosexism, and the driven and uncontrollable sexuality of men. Refined still further, hegemonic masculinity emphasizes practices towards authority, control, competitive individualism, independence, aggressiveness, and the capacity for violence' (cited in Brown 2005: 139).

As traditional manufacturing jobs declined, this closed off opportunities for working-class men to enter long-term and secure paid work. At the same time this was happening, women were increasingly entering the labour market and becoming financially more independent from men. According to Campbell (1993), this 'crisis' for the working-class male ego explained much of the cause of the troubles (e.g. 'joy-riding' and 'riots') on peripheral housing estates in the early 1990s (discussed in Chapter 1). (There is a further issue here in that the expansion of young working-class women entering the labour market also led to the dual bind of women's exploitation at work *and* in the home and community – for a detailed discussion of this see Hamnett et al. 1989).

Throughout the 1990s there was a growing 'moral panic' about the state of (primarily) working-class young men – a panic that took the form of a generalisable 'youth crisis' after 12 February 1993 following the abduction and killing of two-year old James Bulger: Walter Ellis experienced 'apprehension and fear' of children 'that was not there before.... [W]e can never know which of them has the Satan bug inside him'; Beryl Bainbridge saw children whose 'countenance was so devoid of innocence that I was frightened.... Women passing by said...they should have been drowned at birth'; Lynda Lee Potter described a 'nightmarish world...where children are growing up virtually as savages'; Gerald Warner used the Bulger case to argue that 'civilisation' was now 'menaced by adolescents from hell' (cited in Haydon and Scraton 2000: 424–425). The immediate aftermath of Bulger saw the then Home Secretary Michael Howard pursue a 'populist punitive' agenda on crime that included doubling the maximum sentence in a youth offender institution for 15 to 17-year-olds to two years and introducing secure training orders for 12 to 14-year-olds (i.e. a mix of custody in secure training centres and supervision in the community). 'The number of young people serving custodial sentences rose by 122 per cent between 1993 and 1999' (Morgan and Newburn 2007: 1031). This shift in the nature of social policy interventions with young people – from welfare principles to a mix of populist punitivism and moral authoritarianism – has continued apace under New Labour.

Despite New Labour's claim to represent a third way in British politics (between 'Old' Labour and the New Right Conservatives) and its expressed concern for helping young people at risk of social exclusion, young people in Britain – or more specifically, young people from working class and certain black and ethnic minority communities – have faced increasing demonisation and punitive social policies under the governments of Blair and Brown. New Labour's preferred concept of social exclusion – as we saw in the previous chapter – reflects a combination of the moral underclass and social integrationist discourses, and focuses on the cultural failings of individuals (and their communities) as the main barrier to social inclusion. It is largely the behavioural flaws of young people (in particular, their 'risky behaviour' – teenage sex, drugs, truancy, disruptive behaviour in schools, etc.) and their lack of employability skills which are responsible for their social exclusion. These arguments are 'backed up' by various research reports produced by the Social Exclusion Unit (SEU) specifically on children and young people (currently archived at http://archive.cabinetoffice.gov.uk/seu/default.html). The policy focus has been increasingly about activating young people to get into paid work, and to take responsibility for their behaviour. In order to achieve this, there has been an increasing focus on 'casework' with individual young people – particularly through Connexions – to enable them to make more 'responsible' choices. Initially, this involved the New Deal programme to get young people into work, education or training, with those failing to comply with the requirements of New Deal facing sanctions – including the withholding of benefits (France 2007).

New Labour's approach to working with young people has also aimed to address what the SEU identified as the need to co-ordinate children's and young people's services more effectively (reflecting the new managerialism in social policy). This has led to the development of Children and Young People's strategic partnerships involving various service providers – local authorities, health, police, Connexions, Learning and Skills Councils, Sure Start, voluntary bodies, probation, youth offending teams, schools and colleges, Jobcentre Plus and so forth. These partnerships set out the priorities for how services for children and young people should be developed locally, strategically and organisationally, and they are responsible for commissioning services (LCC 2008). To ensure that services are better integrated and more accessible, the government is looking to extend the role of schools, particularly in respect of the delivery of information, advice and guidance. Some fear that creating an enhanced role for schools to support young people will only further alienate those already disillusioned with the school system. At the same time, it will threaten detached youth work with the hardest-to-reach young people – many of whom have been excluded from school or choose not to attend.

Detached youth workers do away with traditional notions of adult authority. They'll ask a young person what sort of learning programmes they want, allowing them to decide what they are going to learn, how they'll learn it and in what way it will be measured. Everything is done from the teenager's point of view. But, above all, what distinguishes these youth workers from others is that they work on young people's territory: on streets and estates, in arcades, pubs, homes and parks. (Shepherd 2008: 3)

Increasingly under New Labour, detached youth workers are being commissioned to work in schools to predetermined outcomes, diverting them 'away from our community-based practice' and threatening 'democratic education with young people' (Graeme Tiffany, formerly a detached youth worker, cited in Shepherd 2008: 3). It is a move that is effectively consistent with other policies aimed at controlling young people's unregulated leisure activities – 'we have already seen how freedom of movement and association in public spaces has been curtailed by the use of curfews and dispersal orders' (Smith 2005: 11). Extended schooling is just another example of 'getting the dirtbags off the street' (Jeffs and Smith 1996).

Alongside these social policy interventions, New Labour have continued to pursue the populist punitive turn in 'youth justice' – the key elements of which were established in their 1997 White Paper *No More Excuses* and the subsequent Crime and Disorder Act 1998 (further developed in succeeding legislation). The particular focus of New Labour's youth justice system has included:

- Abolishing the principle of *doli incapax* and lowering the age at which someone can be criminally liable for their actions from 14-years-old to 10 – a measure the United Nations called a breach of the UN Convention on the Rights of the Child (France 2007).
- Early-intervention prevention schemes with young people considered at risk of offending, parenting programmes and 'safer schools' partnerships (involving police officers in schools) – measures that represent 'an expansion of the criminal justice orbit and risk stigmatizing environments, children, and their families' (Morgan and Newburn 2007: 1036).
- An emphasis on 'anti-social behaviour' and giving local authorities, the police and social landlords the power to impose an anti-social behaviour order (asbo) on anyone over 10-years-old who *may* be considered to have caused alarm, distress or harassment to someone. Asbos prohibit people from behaving in a particular way or from being in a defined public space. The definition of 'anti-social'

is so vague that it is invariably conditional on subjective interpretation. The asbo regime has particularly targeted young people, opening up the possibility for an increase in the number of young offenders being criminalised. There has also been a range of measures introduced to intensify the surveillance and control of young people in their own communities – such as curfews, electronic tagging, CCTV, and the naming and shaming of 'youth offenders' by the courts and local newspapers (France 2007).

• Continuity with the previous Conservative government's commitment to custodial sentences for young offenders. Secure units for juveniles have been expanded – a development that also goes against the UN Convention on the Rights of the Child (France 2007).

Media reporting and New Labour's approach to criminal justice have presented a disproportionately negative portrayal of young people. In May 2005, Professor Rod Morgan (then chairman of the Youth Justice Board and government chief adviser on youth crime) called on politicians and the media to stop describing children as 'yobs', warning that Britain risks demonising a whole generation of young people. This followed references to the need to tackle 'yob culture' (Michael Howard), dispersal orders 'against gangs of yobs' (Tony Blair) and plans to dress young people on community service orders in uniforms (Hazel Blears) (Bright 2005b). Rob Allen, a member of the Youth Justice Board since it was established in 1998, reinforced Morgan's view by attacking the increasing criminalisation of young people involved in minor delinquency, and the excessive use of custodial remands and sentences: '[T]here are some developments of which we really should be ashamed, in particular aspects of the way we lock up children, the demonisation of young people involved in anti-social behaviour and the coarsening of the political and public debate about how to deal with young people in trouble' (Allen, cited in Temko and Doward 2006: 4).

New Labour's response to the youth problem has continued to impact unfavourably on the rights of young people – particularly in terms of their rights of access to public places. Developments in social policy and youth justice, in tandem with the situational crime prevention initiatives described in the previous chapter, are increasingly closing off public spaces that are of such importance to young people – places that 'may be the only spaces they can use outside the family home and school. Limited free youth provision, cost of leisure activity, and age restrictions leave them with limited choice but to use the streets in local neighbourhoods' (France 2007: 100–101). 'Public spaces' are increasingly becoming 'quasi-private' spaces through the development of gated city centre shopping malls, waterfronts and residential communities, patrolled by private security firms who watch out for, and exclude, the riff-raff – and 'where commercial imperatives rule' (France 2007: 101).

The essence of New Labour's youth policy is captured in Henry Giroux's critique on childhood and contemporary culture in western society, *Stealing Innocence*, and what he identifies as a 'growing assault on youth' (Giroux 2000: 10). This attack is evident 'in the indignities youth suffer on a daily basis' largely as a result of the renaissance of their 'surveillance, control and regulation' (Giroux 2000: 10). Today, 'young people are increasingly excluded from public spaces outside of schools that once offered them the opportunity to hang out with relative security… and develop their own talents and sense of self-worth' (Giroux 2000: 10). The streets and public parks are now closed off as places for young people to meet with their peers – representing an attack on their freedom. As Giroux asks, where can young people now go to find 'semiautonomous cultural spheres' (Giroux 2000: 11) – places where they can freely meet with their friends and others, and explore identity?

There is a growing body of research evidence that suggests that living in Britain has become an increasingly unhappy experience for many young people:

- Unicef's assessment of the wellbeing of children and young people in 21 'advanced' nations – covering material well-being, health and safety, educational well-being, family and peer relationships, behaviours and risk, and subjective well-being ('a significant step towards a multi-dimensional overview of the state of childhood' – p. 3) – placed Britain bottom behind the US (Unicef 2007).
- Collishaw et al's assessment of emotional problems amongst 15 to 16 year olds in the UK over a 25-year period – based on an analysis of survey data collected in 1974, 1986 and 1999 – showed how emotional health had declined since 1986. Children in their teens in the 1990s were more likely to experience problems with depression and anxiety (Collishaw et al. 2004).
- The Primary Review's interim report on primary education in Britain identified that children 'are under intense and perhaps excessive pressure from the policy-driven demands of their schools and the commercially-driven values of the wider society' (The

Primary Review 2007: 1). The report argued that educational well-being was being compromised by a narrow and rigid curriculum and national tests. It also detected that 'family life and community are breaking down' in Britain and that for children 'life...is increasingly insecure and dangerous' (The Primary Review 2007: 1).

- Research commissioned by the Nuffield Foundation found a 70 per cent rise in the rate of emotional problems (such as depression and anxiety) experienced by adolescents in Britain since 1974 (Bunting 2004).

- Research commissioned by the Prince's Trust, *Reaching the Hardest to Reach*, found that over one million young people in Britain were outside education, employment or training, and were facing profound social difficulties: 'While disadvantaged 14- to 17-year-olds were optimistic about their chances of getting good, well-paid jobs, these ambitions quickly dissipate as they face the reality of either low-paid, low-skilled jobs or a lack of training opportunities' (cited in Doward 2004: 13).

Teenage mothers in Britain have particularly been subjected to harsh social policy reforms. There has been a profound deterioration in societal attitudes to teenage mothers since the 1980s – they have been portrayed as welfare scroungers and 'promiscuous', and evidence of a decline in moral values (Murray 1990). As Sally Copley, director of policy, research and campaigns at the YWCA England and Wales argues:

> Our government, politicians and media sanction discrimination and disadvantage through perpetuating the belief that teenage mothers are at best ignorant and at worst irresponsible and incapable of being good parents....Teenage mothers, regardless of their background, should be treated as people, not social problems. Root causes – such as social exclusion, poor sex education and lack of educational and vocational opportunities – need to be confronted, not the young mothers themselves. (Cited in Kelly 2004: 2)

Young people have also been particularly affected by the lack of investment in adequate social care. The report *Young Carers*, published in 2005 by The Education Network, revealed that there were at least 175,000 school-age carers in Britain – some as young as five – forced into adopting adult roles looking after other family members (Smithers 2005). Ridge's account of the concerns of children experiencing poverty in Britain offers important insights based on interviews with children and young people living in families in receipt of Income Support. Her assessment stresses the need for politicians and policy makers to look beyond media-induced moral panics that stereotype poor children as victim or villain, and to develop a more insightful understanding of the everyday challenges faced by children who are poor. In particular, she draws attention to how many poor children develop effective strategies for surviving difficult circumstances – for instance, gaining paid employment to support themselves and, in some cases, to support their mothers. This shows that children are not always the passive victims of poverty, but active agents engaged with their circumstances as best they can – including protecting their own families (albeit in a profoundly restrictive structural context). Perhaps the most important lesson from Ridge's study is how modest poor children's expectations are – enough space to live in; better health for a parent or sibling; to spend more time with friends; to participate in social activities in and outside of school; to feel safe and secure (Ridge 2003) – expectations that are well within the capabilities of the British government to meet. Yet despite this, children and young people are continually harmed in Britain due to the refusal of governments to meet these modest expectations.

According to the End Child Poverty coalition, 450,000 of 1.5 million children – almost one in three – were living in poverty in the north-west of England alone by the beginning of the twenty-first century. This compares with the 3.6 million children – 28 per cent – living in poverty in the UK overall. The proportion of children living in poverty in the UK rose from one in ten in 1979 to one in three in 1998 – one of the worst rates of child poverty in the industrialised world (Carter 2005a). As Gordon argues, 'Poverty is currently the world's largest source of social harm; it causes more death, disease, suffering and misery than any other social phenomenon' (Gordon 2004: 251). Although the government set, in 1999, a (modest) target of *halving* child poverty by 2010, in 2008 its own Department for Work and Pensions admitted that this is unlikely to be met (Community Care email news on-line, received 4 March 2008 at 15:17). The social and economic marginalisation of so many poor children and young people reflects what Al Aynsley-Green, the first children's commissioner for England, described as society's 'deep ambivalence' towards children and childhood, and its lack of a child-friendly culture (Ward 2005a: 7).

Exacerbating the class divide
through education

Britain has had a stratified education system throughout modernity. Indeed, it was deliberately patterned in a way that would preserve class differences (Ball 2008). In simple terms, for much of the post-war period this system comprised: public schools and Oxbridge for the elite (leading to the top jobs in government or business); grammar schools and 'red brick' universities for the middle classes (leading to professional or management jobs); and secondary modern schools for the working classes (leading to manual employment). As Byrne argues, despite this stratification, there was the possibility of social mobility for working-class people through education in the post-war era – particularly through the availability of generous grants which made tertiary education more accessible for working-class children (Byrne 2006). However, education policy reforms since the 1980s – reforms which were arguably kick-started by Labour Prime Minister James Callaghan's Ruskin speech in October 1976 – have increasingly closed off such possibilities. Whilst government policy has prioritised greater competition alongside parental choice and voice, in reality the effect has been greater rivalry between education providers and the encouragement of selection – leading to a widening of the class divide (Tomlinson 2001). As Ball explains:

> In a system where many schools now control their own admissions procedures, where there are various, if marginal, forms of selection, and where many 'good schools' have the effect of driving up house prices in their locality, choice making and getting your choice of school are different. There is also a considerable body of evidence that choice systems in themselves promote inequality in as much as 'choice policies' create social spaces within which class strategies and 'opportunistic behaviours' can flourish and within which the middle classes can use their social and cultural skills and capitals advantages to good effect. (Ball 2008: 132–133)

The closing off of possibilities for social mobility is evidenced in a recent study commissioned by the Sutton Trust, an educational charity. This reveals how children born in the 1970s to financially poor families were less likely to escape their parents' class position than those born in the 1950s – largely because education reforms since the late-1980s have disproportionately benefited children from more affluent households. The report argues that: 'The strength of the relationship between educational attainment and family income, especially for access to higher education, is at the heart of Britain's low-mobility culture' (cited in Stewart 2005: 7). One of the authors of the report, Paul Gregg, blamed this widening disparity on New Labour's decision to abolish student maintenance grants in favour of loans (Stewart 2005). A recent report by the Higher Education Funding Council for England (HEFCE) adds weight to the evidence of a widening class divide in the English education system. The report showed that teenagers from well-off backgrounds were six times more likely to go to university than those from deprived areas (Cassidy 2005). According to a report commissioned by the Joseph Rowntree Foundation, 62 per cent of white British boys on free school meals – a measure of deprivation – are in the bottom 10 per cent of performers (Garner 2007: 26). And despite the government pledging £430million on widening participation in higher education for 2006–2007, recent statistics from the Universities and Colleges Admissions Service (Ucas) show that only around 25 per cent of those accepted by universities come from the bottom *four* socio-economic backgrounds (Shepherd 2007) – a factor affected by New Labour's decision to introduce fees and then top-up-fees (Cassidy 2006). A research report produced by Staffordshire University for the Sutton Trust argued that 'students from poor backgrounds are being put off university because they are afraid of getting into debt' (cited in Curtis 2008a: 1). For some commentators, such as Anthony Seldon (an independent-school head), Britain has reached an educational apartheid (Curtis 2008b). As Ball argues, despite the rhetoric,[1] social justice has become peripheral to the purpose of education (Ball 2008).

In addition to its role in widening the class divide, the education system has also been severely and detrimentally affected by the enforcement of the new managerialism and top-down performance management – again, measures arguably set in motion by Callaghan's Ruskin speech. There has been a shift in the loci of power in education – away from the micro level (the classroom, school and local education authority) towards the centre – asserted through the national curriculum, national testing at four Key Stages (7, 11, 14 and 16), league tables and performance indicators, the deprofessionalisation of teachers and the 'reculturing' of school organising towards the business model

---

[1] New Labour's 'commitment' to promote social opportunity through education was highlighted during the 1997 election campaign when Tony Blair was keen to stress: 'To those who say where is Labour's passion for social justice, I say education *is* social justice' (Blair 1997, cited in Beckmann and Cooper 2004: 7).

(Ball 2008). These developments have been responsible for both forging the 'educated subject' (defined *apriori* in benchmark statements – a product of the teaching process) and the 'educating subjects' (the effective proletarianisation of teachers). As Alexiadou argues:

> Teachers are seen as production workers, 'raw material', or part of the 'machinery' of the institution, and their contribution is evaluated along these terms. The expectations on teachers does not exceed that of a mechanical production of a routine type of work, it is more a question of 'reliance'. There is a clear separation between designing a strategy and the execution of the mechanistic aspects of its delivery. This 'industrial' metaphor also reflects a perception of students that is built around production. Students are the 'products' of teacher's work, or the customers that the products have to be sold to. (Alexiadou 2001: 427)

As 'the educated subject now is being constructed by means of articulating the results of an educational regime first, and then evaluating the procedures accordingly' (Fendler, cited in Popkewitz and Brennan 1998: 57), the possibilities of 'becoming' of the human being (the 'educated subject') are increasingly limited and thus, by extension, so too is the kind of society we are creating and living in.

The permeation of the business ethos throughout the education system and the ideological drive towards performance improvement is placing enormous pressures on teachers and pupils. In the case of the former, teacher disaffection, stress-related illness and early retirements have led to a recruitment crisis (Beckmann and Cooper 2004). In respect of the latter, many young people are clearly being harmed by the education system. A report by Mike Tomlinson released in February 2004 argued that millions of school pupils across England and Wales are being put under intolerable pressure because of the constant testing and examinations.

> Between the ages of 15 and 18 pupils can take up to 20 different exams, 12 GCSEs, 5 A/S levels, an intermediary exam launched in 2000, and finally four or more A levels…. One A-level student [from Dulwich College] likened the pressure to being that of a football manager, such was the relentless strain and expectation. (Ahmed and Townsend 2004: 2)

Many parents and pupils not only complain about excessive testing; they also feel that the purpose of education is being narrowly focused more and more on 'tick box' learning to pass assessments (Ahmed and Townsend 2004) at the expense of broader pedagogical aims (such as empathy, empowerment and the enhancement of human wellbeing).

Exacerbating 'social exclusion' through housing policy choices

As we saw in Chapter 1, throughout modernity the affluent middle-classes have always sought to use their assets for residential gain and to segregate themselves from the lower orders. Residential experience impacts more broadly on our social experience – particularly in relation to health, state education, social wellbeing and the environment. Accessing residential advantage has always been a major problem for the most vulnerable in Britain yet the available housing policy choices since the 1980s have aggravated this problem and exacerbated the spatial divide between communities.

Housing policies in the post-war period were far from universalistic and generally prioritised the needs of the most advantaged. The less well off largely remained in a deteriorating private-rented sector – unless they were 'fortunate enough' to be selected for slum clearance between the late 1950s and 1970s (although the most likely alternative housing offered would probably have been either a house on a peripheral housing estate or a high rise flat). Having said this, council housing did (alongside full employment policies) have an important integrative role for working-class communities – albeit communities of largely employed, white, heterosexual nuclear families. Since the 1970s, the character and social base of council housing has changed dramatically – largely as a result of the right-to-buy (alluded to in Chapter 1). The 1974–1979 Labour government allowed some council house sales under a general ministerial consent, but the Thatcher government elected in 1979 'took this one step further with a more active policy of privatisation through demunicipalisation' (Murie 2007: 51). Malpass describes housing policy since 1974 in terms of 'a process of chronic residualization' (Malpass 2005: 163) that has seen council housing (now conceptualised as 'social housing') turned into a tenure increasingly occupied by the least well off. The more affluent sections of the working class have abandoned this tenure and become home owners – a significant number with the help of the right-to-buy. Between 1980 and 1993 alone, the right-to-buy:

> was to remove from council housing some 800,000 households headed by someone in full-time employment at the time of purchase,

and to this total must be added a not insignificant number of other tenants moving into the owner occupied sector by buying on the open market. The majority of these purchasers have been shown to be people sufficiently advanced in their working lives to be able to qualify for large right to buy discounts and/or to be able to afford the costs of mortgage repayments; in the three years to 2001/02 the average weekly income of people moving out of social renting was twice that of tenants in the sector as a whole. (Malpass 2005: 173)

Not only did the economic status of the council-tenant population change, so did the character of the dwelling stock – the houses on the more attractive estates (which had originally been allocated for renting to the 'more deserving', 'hard-working' family) were the ones being bought, leaving behind the least desirable properties (including a disproportionate number of flats). 'The stripping out of much of the best quality and most desirable social rented housing has left remaining and prospective tenants with less choice and fewer options to acquire equivalent accommodation' (Malpass 2005: 174). Amongst those disproportionately disadvantaged by this development are many more elderly and young single people, single parents and their dependent children, people from minority ethnic communities, and people without income from employment due to having caring responsibilities or because they are sick or disabled. For these sections of the 'community', 'social exclusion' has been exacerbated (Malpass 2005).

By the time New Labour was elected in 1997 over two million council properties had been privatised under the right-to-buy or via stock transfer to housing associations (introduced in the late 1980s). The remaining council stock had largely been transformed into 'a welfare sector catering for low-income and benefit-dependent people' (Murie 2007: 52). Labour continued to emphasise home ownership as a central component of its housing policy agenda – although attention was given to the problem of 'social exclusion' (as discussed in the previous chapter). Labour has also pursued the previous governments' privatisation agenda – again through the right-to-buy and stock transfer to housing associations. Local authorities are no longer expected to provide rented housing and those authorities still managing council houses in 2007 have one of three options open to them if they wish to improve their properties: stock transfer (privatisation via housing associations); a Private Finance Initiative (privatisation via a housing consortium 'partnership'); or (in the case of the 'best' management performers) an arm's-length management organisation (or ALMO – reducing local democratic control). Council tenants are able to vote on whatever option is presented to them. To help them 'make up their minds', tenants are generally 'deluged with glossy propaganda – brochures, videos and DVDs' (Mitchell 2005: 23) all putting forward the case *for* transfer. Large sums are also spent on 'independent' consultants, other fees, debt write-off, funding cover for negative equity and grant aid. Where tenants vote against transfer they can expect no additional investment for improvements. In 1987, local authorities owned 90 per cent of all social housing in Britain. Not surprisingly, by 2003 this figure had fallen to less than 66 per cent 'and it is generally expected that the trend will continue' (Malpass 2005: 189).

The privatisation of council housing is problematic. As we saw in Chapter 1, the emergence of council housing in Britain was no coincidence – representing as it did the failure of both the private sector and philanthropic movement to meet the housing needs of the population. Importantly too, council housing represents a valuable public asset managed locally and (to a significant extent) democratically. In contrast, housing associations (now known as Registered Social Landlords) have increasingly become quasi-private sector bodies (rather than quasi-public – see Back and Hamnett 1985) run in a more business-like way and able 'to make decisions that are informed by what is right for the business without having to worry about political pressure from elected members' (Malpass 2005: 194). Major implications of this for tenants has been higher rents (20 per cent on average), and the loss of security of tenure and democratic accountability. As Alan Walter, a Camden council tenant and chair of Defend Council Housing (DCH), argues 'Stock transfer means tenants lose our secure tenancy and pay higher rents. The registered social landlords which take over are, increasingly, multi-million pound national companies run like private businesses' (Walter 2004: 20).

The nature of the housing association movement has changed dramatically since the 1980s. In 1977–1978, when I first worked for a housing association in Portsmouth, the Housing Corporation (the body responsible for the funding and monitoring of housing associations) allocated development funding to 408 associations (Housing Corporation Annual Report 1977–1978, cited in Malpass 2000: 167). Historically, the movement comprised a diversity of organisations of varying scales aimed at meeting a range of needs. Many associations aimed to meet general housing needs whilst others focused on the specific needs of particular groups (including women, older people, young people with support needs, people with disabilities, lesbian, gay, bisexual and transsexual people, and minority ethnic groups). As Malpass argues, the dimensions of diversity within the movement were 'numerous' (Malpass 2000: 9) and associations provided much valuable support by invariably housing groups local authority provision would not prioritise. However, both the role and diversity of the housing association movement has irrevocably changed. In February 2008, the Housing Corporation announced development funding for just 105 'affordable housing developers' (including 13 private developers) – just 25 per cent of the number of associations funded 30 years earlier – with just ten large associations receiving around 20 per cent of the total allocation of £3.3billion (Rogers 2008: 1). A few large associations now monopolise social housing in Britain. Keith Exford, chief executive of Affinity Sutton housing association, predicts the emergence of 'an "elite group" of a dozen associations dominating the development of afford-able homes' (Cooper 2007: 1) – something he supports. 'If we want to play on the biggest stage we have got to be a big organisation' (Exford, cited in Cooper 2007: 1). At the same time, the salaries of housing association chief executives soared in 2007 by an average of 10 per cent (compared with 3 to 4 per cent rises for front-line staff) – with top earners on a quarter of a million pounds (Hilditch 2007).

Local democracy and accountability in the housing system have been marginalised in favour of a managerialist, business agenda – effectively, a victory for neo-liberalism in 'an ideological battle waged by a govern-ment that has a knee-jerk distrust of the public, and puts its faith in the private sector instead' (Mitchell 2005: 23). On one side of this ideological battleground is David Orr, chief executive of the National Housing Federation (the representative body for housing associations), who criti-cises the DCH campaigns against stock transfer for being 'driven by political ideology' (cited in Murray 2007: 18). This criticism fails to acknowledge that the privatisation of council housing (along with other sectors of the British welfare state) was of itself (and continues to be) driven by ideology and prefers to assume instead that the domination of 'social housing' provision by the new-breed of large-scale association represents a 'natural' social order – a 'commonsense' way of welfare organising in a post-industrial society. This of course ignores the his-torical field of council housing (described in Chapter 1) and how its evolution represented a compromise balancing the needs of both the working classes and the capitalist state – a compromise necessitated, as mentioned above, by the failings of both *laissez faire* political economy and the philanthropic housing movement to meet universal housing need. Moreover, the privatisation of (and underinvestment in) council housing since the 1980s, together with the downgrading of tenants' rights and the privileging of an undemocratic social housing sector (the 'big' housing associations), has contributed to rising homelessness and social exclusion in Britain (Burden et al. 2000).

There is of course a fourth option for the future of social housing in Britain, but one the government will not permit. This would allow local authorities to develop, rehabilitate and retain their own housing provision – an option that would be less costly to the public purse:

> If councils retained all their housing revenue without the government siphoning money out (they've taken £13bn over nine years to pay tenants' housing benefit and are still taking around £700 per house for historic debt), retained their own right-to-buy proceeds and added in some borrowing, they could refurbish the stock themselves and even begin to build again. All this would be less expensive if it was done by councils. (Mitchell 2005: 23)

The fact that local authorities can provide, manage and maintain housing stock cheaper than housing associations, largely because of the lower interest rates charged to government bodies, but are not allowed to, not only 'demonstrates contempt for local democracy' (Mitchell 2005: 23) but also furthers the interests of capital accumulation (in terms of returns for finance investors, consultants, developers and chief executives) over those of social housing residents and those in housing need.

At the same time, the increasing reliance in British housing policy on owner occupation comes at a time of significant financial risk for many given the uncertainty of 'an officially sanctioned flexible, insecure labour market' (Malpass 2005: 215). In this scenario, those in well-paid secure jobs not only gain access to better quality homes in pleasant environments but gain further from increased spending power (through equity withdrawal) and access to better schools, health and other public services. For other owner occupiers, home ownership and access to other public services is increasingly associated with risk and uncertainty. Rising interest rates following the 2007 global liquidity crisis caused by excessive mortgage defaults in the US – coming on top of years of 'easy credit' for house purchase in Britain, such as loans representing 130 per cent of the property's value offered by Northern Rock (Inman and Balkrishnan 2007: 31) – has intensified the risk for many. In 2008, access to homeownership for first-time buyers in employment has become more difficult 'to grasp than ever' (Balakrishnan

2008: 29). For non earners and those with the lowest incomes in the most insecure jobs, the situation is even more hazardous with reliance on residualised social housing and other public services. And then there is the increasing risk of homelessness, with the number of 'official' homeless households living in temporary accommodation at the end of September 2005 standing at 101,020 – more than double the figure when New Labour were elected in 1997. Moreover, more than 782,000 occupied homes are officially unfit for human habitation and 500,000 households (including 900,000 children) are living in overcrowded conditions (Shelter 2005: 1). As Malpass concludes:

> the intractability of the problems associated with a deeply residualized public sector and an unstable and highly unequal private market should give policy makers reasons to ponder. The prospects for the future appear to imply a self-reinforcing spiral in which the housing market amplifies the widening inequalities rooted in the labour market…. As a model for a reformed welfare state it leaves a lot to be desired. (Malpass 2005: 216–217)

It is a system that continues to reflect profound social divisions rooted in our communities whilst providing or denying (depending on your residential situation) further sources of opportunity for the advancement of social wellbeing.

Differential experiences of health and social care

Health protection for social wellbeing has become increasingly precarious for many in contemporary times. The post-war ideal of a universal and fully comprehensive health service in Britain, free at the point of delivery, has been superseded by a new political consensus on health care built on the neo-liberal ideological preference for competition between service providers, greater management freedoms and enhanced opportunities for private sector involvement. Health services are increasingly being exposed to the business model where 'Excellence in financial management is the prerequisite for high quality sustainable services' (Patricia Hewitt, Secretary of State for Health, cited in Carvel 2006: 1). The extension of the business ethos to health care organising has intensified rationing in the National Health Service (NHS) and social harm for many – for example, the Stroke Association estimate that around 5,000 people in England and Wales are dying prematurely each year after a stroke because of a lack of appropriate care (Meikle 2005). Additionally, drugs helpful for patients in the earliest stages of Alzheimer's disease and other forms of dementia are no longer to be provided by the NHS because they are not considered 'cost effective enough' by the National Institute for Health and Clinical Excellence (Nice). Dr Cornelius Katona, honorary consultant in old-age psychiatry and dean of the Kent Institute of Medicine and Health Sciences, highlights the social harms this judgement will have on older people and their carers:

It is clear that the quality of life gained in later years is being valued less highly than those years in middle age. The recommendation from Nice was driven by a wish to cut costs, because they admitted the drugs were clinically effective…. This will be devastating for the patients and their carers. (Cited in Revill 2005: 9)

The quality of life for some in early years is similarly devalued by an NHS system which prioritises what is effectively *cost-cutting* rather than cost effectiveness. In March 2005, it was announced that Great Ormond Street children's hospital in London had to close up to one-fifth of its beds due to severe financial constraints and 'cancel operations and turn away dozens of critically ill children' (Revill and Hinsliff 2005: 1).

Alongside these financial constraints, and in the wake of the Wanless Report and the government's subsequent response to it entitled *Choosing health* (both 2004 – see Klein 2005), there has also been greater emphasis on individuals taking more responsibility for their own health – that is, the 'self care agenda':

The self care agenda focuses on the contribution of patients (and their carers) to their own health and well-being. Essentially this means individuals taking responsibility for staying fit and maintaining good physical and mental health; meeting social, emotional, and psychological needs; preventing illness or accidents; caring for minor ailments and long-term conditions; and maintaining health and well-being after an acute illness or discharge from hospital. (Peckham 2007: 37)

Supporting individuals to opt for healthier lifestyles, as envisaged in *Choosing health*, seems eminently sensible. However, it fails to acknowledge inequality as a significant factor in determining health experience – evident in the differential rate of premature mortality and morbidity by social class (Townsend et al. 1992). Health inequalities by social class worsened under New Labour's first decade in government (Andalo 2008: 7).

Concerns have also been raised about the effect of organisational changes on accountability in the NHS. An emerging consensus appears to have been forged around the future of health provision – with the state increasingly withdrawing from the direct provision of care in favour of greater competition between a diverse range of service providers and greater management freedom to work autonomously and to raise private finance. Dexter Whitfield, of the Centre for Public Services, calls on government to reverse its pro-market health policies, which he sees as a threat to job security, universalism, equity and democratic accountability (Ruane 2005).

Chris Jones et al. also see pro-market policies as having profoundly harmful effects on social care work:

> [O]ur work is shaped by managerialism, by the fragmentation of services, by financial restrictions and lack of resources, by increased bureaucracy and workloads, by the domination of care-management approaches, with their associated performance indicators, and by the increased use of the private sector. ... The main concern of too many social work managers today is the control of budgets rather than the welfare of service users, while worker-client relationships are increasingly characterised by control and supervision rather than care. (Jones et al. 2006: 3)

Rather than being empowered to make judgements and take decisions about their client's wellbeing, care workers are increasingly inhibited by managerialism: 'Care workers often feel unable to provide decent care to people because of a fear of rules, ... being sacked for not following policy, and the failure of managers to back risk taking' (Fanshawe 2007: 2). Part of the problem is caused by the way funding for social care is split between local government and the NHS.

> One care worker I spoke to told me: 'A disabled woman fell out of her wheelchair, but the support staff were not funded or insured to assist her back into it. ... [In another case] a man with progressive MS was living independently, so the staff were not funded to provide personal care. When he soiled himself, they were, strictly speaking, not supposed to help him'. (Fanshawe 2007: 2)

The anti-social activities of private corporations and the rise of consumer society

Influential corporate interests increasingly intrude into all aspects of our lives both through their interference in social policy developments, and through fostering and sustaining the consumer society. The avenues for these intrusions have been paved by global institutions acting in the interests of powerful (often US) corporations: for instance, directives from the World Trade Organisation (WTO) such as the General Agreement on Trade in Services (GATS) place strict constraints on national governments in relation to their welfare systems; the imposition of these restrictions, whilst justified in the name of social justice, simply serve the interests of powerful financial markets by opening up opportunities for private sector involvement in the delivery of public services (as we saw above in our discussion of welfare reforms). 'Influential Third Way thinkers... support the arguments... that social justice is best served by going with the logic of global markets, and adopting national and international policies which *promote* the interests and strategies of multinational companies' (Jordan 2006: 90 – emphasis in original).

In Britain, this approach has facilitated greater opportunity for private sector involvement in the delivery of health, education and social care systems – specifically in respect of the way new hospitals, schools and care homes have been funded and managed. Through the GATS, powerful western business and financial interests collude with governments to generate 'an opportunity to link domestic social policy with the strategies of global corporate businesses, gaining advantage in new world markets' (Jordan 2006: 91–92). Liberalisation programmes pursued in health care and education through the GATS has encouraged these sectors to function more like markets – opening up possibilities for a range of consultants, professional advisers and corporate investors to make highly lucrative profits (Byrne 2006).

Those who can afford it are encouraged to take out private insurance schemes to cover their own and their family's health risks. Those who cannot afford it are left to rely on an increasingly residualised and rationed state health-care sector (as we saw above). Similarly, in education, where the more resourceful use their autonomy and freedom to escape the less successful state schools for their children, placing them instead in those schools which 'perform' – again, leaving the children of disadvantaged communities reliant on the 'worst' schools. The social democratic vision of health and education – that is, universal and comprehensive provision that supports full social participation for all citizens – has been destroyed and with this life chances have been further polarised. Again, these changes are the source of profound social harms for the least advantaged. As Jordan argues:

> [T]here are questions about whether autonomy and choice for the sake of private advantage can be the basis of a public culture, and especially of democratic citizenship. … The business agenda … discounts membership and belonging and promotes the 'rational egoism' of micro-economic models. This cannot address issues such as 'community cohesion' which have troubled the UK government … ; nor can it promote 'civil renewal' and democratic participation … . (Jordan 2006: 118)

Corporate-state induced individualism has led to the corrosion of cooperation and commitment to others. As Durkheim warned, 'individualism could turn sour unless it was adequately balanced by collective solidarities' (Jordan 2006: 167).

Parallel to the decline in social solidarity in Britain is the rise in individualistic self-interest and the ascendancy of the consumer society (and with it, rising levels of debt). Herbert Marcuse, back in the 1950s, perceived the damaging effects of consumer society on freedom and possibilities for controlling one's own destiny – for the consumer society shapes 'aspirations, hopes, fears, and values, and even manipulates vital needs' (Kellner 1991: xxvii).

> For Marcuse, commodities and consumption play a far greater role in contemporary capitalist society than that envisaged by Marx and most orthodox Marxists. Marcuse was one of the first critical theorists to analyze the consumer society through analyzing how consumerism, advertising, mass culture, and ideology integrate individuals into and stabilize the capitalist system. In describing how needs are produced which integrate individuals into a whole universe of thought, behavior, and satisfaction, he distinguishes between true and false needs … . (Kellner 1991: xxx)

Marcuse (1991) believed that the production of 'false needs' had an insidious hold over people's consciousness and idea of status, and served to inhibit critical thought and resistance. His insight is shared by Smart who argues: 'Ours is a consumer society in so far as identity and status are acquired, and social inclusion or integration is achieved, through participation in consumer activity' (Smart 2003: 57). In consumer societies, identity is increasingly constructed by what we consume rather than other capabilities and senses (such as critical reasoning or the desire for freedom from domination). Through modern advertising, salesmanship and the increasing availability of credit, people are being seduced further and further into the world of consumption.

> In respect of consumption, acceleration in the pace or speed with which things are consumed through the market system has been achieved by the deployment of advertising, marketing and branding techniques and strategies. The objective of these is both to promote different, and forever changing, fashions and styles in relation to virtually all goods and services and, no less significantly, to reproduce consumers ever eager to believe that their fantasies can be fulfilled. (Smart 2003: 158)

The reproduction of consumers in this way means that needs or desires are no longer authentic – we become the creation of the consumption industry or, as Marcuse (1991) would argue, 'one-dimensional man' (with harmful consequences):

> One-dimensional man does not know its true needs because its needs are not its own – they are administered, superimposed, and heter-onomous; it is not able to resist domination, nor to act autonomously, for it identifies with public behavior and imitates and submits to the powers that be. Lacking the power of authentic self-activity, one-dimensional man submits to increasingly total domination. (Kellner 1991: xxviii)

Social status is increasingly signified by our capacity to consume the latest technological gadget and the right designer labels. In his book *The Challenge of Affluence* (2006) Avner Offer argues that over the past 25 years this development has convinced people that 'there is no alterna-tive to dual-income workaholic consumerism' (James 2006: 28). Consumption – in the form of an increasing range of goods (and better upgrades) considered culturally indispensable; a presentable house in a secure neighbourhood with access to 'good' schools; and a car for every active adult – becomes a necessity and, therefore, dual-income earning becomes unavoidable. 'As status consumption grew, the need to work increased…driving up the number of hours needed to work to succeed' (James 2006: 28). This clearly has implications for other ways of being – for example, spending time with family, friends and children; engaging in meaningful leisure time or political and community activities; caring for others. It also contributes to marital stress, family collapse and an increase in anxiety and mental illness. Oliver James identifies an 'affluenza virus' in British society – a result of 'placing a high value on money, possessions, appearances (social and physical) and fame' (James 2007: 30). He suggests that studies prove that 'people who strongly subscribe to virus values are at significantly greater risk of depression, anxiety, substance abuse and personality disorder' (James 2007: 30). Various research projects have shown that while the majority of people in western societies have grown more affluent over the past 20 years or so, they have not become any happier (Arnot 2006: 11). Such evidence has led some economists to call on governments to concentrate less on economic growth and more on the social wellbeing of their citizens. As Andrew Oswald argues:

> If you're poor, and can't feed your children, theories about the economics of happiness don't matter. But in America and western Europe, a lot of us don't need a TV wider than the one we have, or a third car. ... We're stuck with thinking that applied in 1945, when we needed economic growth to supply us with basic things. (Oswald, cited in Arnot 2006: 11)

This change in the character of the economic system is recognised in Benjamin R. Barber's critique of rampant consumerism in contemporary society. Barber sees a transformation in the nature of capitalism from a system built by 'Protestantism's productive winners' (Barber 2007: 53) committed to hard work in pursuit of meeting authentic needs to 'today's newfound land of consumerist losers driven as much by an ethos of infantilism' (Barber 2007: 53) where the focus is on stimulating consumer wants for things people do not need.

A major social harm resulting from the drive to consume is debt. While we all possess human agency and the ability to resist being infantilised into consuming – it is arguable that escalation into debt cannot be entirely blamed on the individual. As Smart argues, 'While responsibility lies in part with the unrestrained consumption of those consumers who get into unmanageable levels of debt, the aggressive marketing of credit card companies and easy availability of credit undoubtedly contribute significantly to rising levels of indebtedness' (Smart 2003: 70). *New Statesman* arts editor Rosie Millard confessed herself to be part of the growing breed of heavily indebted professionals – 'a trend spreading slowly and surely among British consumers' (Ward 2005b: 5).

Britain's debt mountain totals £1 trillion, including about £55bn on credit cards. Consumer advice and debt counselling bodies make clear that, while there are companies which are attempting to lend cash at extortionate rates to those on the very lowest incomes, the real targets of the banks and credit card firms are the middle classes.... Leaflets offering loans for Caribbean holidays or home improvements on a Palladian scale are taking advantage of a now-ingrained consumer psychology to 'have it now, pay tomorrow'. (Ward 2005b: 5)

A study by the Financial Services Authority (FSA) and Bristol University published in March 2006 found what it called 'a lost generation' of 18- to 40-year-olds 'unable to cope with debts and soaring house prices' (Collinson 2006: 1). The FSA chief executive, John Tiner, argued:

There is an urgent and serious need to help the young. They are the first generation to be leaving college with massive debts, and while housing has always been a challenge, it's become extremely difficult for young people in parts of the country. Yet at the same time the young have become serious consumers. It was difficult for an 18-year-old to get a credit card 20 years ago but today it is relatively easy. (Cited in Collinson 2006: 1)

The continuous endorsement for individualised consumption sits uneasily alongside notions of collective values: how can we be concerned with the needs of 'others' when we are so absorbed with our own financial risk taking? Martin Kettle describes this development as 'disintegration – we are separating into our component parts, losing the coherence and integrity of many of our common experiences. ... [T]he inhabitants and communities of this country have gone their separate ways' (Kettle 2005: 22) – with some heading to Selfridge's for lunch to consume a sandwich for £85! (Kennedy 2006).

Increasingly, marketing and advertising agencies are targeting the very young, sometimes deploying children's cartoon characters to sell their products. The encouragement for children to consume not only exploits a vulnerable group but is particularly insensitive to the needs of low-income parents. Worse, part of this marketing impetus involves children being sexualised earlier and earlier in the drive to push consumption. Megan Bruns of Kidscape, the charity concerned with keeping children safe, identifies:

[A] 'distressing trend' for girls as young as seven or eight to be encouraged to enact identities for which they simply aren't prepared: mainstream retailers offering padded bras and thongs to prepubescents until campaigners made them think again; consumer magazines bought by the barely adolescent dispensing tips on tarting up and chasing boys. (Cited in Hill 2003: 2)

Additionally,

Awareness of global emblems is already strongly implanted in the very young. ... [T]he International Journal of Advertising and Marketing to Children reported that 31% of three-year-olds remember having seen the Coca-Cola logo, 69% McDonald's and 66% that for Kinder confectionary. Meanwhile, according to teachers surveyed for a Basic Skills Agency report, about half of four- and five-year-olds entering school for the first time cannot recognise their own names – or speak in a way understandable to others or count up to five. Could these things be connected? Could it be that their induction into consumer society is making our children fat, dull, prematurely obsessed with shopping and sex and that the situation is getting worse? (Hill 2003: 3)

There is also a growing concern about the loss of childhood in Britain's consumer society:

Death of Childhood theories gained currency in the 80s as liberated market forces addressed new categories of childhood and moral conservatives worried that this was one of many factors forcing kids to grow up too soon. For example, Eileen Wojciechowska of Family and Youth Concern is enraged by the 'suggestive dancing' of little girls in adverts. (Hill 2003: 3)

In October 2006 it was reported that Tesco had been forced to remove a pole-dancing kit from the toys and games section of its website after it was accused of 'destroying children's innocence':

The Tesco Direct site advertises the kit with the words, 'Unleash the sex kitten inside... simply extend the Peekaboo pole inside the tube, slip on the sexy tunes and away you go!... Soon you'll be flaunting it to the world and earning a fortune in Peekaboo Dance Dollars'. The £49.97 kit comprises a chrome pole extendible to 8ft 6ins, a 'sexy dance garter' and a DVD demonstrating suggestive dance moves. (Fernandez 2006: 1)

Dr Adrian Rogers of the family campaigning group Family Focus argued that the kit would:

> destroy children's lives. ... This will be sold to four, five and six-year olds. This is a most dangerous toy that will contribute towards destroying children's innocence. ... Children are being encouraged to dance round a pole which is interpreted in the adult world as a phallic symbol. It ought to be stopped, it really requires the intervention of members of Parliament. This should only be available to the most depraved people who want to corrupt their children. (Cited in Fernandez 2006: 1)

The Tesco case followed those of Asda – 'forced to remove from sale pink and black lace lingerie, including a push-up bra to girls as young as nine' – and Next – who 'had to remove t-shirts on sale for girls as young as six with the slogan "so many boys, so little time"' (Fernandez 2006: 2).

Beyond corrupting childhood, there is evidence to show how giant supermarket chains are threatening community wellbeing in other ways – for example, threatening other independent markets (pharmacies, news agencies, legal and financial services, smaller traders and so forth); engaging in land banking and collusion with local planning systems; and exerting excessive control over their supply chain. Overall, giant supermarket chains effectively operate as local monopolies and, thereby, have a profound bearing on the social fabric of local communities (Simms 2007). Despite evidence marshalled by the New Economics Foundation 'that the rise of the supermarkets has been accompanied by the collapse of thousands of independent shops' (Conn 2007: 1) these same private corporations have been given a key role in New Labour's urban regeneration strategy via the 'Underserved Markets' project. Such a development reflects what Hywel Williams sees as the 'power of capital over New Labour ... Britain's most consistently business-friendly party' (Williams 2006: 23).

It has also become increasingly accepted that unfettered consumerism is contributing towards profound environmental damage that can no longer be ignored. As Caroline Lucas has argued: 'We need to change the aims of our economic system so it places less emphasis on consumption and over-employment, and more on creating meaningful work' (Lucas 2005: 16). Whilst New Labour was pursuing its dubious 'war on terror', the government has paid little more than lip service to what the scientific community is now clear on – that climate change is now one of the biggest threats to civilization. The government's scientific adviser, Sir David King, warned that climate change poses a 'greater threat than terrorism' (cited in Lucas 2005: 16). However, 'The government has refused to implement key EU legislation on emissions reduction, and is promoting a big expansion of our aviation industry – the fastest-growing source of greenhouse gas emissions' (Lucas 2005: 16). Instead, government ideology persists in prioritising economic growth over environmental safety.

We can see, therefore, that the unfettered rise of the consumer society and the prioritisation of economic growth over other societal values are having profoundly damaging consequences for community safety, cohesion and wellbeing. Countering these developments will require a change in ideology at the heart of government – a change that would effectively represent:

> a radical shift in the way we run our economy and measure progress. It's time to discard the outdated notion that more economic growth automatically equals greater wellbeing. Mounting evidence suggests that after basic needs have been met, more material growth doesn't make us happier – the UK's economic output has doubled in the past 30 years, but levels of life satisfaction remain unchanged. (Lucas 2005: 16)

International psychological research on subjective wellbeing (or self-assessed happiness) reveals that, throughout the affluent developed countries, 'individuals feel no happier than they did 40 years ago, despite substantial rises in GDP' (Jordan 2005: 429). This presents a strong challenge to the neo-liberal orthodoxy on wellbeing: 'Economists such as Richard Layard (2003, 2005) now accept many of the arguments of social theorists and researchers such as Robert E. Lane (1991, 2000) and Michael Pusey (2003), that competition and rivalry in market societies with privatized public sectors lead to "stalled well-being"' (Jordan 2005: 429).

These criticisms of neo-liberal market assumptions lend support to a different view of the role of the state:

> A fundamental shift in the primary aim of government – from maximising gross national product to maximising gross national wellbeing – would bring real quality of life improvements as well as moving the UK towards a sustainable future. Immediate rewards

would include revitalising local communities, for example, and freeing up more time to spend with friends and family. (Lucas 2005: 16)

By adopting a different role to that prescribed by the neo-liberal paradigm, governments may find a way of fostering healthier community relations – safer and more cohesive societies based on trust, solidarity and less moral indifference to the suffering of others.

The 'war-on-terror' and its domestic impact

New Labour's engagement in the 'war on terror' and invasion of Iraq holds profound implications for community cohesion and safety domestically. The communities of Iraq continue to experience the human costs of war in terms of killings and injuries, mental and emotional turmoil, poverty and hunger, poor sanitation and living environments, and a lack of adequate health and welfare provision. Children in Iraq have been hit hard by the humanitarian crisis there – more and more are born underweight, lack basic amenities or are homeless, and are suffering ill-health; many are showing learning difficulties (Steele 2007). At home, community tensions have been provoked further by the government's engagement in the war on Iraq and 'suspect terrorists'. Moreover, this war and the community tensions it has fuelled have legitimated a range of legal measures which have undermined civil and human rights in Britain.

The reason given by the government for the war was that 'Iraq posed a threat to the west by virtue of its programme on weapons of mass destruction and (latterly) by virtue of its links with international terrorism. Both of these justifications were categorically false' (Miller 2004: 3). In the September 2002 dossier – *Iraq's Weapons of Mass Destruction: The Assessment of the British Government* – the government claimed that weapons of mass destruction could be 'ready within 45 minutes of an order to use them' (cited in Miller 2004: 3) and, therefore, that a pre-emptive attack on Iraq was necessary. However, government sources at this time had evidence that 90–95 per cent of Iraq's chemical and biological agents had been destroyed whilst most of what was left would have degraded to uselessness (except for a small quantity of mustard gas). Neither did Iraq have long-range ballistic missiles. The original intelligence was, according to John Scarlett of the Joint Intelligence Committee, that battlefield mortar shells or small calibre weaponry could be deployed in 45 minutes. 'Again, both Blair and [Alastair] Campbell were in a position to know this since it was their own intelligence' (Miller 2004: 4).

The attack on Iraq shows the integration of propaganda and lying into the core of government strategy. ... Most crucially the Iraq lie shows the immense gulf between the democratic wishes of the population and the priorities of the political elite. The elite can simply ignore the will of the people of the UK and the majority of global opinion. It can control or bypass the institutions of democracy ... by means both of deception and the long-term sapping of their practical democratic power. It shows that democracy in both the US and UK is institutionally corrupt, and that there is a need for fundamental changes in the system of national and global governance for them to be objectively recognisable as democratic. (Miller 2004: 5–6)

One of the few winners from the war in Iraq are US corporations who stand to gain from oil extraction contracts – otherwise known as 'Production Sharing Agreements' (PSAs). The PSAs, 'lasting for up to 30 years, will divert up to 75 per cent of Iraqi oil revenues to Western drilling companies until their initial investment costs have been recouped' (*The Independent* Leading Article, 7 January 2007). This follows the US government denying the Iraqi state the ability to award preferential contracts to Iraqi companies for reconstruction work after the war. 'Instead, US companies were awarded contracts totalling more than $50bn' (*The Independent* Leading Article, 7 January 2007). These developments lend support to the argument that the invasion of Iraq served US geo-political and economic interests in the region. Jordan supports this view:

[T]he toppling of Saddam Hussein in Iraq was motivated at least partly by the goal of creating a model state in that region, which exemplifies the advantages of a fully open set of infrastructural services. Iraq was supposed to supply this opportunity, first by the post-war reconstruction process (contracted out almost exclusively to US-based companies), and then through the privatization of all the rest of its resources and services. (Jordan 2006: 91)

Bush maintained that he went to war in Iraq to fight threats to the ' "values of civilised nations": terror, cruelty, barbarism and extremism' (cited in Monbiot 2006: 27). Yet, in exercising this war, the US itself engaged in systematic terror, cruelty, barbarism and extremism:

The Detainee Abuse and Accountability Project (DAA), a coalition of academics and human-rights groups, has documented the abuse or killing of 460 inmates of US military prisons in Afghanistan, Iraq and at Guantánamo Bay. This, it says, is necessarily a conservative figure: many cases will remain unrecorded. The prisoners were beaten, raped, forced to abuse themselves, forced to maintain 'stress positions', and subjected to prolonged sleep deprivation and mock executions. ... Alfred McCoy, professor of history at the University of Wisconsin-Madison, argues that the photographs released from Abu Ghraib prison in Iraq reflect standard CIA torture techniques: 'stress positions, sensory deprivation, and sexual humiliation'. (Monbiot 2006: 27)

Precedence for assessing the British and US invasion of Iraq is to be found in the Nuremberg trials of Nazis at the end of the Second World War. The judges in these trials stated that: 'To initiate a war of aggression is not an international crime; it is the supreme international crime differing only from other war crimes in that it contains within itself the accumulated evil of the whole' (cited in Pilger 2004b: 29). Moreover, 'in stating this guiding principle of international law, the judges specifically rejected German arguments of the "necessity" for pre-emptive attacks against other countries' (Pilger 2004b: 29). Coming on top of the death of around 500,000 children caused by sanctions imposed on Iraq in 1990, together with British involvement in the systematic bombing of Iraq (a country Britain was not at war with) during the 12 years of sanctions, the illegal invasion of Iraq raises questions about the legitimacy of Britain's political elite. It also raises the distinct probability that community cohesion and the cessation of the terrorist threat in Britain may not be realised until Blair and his fellow conspirators are made to account for their actions. As Pilger argues:

[O]n the prima facie evidence, Blair is a war criminal, and all those who have been, in one form or another, accessories should be reported to the International Criminal Court. Not only did they promote a charade of pretexts few now take seriously, they brought terrorism and death to Iraq. A growing body of legal opinion around the world agrees that the new court has a duty, as Eric Herring of Bristol University wrote, to investigate 'not only the regime, but also the UN bombing and sanctions which violated the human rights of Iraqis on a vast scale'. Add the present piratical war, whose spectre is the uniting of Arab nationalism with militant Islam. The whirlwind reaped by Blair and Bush is just beginning. Such is the magnitude of their crime. (Pilger 2004b: 33)

Pilger's assessment is shared by Richard Gott (2005) who believes Blair should be jailed and Harold Pinter who, in his 2005 Nobel acceptance speech, argued:

> We have brought torture, cluster bombs, depleted uranium, innumerable acts of random murder, misery, degradation and death to the Iraqi people and call it 'bringing freedom and democracy to the Middle East'. How many people do you have to kill before you qualify to be described as a mass murderer and a war criminal?... [I]t is just that Bush and Blair be arraigned before the International Criminal Court of Justice. (Pinter 2005: 12)

Blair's own violation of human rights includes his justification of Guantánamo as a necessary deterrent against threats to community safety in Britain – 'We hear an immense amount about their human rights and their civil liberties. But there are also human rights of the rest of us to live in safety' (Blair, cited in Brown and Morris 2006: 2). In contrast, the Commons Foreign Affairs Committee argued that the camp 'diminishes the moral authority of the US and hinders the war on terrorism' (cited in Brown and Morris 2006: 2). The Committee also expressed serious concerns about rendition (the use of British airports and airspace to transport prisoners for interrogation and possible torture in other countries) and abuses against Iraqi prisoners by coalition troops in Iraq (Brown and Morris 2006).

A report by the Joint Intelligence and Security Committee (JISC) had warned Blair before the war, in February 2003, that the terrorist threat to western interests 'would be heightened by military action against Iraq' (JISC 2003: 34). Evidence also suggests that Blair's government was warned by the Joint Terrorist Analysis Centre (JTAC) in June 2005 that the conflict in Iraq could provoke terrorist acts in Britain and 'compound anger among young British Muslims' (Norton-Taylor et al. 2005: 8). Once started, the conflict compounded anger among many thousands of non-Muslims – evident on 15 February 2003, when millions joined demonstrations against the war throughout the world. A report published by Chatham House and the Economic and Social Research Council also argued that the UK was at particular risk of terrorist attack because it had *inter alia* 'deployed armed forces in the military campaigns to topple the Taleban regime in Afghanistan and in Iraq' (Gregory and Wilkinson 2005: 2). Moreover, the report argued:

> There is no doubt that the situation over Iraq has imposed particular difficulties for the UK, and for the wider coalition against terrorism.

It gave a boost to the Al-Qaeda network's propaganda, recruitment and fundraising, caused a major split in the coalition, provided an ideal targeting and training area for Al-Qaeda-linked terrorists, and deflected resources and assistance that could have been deployed to assist the Karzai government and to bring bin Laden to justice. Riding pillion with a powerful ally has proved costly in terms of British and US military lives, Iraqi lives, military expenditure, and the damage caused to the counter-terrorism campaign. (Gregory and Wilkinson 2005: 3)

A corollary of the war on terror has been the erosion of civil, human and democratic rights in Britain. Public trust in 'representative democracy' is eroding with people increasingly feeling denied any real political choice. National turnout in the 2001 election fell from 71 per cent in 1997 to 59.4 per cent – the lowest figure since 1918. A study by the BBC in 2002 found that two-thirds of the population felt unrepresented by the political system and powerless to make any difference in respect of how their lives are managed (Addley 2003) – reflecting Marx's (1976) classic notion of alienation. New Labour was re-elected in May 2005 with 35.2 per cent of the turnout vote of 61 per cent – effectively, with only the expressed support of one-in-five of those eligible to vote. This is hardly a mandate to govern.

The growing unease about the state of governance and accountability in Britain is no more evident than in concerns raised since Blair's premiership and its impact on human rights. Under Blair, the state steadily gained arbitrary powers at the expense of civil liberties and freedoms. New Labour have used these powers against John Catt (stopped under section 44 of the Terrorism Act 2000 for wearing a T-shirt accusing Blair and Bush of war crimes); Walter Wolfgang (detained briefly under section 44 of the Terrorism Act 2000 following shouting 'That's a lie' at Jack Straw during a Labour Party conference – for which he was also violently ejected from the conference hall); Maya Evans (arrested under the Serious Organised Crime and Police Act 2005 for standing on the Cenotaph in Whitehall and reading out a list of soldiers killed in Iraq); and Helen John and Sylvia Boyes (arrested under the Serious Organised Crime and Police Act 2005 for walking across the sentry line at the US military base in Menwith Hill in North Yorkshire). As Shami Chakrabarti, Director of Liberty, argues: 'Just when our politicians lament the demise of participatory democracy they increasingly criminalise both free speech and protest' (cited in Morris and Brown 2006: 2).

The 'war-on-terror' and the subsequent illiberal reforms at home described clearly represent a grave threat to community cohesion, and the safety and wellbeing of all of us, due to the negation of our legal and human rights. Vast swathes of legal protection against threats to personal freedom and privacy are being removed by government – justified as necessary to defend us from threats of terrorism, crime and 'anti-social behaviour'.

Moral indifference to the suffering of others

Economic change and social policy choices since the 1980s have contributed to the surfacing of a less supportive society and increasing exposure to risk – where individual self-reliance is expected to substitute for collective welfare. Accompanying this change appears to have been a growth in moral indifference to the suffering of others. The concept of moral indifference has been alluded to by Bauman and explored by Simon Pemberton who states: 'The concept of moral indifference seeks to capture the moral silence/inactivity of capitalist societies to the human suffering caused by their organisation' (Pemberton 2004: 67). Those most disadvantaged by neo-liberal reforms have borne the brunt of this indifference – 'the plight of the losers has become increasingly dire, as collective responsibility for these people evaporates: the welfare system is exchanged for the criminal justice system, as a means of dealing with them' (Pemberton 2004: 80). Increasingly, the most vulnerable – including mentally-ill people, and those who have experienced sexual and violent abuse – are likely to be incarcerated rather than cared for (Corston 2006). Each year in Britain, 200 mentally-ill people held in police cells because there is no place in the health care system for them commit suicide within 48 hours of release (Johnson 2007). In the absence of any meaningful political commitment to social justice, the most impoverished and vulnerable in society are becoming increasingly exposed to criminal justice sanctions. As Squires observes:

> The ensuing criminalization of social policy suggests a clear shift in priorities. It goes beyond a simple recognition that crime and disorder policy objectives might be achieved by a variety of ways and means to suggest that the maintenance of social order and control may have superseded the more familiar objectives of housing, education, youth, health, career and welfare service agencies. (Squires 2006b: 154)

Community safety has replaced the more traditional social policy themes of more comprehensive housing, education, youth work, health care and social protection provision as the key political manifesto issue – community safety, that is, in the sense of 'the guardianship of "law and order", increasingly narrowed down to the promise of personal safety... [and] declaring war on crime and more generally on "disturbances of public order"' (Bauman 2006: 144–145). The moral indifference within government to supporting people establish firmer foundations for their lives inhibits possibilities for generating more progressive social policy solutions to social problems.

According to Wilkinson's research, moral indifference to vulnerable communities is more prevalent in vastly unequal societies. 'The tendency is for societies with bigger inequalities to show more discrimination against vulnerable groups' (Wilkinson 2005: 28). This tendency can clearly take on a 'race' dimension, with implications for community cohesion.

> Inequality seems to shift the whole distribution of social relationships away from the most affectionate end toward the more conflictual end, so that, given what we know from the available data, we might also expect people in more unequal societies would turn out to be less helpful to strangers..., and that there would be more conflict... and more prejudice against disadvantaged groups. (Wilkinson 2005: 56)

Extreme moral indifference to racism within the UK criminal justice system was evident in the inquiry into the death of Zahid Mubarek at Feltham young offenders institute – battered to death with a table leg by his racist cellmate Robert Stewart. 'The inquiry has heard claims that prison officers placed Zahid with a white racist for their perverted pleasure.... "The intention was to see whether or not the two fell out and came to blows. Officers were betting on the outcome", Mr Keys [a Prison Officers' Association official] said' (Carter 2005b: 12).

Moral indifference to the suffering of the vulnerable is also evident in the treatment of Michelle Wood in January 2003 following her arrest and subsequent release without charge by Lincolnshire police:

> A confused and hungry heroin addict, dressed in soaked clothes and with no money, bus ticket or mobile phone, was callously dumped on a near-freezing roadside by two police officers.... Michelle Wood, a mother of three aged 25, died of hypothermia in a nearby field.... The sergeant had instructed the two constables to take Ms Wood to the boundary [between the Lincolnshire and Humberside police force] and leave her there. They had done what they were told, against all their training in their duty of care. (Wainwright 2005: 11)

Conclusions

It has been increasingly argued that parliaments of nation states are no longer able to act autonomously in the interest of their citizens. As Günter Grass puts it, 'Democracy has become a pawn to the dictates of globally volatile capital' (Grass 2005: 4). For Grass, the political system no longer protects civil rights as a priority; instead, it 'now only serves the so-called free-market economy in line with the neoliberal Zeitgeist' (Grass 2005: 5). At the same time, as we have argued throughout this chapter, the market system has been allowed to commit grave social harms – a view supported by Grass:

> We all are witness to the fact that production is being destroyed worldwide, that so-called hostile and friendly takeovers are destroying thousands of jobs, that the mere announcement of rationalisation measures, such as the dismissal of workers and employees, makes share prices rise, and this is regarded unthinkingly as the price to be paid for 'living in freedom'. (Grass 2005: 5)

Those who dare to criticise these developments as socially unjust are:

> at best ridiculed by slick young journalists as 'social romantics'…. Questions asked as to the reasons for the growing gap between rich and poor are dismissed as 'the politics of envy'. The desire for justice is ridiculed as utopian. The concept of 'solidarity' is relegated to the dictionary's list of 'foreign words'. (Grass 2005: 5)

Grass argues that the greatest threat to social wellbeing is the seeming impotency of contemporary politics to protect citizens from exposure to the dictates of the economy. As Beck explains, we now live in a 'political economy of insecurity' (Beck 2000, cited in Smart 2003: 153) – an insecurity which Bourdieu sees as having grave consequences for collective action in defence of social justice. For Bourdieu, the rise in insecurity in society is leading to:

> the destruction of existence, which is deprived among other things of its temporal structures, and the ensuing deterioration of the whole relationship to the world, time and space. Casualization profoundly affects the person who suffers it: by making the whole future uncertain, it prevents all rational anticipation and, in particular, the basic belief and hope in the future that one needs in order to rebel,

especially collectively, against present conditions, even the most intolerable. (Bourdieu 2004: 82)

Insecurity not only works against the most disadvantaged in society – expressed in terms of premature death and morbidity, psychosocial problems (depression and anxiety), suicide and alcoholism, and violence and crime (Wilkinson 2005) – but also, as Bourdieu argues, against political engagement and, consequently, democracy itself. Grass warns of the emergence of 'a new totalitarianism, backed as it is by the world's last remaining ideology…. As conscious democrats, we should freely resist the power of capital, which sees mankind as nothing more than something which consumes and produces' (Grass 2005: 5).

Crucially, therefore, before we can generate the societal preconditions whereby universal and egalitarian notions of community safety and wellbeing can be genuinely fostered we need, first, to reclaim democracy – to reclaim the social, civil and human rights upon which social wellbeing, economic security and active political engagement can thrive. The way to do this is to challenge the dominant assumptions on community safety, cohesion and wellbeing within the neo-liberal discourse, and to expose how these serve to socially construct a disproportionate understanding in mainstream thinking about the major risks we are facing in society. We also need to expose how this dominant discourse continues to camouflage more serious social harms wrought by the anti-social policies and practices of both governments and private corporations.

Local antagonisms within communities are problematic for those on the sharp end of day-to-day hostilities. We do not dispute that. However, we would argue that the greater threat to community safety, cohesion and wellbeing is the oppressive social environment in which we live and which inhibits possibilities for realising our full human development and happiness. This inhibition has been exacerbated in Britain due to the destructive tendencies within the neo-liberal ideological project of the past 30 years. In the name of progress, neo-liberal policies of widespread privatisation and structural adjustment have been applied throughout the world – with devastating effects in terms of poverty, social breakdown, and human and ecological devastation (Kingsnorth 2004). More specifically with regard to Britain, as we have seen, society has become a more risky, dangerous and divisive place as a consequence of the devastation inflicted on social solidarities (with the attendant rise in moral indifference to the suffering of others), the erosion of political and human rights, the fetishisation of consumerism, and state crimes of aggression. Attending to these contextual realities would present possibilities for reconstructing the societal preconditions needed for individual self-determination and social wellbeing to be realised. Instead, however, New Labour has doggedly pushed on with a policy agenda designed to favour the interests of finance capital (capital accumulation) whilst seeking to heal the antagonisms in society they themselves have largely created (legitimisation). In respect of the latter, New Labour has drawn heavily on the values of communitarianism, discussed at length in Chapter 2, for these appear to offer a blueprint (which can be presented as 'rational' and 'commonsensical') for society to live in 'safety' – harmonious, unified and cohesive, free from conflict.

The likelihood of New Labour's strategy on community safety and cohesion succeeding is doubtful – largely because it is based on a false notion of community as a site where shared values, unity and cohesion can, with external intervention (education and treatment), be gener-ated. Communities cannot be and, as history suggests (illustrated in Chapter 1), have never been like this. Communities consist of differ-ence and diversity, and whilst attempts might be made (e.g. through the new networks and partnerships that are being set up to administer local regeneration schemes) to generate a 'commonsense' understanding of mainstream 'community values' individuals are expected to comply with, many will remain feeling isolated and disconnected (and even hostile to) these values. In such a context, the ability to take charge of one's own fate and achieve social wellbeing is denied. As we have seen throughout the course of this book, this denial of wellbeing has par-ticularly generated profound social harms for the most vulnerable in society – for example, young working-class people, the sick and disa-bled, unskilled labourers and certain ethnic-minority groups. Increasingly too, British society has become a more dangerous place for many more of us because of the breakdown in social solidarity, the rise of consumerism, the erosion of civil and human rights, and the crimes of the powerful.

In the final chapter that follows we look to establish a set of key principles upon which to compose the kind of social context that would enable individuals and communities to realise their full potential and attain social wellbeing. Drawing on critical theories of community which emphasise notions of conscientisation and counter-hegemonic strategies in pursuance of radical social change – notions which stress the transformative capacities of 'community' (discussed in Chapter 2) – we consider practical possibilities for transcending the established order of things and generating a progressive kind of politics that would allow meaningful community participation and genuine opportunities for people to influence the structural forces shaping their worlds. In doing this, we offer a different understanding to that of the communitarian position about the kind of societal preconditions needed for nurturing community wellbeing for all.

5
Summary and Conclusions – Community Wellbeing for All?

In this final chapter we conclude with a consideration of the possibilities for developing a more universalised vision of community wellbeing. We do this by imagining the kind of societal context needed to enable individuals to develop their capacity to engage freely in society as healthy, autonomous beings. We also consider the practical means by which we can transcend the established state of affairs and arrive at a more progressive basis for democratic decision making where community involvement is more meaningful and where real possibilities exist for enhancing the wellbeing of the many. In thinking about the way such a basis for society and politics might be reached, we draw on critical theories of community which emphasise the concept's transformative capacity and its utility as a counter discourse to the neo-liberal and communitarian principles adopted by New Labour. Before embarking on this endeavour, however, we set out a brief summary of the main argument developed throughout this book in order to define the bedrock or platform upon which any future arrangement for maximising social wellbeing will need to evolve.

Summary of the argument

As we have seen, throughout modernity in Britain the relatively privileged have remained fixated with threats to their property and bodies from 'dangerous Others' (strangers apart) and preoccupied with finding the most effective means possible to counter these threats. As we saw in Chapter 1, from the nineteenth century the British state increasingly intervened in social and economic affairs in order to address risks largely perceived by the powerful – for example, the spread of disease from the slums; threats to profit in peacetime and to the military in wartime from an unhealthy and uneducated working class; social instability and threats to property and body from a morally corrupt and lawless underclass; and political instability from a radicalised workers' movement. In relative terms, these anxieties and the policies they spawned have largely been (and continue to be) represented in a disproportionate and misleading way, overshadowing more serious threats to social wellbeing faced by the least powerful.

As we also saw in Chapter 1, throughout modernity communities in industrial Britain have been divided socially and spatially – an enduring feature of which has been conflict (based largely around class, 'race', gender, disability and sexuality). These divisions and tensions are an inherent feature of industrial capitalism, and responsible for the disproportionate suffering experienced by the least advantaged – due largely to the perilous state of labour markets, social protection systems, state education and health care provision, and housing and neighbourhood circumstances. These divisions and social harms have, as we saw in the previous chapter, become more pronounced with post-industrialism.

There was a brief time under Keynesian welfarism (the period following the end of the Second World War up to the late 1970s) when the social wellbeing of many individuals in working-class communities improved as a result of both economic demand management and advances in collective social welfare – although it is acknowledged that people's experiences were differentiated by class, 'race', gender, disability and sexuality. Since around 1976, however, there has been a discernible shift in social policy emphasis with a return to incentivising individualised solutions to economic and social problems. Since that time, governments have increasingly sought to privilege the economic over the social. As a consequence, the contextual circumstances shaping human relations – in particular, the conditions within which disadvantaged communities have to contend with the everyday risks forced upon them (the poverty, the inequality, the exploitation, the morbidity, the bad housing conditions and difficult neighbourhood circumstances, the lack of social support, the racism, the oppressive policing, the failing education system, the general sense of hopelessness, and their effective disenfranchisement) – has become increasingly unsupportive (with profound implications for community wellbeing). Those who fail to rise above these difficult circumstances are increasingly likely to be criminalised rather than cared for. New Labour added 3,000 criminal offences to the statute book during its first ten years in government (Bunting 2007). At the same time, the nationalistic and neo-imperialistic discourse within both New Labour's race relations and foreign affairs agendas, with their intolerant stance towards the defective cultures of 'dangerous Others' (discussed in Chapters 3 and 4), is further marginalising ethnic minority communities. More broadly, foreigners (immigrants, refugees and asylum seekers) have been increasingly demonised by politicians of all hues (as well as the media) as not only 'scroungers' but, since 11 September and 7 July, as potential 'terrorists'. These developments serve not only to alienate working class and ethnic minority communities in Britain. They also serve to distract attention away from the British state's blameworthiness in respect of its failure to protect the social wellbeing of its citizens at home, and its collusion in the illegal and immoral assault on the sovereign state of Iraq abroad.

In pursuing its punitive turn in social policy, New Labour have been keen to embrace, as we have seen, the notion of 'community' for it provides them (as it provided previous governments) with a useful conceptual device or discourse for legitimising its policies by engendering the appearance of consent (underpinned by notions of 'direct democracy', 'shared values' and 'harmony and unity' – the antithesis to 'conflict') whilst privileging the status quo. However, as we showed in Chapter 2, 'community' and 'conflict' remain contested concepts. In contrast to the communitarian notions shaping New Labour thinking – that is, that community serves as a counterweight to conflict (where 'conflict' is seen as something bad) – community can also be seen as a site upon which to forge alternative institutional arrangements for maximising social wellbeing for all – that is, a site upon which to mobilise social solidarity and engage in conflict in pursuance of social change (where 'conflict' is seen as something good). Used in this way, community offers a position from where genuine possibilities exist to reopen a broad debate within the public sphere about the true nature of neoliberalism and its effects on social justice, democracy and community wellbeing – something that has increasingly been stifled in recent years by government and unaccountable global institutions (aided by a complicit media).

A wider public debate on community wellbeing for all might ask such questions as: is the fundamental threat to community wellbeing *cultural* (i.e. the cultural deficit of flawed communities – i.e. dysfunctional parenting, workshy, feral youth and a crisis of national identity) – or is it *structural* (i.e. widening social inequality, the loss of social solidarity and racism)? In the case of New Labour, as we discovered in Chapter 3, because of their preoccupation with communitarian values their policy emphasis has clearly focused on the former as the key area in need of attention. In contrast, in this book we clearly argue the case for the latter and the need to restore solidaristic social relations; we argue the need to allow people to recognise the benefits of such relations as against the disbenefits of reliance on individualistic endeavour. Here, I would commend the observations from my own housing research, alluded to in the introduction, and the contribution of a cross-national comparative perspective for identifying social, political and economic benefits derivable from solidaristic approaches to welfare organising that are largely absent in more marketised welfare systems. Such observations are supported by Jordan who argues the need for a paradigm shift in the direction of social policy towards one that would attend 'to the contextual, cultural, convivial and co-operative elements in social relations' (Jordan 2005: 440).

In the next section, we look to describe the kind of societal preconditions necessary to enable individuals to develop their capacity to engage as fully and freely as possible in society, as healthy, autonomous beings, and in a way that will allow greater possibilities for attaining community wellbeing. We then move on to consider some practical means by which we can rise above the established social order and arrive at a more progressive basis of democratic decision making where community engagement becomes meaningful, and where genuine possibilities emerge for influencing the social and political basis upon which the wellbeing of the many will be determined.

A social context for determining the wellbeing of the many

A basic premise underlying the key thesis of this book is that the community wellbeing of the many requires social policy developments to emerge from within a social context where the discourse of social problems reflects the broad agenda of diverse needs, articulated and defined by a similarly broad constituency of individuals and groups. For such societal preconditions to become reality requires the facilitation of a form of dialogue that recognises contextuality and promotes greater mutual understanding. As Jonathan Rutherford argues:

> The common good which we can bring into social existence through political thought hinges on the capacity to grant each other recognition. The giving of recognition and the need to be recognised by others is fundamental to our existence. It confers self-esteem in which lies the wish for a good life in which others are esteemed. Mutual recognition of difference marks a respect for the integrity of

others. Its absence through oppression, bad faith, exploitation, the utilisation of power in pursuit of self or sectional interest represents the dissolution of meaningfulness. (Rutherford 2007b: 154)

Of relevance here is Rawls' (1971) notion of self-respect, discussed in Chapter 3, as a prerequisite for living a full and meaningful life in co-operation with others – and therefore a right that the social institutions of society should support as an entitlement of citizenship and social justice. As Bunting sees it, '[R]espect and status are at the core of a sense of self, as essential to our wellbeing as meat and drink. We all need them, and without them (research has established) we all live shorter, unhappier lives' (Bunting 2007: 25). A combination of the erosion of social protection and the intensification of 'a culture of hypermaterial-ism…obsessed with high-status possessions' (Bunting 2007: 25) over the past 30 years has meant that the attainment of self-respect and status remains beyond the reach of the many.

As various commentators from the radical Left have stressed, social policy developments have failed to address the structural barriers preventing the socially, politically and economically marginalised from attaining self-respect and social wellbeing – suggesting the need for a ' "radical extension" of Marshall's triad [of citizenship rights] to embrace other categories of rights' (Lister 1997: 30). A useful starting point for identifying what these rights might be – and by extension, the kind of social environment within which community wellbeing might flourish – remains Doyal and Gough's thesis on the societal preconditions for the satisfaction of human need – alluded to in the previous chapter. Central to their argument is the notion that social rights are a necessary precondition for the effective exercise of civil and political rights essential for individual autonomy, and that societies cannot be morally indifferent to the needs of others. This is not only because it is morally wrong to ignore human suffering – something that 'accounts for the lasting popularity of the rhetoric of justice and equality' (Doyal and Gough 1991: 99) – but also because it is morally inconsistent to expect individuals to assume their duties as citizens without them having an entitlement of need-satisfaction necessary for them to be able to do this. If individuals are required to meet their reciprocal moral responsibilities within society – as expected by New Labour – then that society has a duty to ensure equal levels of need-satisfaction. 'When this does not occur, the disadvantaged suffer not because they *have* less than others but because they can *participate* less in their respective form of life. It is their impaired agency rather than their inequality as such that should be the focus of our moral concern' (Doyal and Gough 1991: 95–96 – emphasis in original).

Meaningful participation in society will require people not only having rights to basic need satisfaction (e.g. for sustenance) but also need-satisfaction up to an optimal level – 'the needs of *all* people should be satisfied to the *optimum* extent' (Doyal and Gough 1991: 111 – emphasis in original). This vision of a society where healthy and autonomous humans are free to explore their optimum creativity – where community wellbeing can flourish – will require a more equitable share of resources *and* wider access to political decision-making processes – including meaningful participation in decisions made about how needs are to be fulfilled. 'It is for this reason that the problems of welfare provision and effective democracy are inextricably linked' (Doyal and Gough 1991: 4).

Doyal and Gough argue that the most appropriate and effective way of optimising community wellbeing and need-satisfaction is through informed communication between all relevant stakeholders – effectively, democratic participation in the making and implementation of social policy. 'In short, what is required for the optimisation of need-satisfaction is a "dual strategy" incorporating both the generality of the state and the particularity of civil society' (Doyal and Gough 1991: 297). State planning is necessary to guarantee universal access to necessary services and resources, and state legislation is needed to ensure that the procedural preconditions for full democratic participation are in place. In respect of the latter, Doyal and Gough argue 'individual autonomy cannot be optimised without the opportunity for participation not just in the polity but in the economy and other aspects of civil society as well' (Doyal and Gough 1991: 299). Held shares a similar perspective in calling for a constitution and bill of rights that would:

> involve not only equal rights to cast a vote, but also equal rights to enjoy the conditions for effective participation, enlightened understanding and the setting of the political agenda. Such broad 'state' rights would, in turn, entail a broad bundle of social rights linked to reproduction, childcare, health and education, as well as economic rights to ensure adequate economic and financial resources for democratic autonomy. (Held 1987, cited in Doyal and Gough 1991: 301–302)

However, there remains the question of how to establish the conditions by which effective participation in decision making, based on enlightened understanding, becomes a possibility. As we saw in Chapter 2 and despite their limitations, principles upon which to build more meaningful forms of political participation lie in Habermas' (1981) concept of 'ideal speech situations' (i.e. permanent channels of communication where political dialogue and engagement occurs without predetermined expectations on either what can and cannot be debated, or what the outcome of the discussion will be) and Freire's (1996) 'critical pedagogy' (which offers a set of instruments for enabling oppressed communities to develop their critical awareness of their social context and to understand how to change it). Both approaches contrast profoundly with state-sponsored community involvement. However, questions remain about the degree to which it is genuinely possible for individuals to engage in meaningful dialogue and communication that is untarnished by either lack of understanding (or understanding based on populist authoritarianism) or ideological and cultural invasion. Notwithstanding such reservations, Habermas and Freire both underline the importance of non-coerced, ongoing, critical questioning, free of preconceived outcomes, and the need for permanent structures and procedures to be set in place for this to happen. They stress the significance of critical community engagement – free from the kind of preconceived moral judgements associated with mainstream communitarian paradigms of community participation – where individuals are permitted to question normative propositions. The style of dialogue proposed is one in which participants critically consider through discourse a range of competing positions presented by others before arriving at a judgement based on consensus. In the next section we offer an example of how such a mode of dialogue or exchange of ideas might be facilitated in practice – and what implications this might have for generating a more progressive basis of democratic decision making with genuine opportunities for promoting the social wellbeing of the many.

Democratic decision making and meaningful community engagement in practice

A means of generating the kind of critical democratic dialogue imagined by Freire and Habermas can be found in Niels Åkerstrøm Andersen's (2003) account of the discourse analyses of Michel Foucault, Reinhart Koselleck, Ernesto Laclau with Chantal Mouffe, and Niklas Luhmann. As I have suggested elsewhere (Cooper 2005), Andersen's synthesis of the theoretical contributions of these writers offers a practical approach to deconstructing normative understandings and subjecting these to critical scrutiny – thereby offering possibilities for facilitating more meaningful insights into the nature of social relationships and, for the purpose of this book, for generating a more progressive vision of social wellbeing.

First, Andersen suggests that Foucault's *Archaeology of Knowledge* (2005) sets out a clear framework for critically analysing moral interpretations: that is, who or what determines what is morally good and acceptable and, as a consequence, what is 'evil' and unacceptable? And what knowledge sources and discourses (ideas and ways of communicating) have been excluded from such determinations? And how are the subjects of dominant discourses represented – are they victims in need of assistance, or criminal deviants in need of treatment or punishment? And what are the effects of these representations in terms of social policy responses – welfare support and inclusion, or criminalisation and exclusion? And finally, what are the outcomes of these representations and policy responses in terms of winners and losers – who gains most from such discursive practices and who loses out? Have they led to general improvements in social wellbeing for the many or have they served to protect the privileges maintained by existing power relationships? In this way, Foucault offers an approach to deconstructing moral judgements of people and behaviour, and assessing who gains most (as included insiders) and who loses out (as excluded outsiders) from the policies these generate. In relation to community safety, for instance, we can ask why has the focus of attention spotlighted the misdemeanours of the relatively powerless whilst giving little or no weight to the indiscretions of the powerful or the difficult social circumstances within which many people struggle for survival? And who has gained most from this focus, and who has lost out?

Second, Andersen describes Koselleck's exploration of the history of concepts – developed at the end of the 1950s and set out in *Geschichtliche Grundbegriffe, Historisches Lexikon zur politisch-sozialen Sprache in Deutschland* (Brunner et al. 1990) – which he sees as setting out a terrain upon which counter positions to dominant discourses can be built. Koselleck emphasised both the contestability of ideas and their centrality to social and political action, focusing attention on to the ambiguity of concepts (meaning that they can never offer a completely true representation of their subject – otherwise, they would not be concepts) and, therefore, the potential for counter discourses around which alternative ideas can be formulated. For Koselleck, the presentation of concepts effectively generates a site for 'a semantic battle about the political and

social; a battle about the definition, defence and occupation of conceptually composed positions' (Andersen 2003: 34). There are always possibilities, therefore, for resisting dominant discourses through counter
concepts. For example, in relation to community safety's focus on the
indiscretions committed by the relatively powerless, it is also possible to
generate counter ideas that expose the structural context in which
social relations are played out – such as 'race', class and gender – or to
focus on more proportionate notions of threats to safety such as harms
generated by the activities of the powerful (e.g. environmental pollution and welfare retrenchment).

Third, Andersen outlines the ideas of Laclau and Mouffe (2001), set
out in *Hegemony and Socialist Strategy*, to identify how organised resistance to dominating discourses and concepts might be realised in practice. Laclau and Mouffe argue that hegemonic consent can never be fully
secured because hegemony is something contingent which has to be
constantly strived for – a 'battle of fixating' (cited in Andersen 2003: 55).
Consequently, there is always potential for counter-hegemonic projects
against dominating discourses which allow underlying mainstream
assumptions to be challenged. In the case of community safety, this battle of fixating can float between, on the one hand, a discourse emphasising threats from 'yobs', 'welfare fraudsters', 'dysfunctional parents',
'radical Muslims', 'political dissenters' and 'deviant sub-cultures' (simultaneously establishing the identities of both the 'dangerous Other' to be
excluded and the 'respectable insider' to be included) and, on the other
hand, a counter discourse stressing threats to community wellbeing
from structural forces and the actions of the powerful (simultaneously
establishing a counter position from which to mobilise resistance). This
comes close to Foucault's notion that 'there are no relations of power
without resistance' (cited in Gordeon 1980: 142). The possibilities exist,
therefore, for counter hegemonic projects to develop wherever dominating discourses seek to impose discipline and control.

Finally, Andersen refers to Luhmann's (1995) general treatise on social
systems which he sees as presenting a framework for scrutinising the
motives of social institutions and bringing these bodies to account. Of
particular interest here is the way 'function systems' of modern society
(e.g. scientific, political, social, economic, educational, judicial and
media systems) observe and explain 'social reality'. Luhmann intro-
duces the idea of 'observations' as 'operations' that 'do not refer to conscious subjects but to differences' (Andersen 2003: 64). In other words,
an observation is defined as a specific operation that involves the selection of distinctions – that is, we cannot observe social phenomenon

and make judgements about its essence without first having selected a means of distinguishing. Ways of distinguishing – seeing and naming something in the world – always accord with particular judgements. Consequently, what is named will always possess characteristics which are not indicated because other options of distinguishing were not chosen – in other words, in all observations there will be blind spots. Luhmann seeks to illuminate these blind spots and expose the way social systems select 'distinctions that fundamentally decide what can appear in society and how' (Andersen 2003: 65). The way to do this is to conduct second-order observations of the way social systems observe. This will reveal how those systems only observe what their choice of distinction permits them to see. Doing this requires self-restriction and precision of observation on behalf of the second-order observer. It may involve asking such questions as: why was a particular distinction chosen in preference to a different one, and what was the implication of that choice? (Andersen 2003). This allows social phenomena to be understood within a broader context – beyond the limited perspective drawn from observations made from a particular choice of distinction. In this way, social systems can be brought to account for the way they *choose* to observe and, subsequently, for the way they explain 'social reality'. For example, in the case of community safety, why does the criminal justice system distinguish 'yob culture' as one of the primary threats to communities rather than welfare retrenchment and disadvantaged young people's lack of social opportunity?

In conclusion, Andersen's framework offers an appropriate toolbox for academics, community workers and other welfare practitioners to both research and work with communities in ways that facilitate:

- the unravelling and scrutinising of dominant discourses (to appraise the 'truths' they stake claim to and whose interests these serve);
- the generation of counter discourses (that expose the contradictions within dominant discourses and convey alternative 'truths' that may serve the interests of a broader constituency);
- the identification of possibilities for counter-hegemonic projects and the potential sites of conflict for engaging in these; and
- the development of strategies for exposing the limited assumptions underpinning the activities of social institutions and calling these to account.

Bamber and Murphy (1999) outline an example of such an approach from their experience of critical youth work. They describe a 'holistic project' for youth work – one that strives to help young people to become (in Freire's term) 'fully human' – which takes as its starting point 'the interests and inclinations of groups of young people' (Bamber and Murphy 1999: 231) themselves (although the agenda will be subject to negotiation to counter populist authoritarian claims based, for example, on racist preconceptions). Central to this project is attending to the issue of 'power' and exposing 'the capacity of a select few to influence the manner in which the many make sense of the world' (Bamber and Murphy 1999: 231) – that is, addressing how 'people's awareness is socially constructed' through what Gramsci (1971) termed 'hegemony' (Bamber and Murphy 1999: 232). More specifically, critical youth work practice seeks to help people both understand their situation (e.g. their disadvantage) and to challenge it through a three-stage process:

- Stage one: developing a group's critical awareness of an issue or problem through open dialogue and counterarguments (supported by evidence and logical argument).
- Stage two: developing a sense of the group's shared commitment to deal with the issue (is there a consensus in favour of doing something?).
- Stage three (where a consensus in support of action exists): planning for and mobilizing action to deal with the issue or problem – reflecting on and learning from the outcome of this action (clarifying what can be done realistically).

In relation to community wellbeing, working with communities in this way opens up possibilities for exploring the social context shaping people's experiences and lived realities, and generating a broader perspective on their sense of wellbeing that takes account of such issues as relationships in the workplace, social protection and health care, housing and the local environment, education and training, sense of personal safety and security, and opportunities to influence decision-making processes. Working in this way, possibilities emerge for forging networks and constituencies of support for alternative social policy arrangements in a range of settings to deal more effectively with these issues – issues that have substantive implications for social wellbeing. Drawing on Foucault's (1979) notion that where there is power there is resistance, addressing these matters will require counter-hegemonic strategies located at various sites: in trade unions (to protect the wellbeing of workers and public services); in welfare campaigns (to maintain adequate social protection and health care); in town and country planning processes (to deliver affordable housing and transport in healthy environments); in schools and further education (to maintain a social and political role for education in relation to social justice and democracy); in the criminal justice system (to voice our concerns about threats to our sense of personal wellbeing); and in politics (through engagement in formal and informal political movements). This is an approach advocated in the critical cultural studies' theories of Stuart Hall (see Morley and Chen 1996). As Giroux observes:

> Hall's writing has always refused to limit the sites of education and politics to those 'privileged' by the advocates of 'genuine' politics. Organizing labor unions, demonstrating in the streets for legislation to curb corporate crimes, and organizing workers to promote radical forms of social policy are important forms of political practice, but working in the public [i.e. state] schools, the television industry, law firms, museums, or a vast number of other public spheres does not constitute for Hall a less reputable or less important form of political work. In fact, Hall continually has called for intellectuals to 'address the central, urgent, and most disturbing questions of society and a culture in the most rigorous intellectual way we have available.' He has urged cultural workers to take up this challenge in a variety of educational sites, and in doing so he has opened up the possibility for working within dominant institutions while challenging their authority and cultural practices. For Hall, the context of such work demands confronting a major paradox in capitalist societies – that of using the very authority vested in institutions such as schools to work against the grain of such authority. (Giroux 2000: 171–172)

This way of working is also consistent with Freire's belief that the process of critical dialogue should occur within and across a range of public sites – offering prospects for what Giroux sees as 'new political realities and projects' (Giroux 2000: 155). Indeed, one of the great ironies within New Labour's communitarian agenda is that whilst it has clearly sought to widen the surveillance gaze of the state throughout society through using 'community' as a site of governance and control (discussed in Chapter 2), in doing this they have inadvertently opened up possibilities for new sites of resistance to emerge. This irony is not lost on John Clarke who identifies instabilities and contradictions within the new system of welfare organising due to its 'incompatible models of governing – oscillating between centralizing and decentralizing tendencies, between competition and collaboration, and regularly unsettled by shifting political objectives' (Clarke 2004: 123). In this context:

> [T]he potential sites of contention and instability are simultaneously multiplied and localized. The proliferation of agencies involved in policy, process and practice of services, and the number of 'authorized' decision-making settings (local management, partnership steering bodies, community participation, contracting bodies etc.), mean that the potential sites where conflicts may occur – or be articulated – have increased. (Clarke 2004: 123)

There is still a role for human agency and the potential to act 'in and against the state' in pursuit of social justice. In addition, by embracing the notion of community involvement in social programmes, the government has generated potential sites of conflict it clearly did not intend. Despite New Labour's communitarian notion of community involvement (i.e. the involvement of 'respectable', 'law-abiding', 'active citizens' living in harmony in accordance with particular moral values) and the fact that more often than not it is 'responsible', middle-aged white people who dominate community involvement processes in practice, 'community' remains, as we saw in Chapter 2, a contested concept. 'Despite the organicist imagery, "communities" are contested and changeable constructions (rather than naturally occurring entities). They have shifting and contested memberships which imply problems of activism, leadership and representation (especially when what governance systems seek are "responsible" representatives)' (Clarke 2004: 124). As Clarke suggests, the 'active citizen' may turn into an 'activist citizen'.

Connecting with the global

It is increasingly recognised that achieving a more visionary, humanistic and solidaristic model of human wellbeing cannot rely on community engagement at the local level alone. As Newman and Mahoney argue, this level of involvement invariably: 'produces a form of participative politics that limits people (in the form of apparently neatly differentiated "communities") to local forms of engagement, cutting local constituencies off from national and global public policy issues that impinge on – and indeed serve to generate – such locales' (Newman and Mahoney 2007: 62).

As we have seen throughout the course of this book, it is the pursuit of the same ideological configuration – liberalised markets and an imposed neo-liberal social order – that has inflicted social harms on both the global level (through structural adjustment programmes and the 'war on terror') and the local (through economic restructuring and welfare retrenchment).

The local and the global have become increasingly entangled, with social wellbeing at the local level increasingly dependent on decisions made by supranational institutions (the World Bank [WB], the World Trade Organisation [WTO], the International Monetary Fund [IMF] and so forth) and powerful international leaders (especially the US leadership) at the global level. In such a context, it seems unlikely that the challenge of community wellbeing for the disadvantaged – that is, the need for political voice, civil and human rights, and adequate social protection and opportunity – can be truly addressed without, at the same time, democratising decision-making processes at the global level. Political strategies at the local level, therefore, need to engage with social movements that challenge the legitimacy of these supranational organisations who, in imposing their ideological agenda, reap destruction worldwide.

Whilst Naomi Klein rightly warns us that any attempt 'to hold ideologies to account for the crimes committed by their followers must be approached with caution' (Klein 2007: 19), at the same time it is also the case that:

> [C]ertain ideologies are a danger to the public and need to be identified as such. These are the closed fundamental doctrines that cannot coexist with other belief systems; their followers deplore diversity and demand an absolute free hand to implement their perfect system. The world as it is must be erased to make way for their purist invention. (Klein 2007: 19)

The authoritarianism of Soviet communism and German National Socialism has already been brought to account.

> But what of the contemporary crusade to liberate world markets? The coups, wars and slaughters to install and maintain pro-corporate regimes have never been treated as capitalist crimes.... If the most committed opponents of the corporatist economic model are systematically eliminated, whether in Argentina in the seventies or in Iraq today, that suppression is explained as part of the dirty fight against Communism or terrorism – almost never as the fight for the advancement of capitalism. (Klein 2007: 20)

It is the extreme policies of the neo-liberal globalisation agenda – policies that interfere increasingly in almost every area of our lives via the media, advertising, economic restructuring, regressive social policies, illegal wars and environmental pollution – that poses the greatest threat to community wellbeing and world stability.

At the same time, however, as Hardt and Negri argue, by colonising and interconnecting more and more areas of people's lives ever more deeply, neo-liberal globalisation is unwittingly generating the sites from which democratic alternatives to the present world order might be forged:

> You might say, simplifying a great deal, that there are two faces to globalization. On one face, Empire spreads globally its network of hierarchies and divisions that maintain order through new mechanisms of control and constant conflict. Globalization, however, is also the creation of new circuits of cooperation and collaboration that stretch across nations and continents and allow an unlimited number of encounters. This second face of globalization is not a matter of everyone in the world becoming the same; rather it provides the possibility that, while remaining different, we discover the commonality that enables us to communicate and act together. (Hardt and Negri 2005: xiii)

Monbiot identifies similar contradictions within the discourse of the neo-liberal globalisation thesis. As he argues:

> Corporate and financial globalization, designed and executed by a minority seeking to enhance its wealth and power, is compelling the people it oppresses to acknowledge their commonality. Globalization is establishing a single, planetary class interest, as the same forces and the same institutions threaten the welfare of the people of all nations. ... Simultaneously, it has placed within our hands the weapons we require to overthrow the people who have engineered it and assert our common interest. By crushing the grand ideologies which divided the world, it has evacuated the political space in which a new, global politics can grow. ... The global dictatorship of vested interests has created the means of its own destruction. (Monbiot 2003: 8–9)

Neo-liberal globalisation is not inescapable and all-powerful, and resistance movements against its effects are emerging. As Hardt and Negri observe:

> Today there are innumerable protests throughout the world against the inequalities, injustices, and undemocratic characteristics of the

global system, and these protests are increasingly organized in powerful, sustained movements.... [F]or decades groups in the dominant and subordinated parts of the world have posed grievances against the global system on political, legal and economic issues. (Hardt and Negri 2005: 268)

Bringing these protest movements together as a broad global justice coalition would clearly improve their potential for effecting change and bringing into being a manifesto for a new world order – one offering prospects for greater social justice and human wellbeing for the many (Kingsnorth 2004). Hardt and Negri suggest organising such a coalition around a contemporary version of the *cahiers de doléances* – the lists of grievances that were compiled in France on the invitation of Louis XVI in return for the right to impose new taxes.[1] On a global level, Hardt and Negri suggest that a contemporary version of this list would address three themes: 'the critique of existing forms of representation, the protest against poverty, and the opposition to war' (Hardt and Negri 2005: 269–270). Mainstream political and economic representation is flawed both at home (through the paucity of choice offered by electoral systems and the erosion of trade union powers) and globally (through the disproportionate influence of the US on supranational institutions and militarily). Coinciding with this are growing criticisms about the erosion of civil rights domestically and the lack of an adequate international structure to enforce human rights globally (Hardt and Negri 2005). Although the establishment of the International Criminal Court (ICC) in 2002 suggests 'the possibility of a global system of justice that serves to protect the rights of all equally' (Hardt and Negri 2005: 276)

---

[1] By the time of the meeting of the Estates General at Versailles in May 1789, more than 40,000 lists had been compiled from all over the country addressing such issues as personal liberties (relating to fair trials, freedom of expression and limits to abusive powers). The estate of the Nobility of Blois called on the King to address 'a number of instances in which natural liberty is abridged' – including 'The abuse of police regulations, which every year, in an arbitrary manner and without regular process, thrusts a number of artisans and useful citizens into prisons, work-houses and places of detention, often for trivial faults and even upon simple suspicion' (Stewart 1951: 2). It also called on the King to establish a commission composed of 'citizens of all orders' to 'formulate a plan of national education for the benefit of all classes of society' (Stewart 1951: 3). The Third Estate of the Dourdon called on the King to allow a broad constituency to deliberate 'in common' concerning social needs (Stewart 1951: 4). These grievances would not be out of place in contemporary Britain.

the most powerful country in the world – the US – has refused to ratify the statute of the court and therefore remains outside its jurisdiction. This clearly 'undercuts all the attempts to institute a supranational or global system of justice' (Hardt and Negri 2005: 276).

The degree of global poverty is reflected in the World Bank's assessment that half the population of the globe live on less than $2 a day (a fifth on less than $1) – and that this lack of resources translates into a lack of health care, education, social and political representation, and premature death. Poverty is distributed unevenly both geographically and along the lines of class, 'race', ethnicity and gender. Underpinning poverty and inequality globally and locally is the neo-liberal assumption that politics can do less and less to regulate economic activity because of the mobility of capital. As a consequence, neo-liberal states 'conform to and even anticipate the needs of capital' (Hardt and Negri 2005: 279). National policies are increasingly driven by directives from supranational bodies such as the General Agreement on Trade in Services of the WTO which acts as one of the main mechanisms for the liberalization of public services (Beckmann and Cooper 2004). As Hardt and Negri argue, under neo-liberalism, broader societal interests 'take a backseat to those of capital' (Hardt and Negri 2005: 279).

In addition to previous biopolitical global grievances – that is, ecological problems and threats to the environment; struggles around 'race' and gender issues (including those of indigenous populations); the control of scientific knowledge and patents (such as those related to genetically modified foods and pharmaceuticals) – the 'war on terror', following 11 September 2001, focused concern on to 'the global state of war … [and] the ultimate biopolitical grievance, against destruction and death' (Hardt and Negri 2005: 284). The global protest against the war reached a peak on 15 February 2003, with massive demonstrations coordinated in cities across the globe. 'The other grievances have not gone away, and they will all reappear forcefully in time, but now war has been added to each struggle as the common, fundamental grievance' (Hardt and Negri 2005: 284).

Due to these numerous grievances against the present global order, a perceived need for democracy on a global scale is becoming more widely acknowledged and articulated. 'The common currency that runs throughout so many struggles and movements for liberation across the world today … is the desire for democracy' (Hardt and Negri 2005: xvi). Examples of such struggles include the *A World to Win* campaign against global capitalism (see http://www.aworldtowin.net/) and *Statewatch*, who continue to monitor the effect of state activities on civil liberties (see http://www.statewatch.org/). Giroux argues that intellectuals have a role and responsibility here too to facilitate the exposure and transformation of 'the oppressive conditions through which individuals and groups are constructed and differentiated' (Giroux 2000: 136), and to help identify the circumstances necessary for individuals and communities to take control over the structural forces shaping their life chances.

Conclusions

This book set out to interrogate vying concepts in relation to community, social wellbeing, community safety and community cohesion, and to analyse how dominant ideas in relation to these themes have shaped social policy developments in Britain over time – including an assessment of the practical consequences of these policies. What becomes apparent from this discussion is that the dominant discourse in relation to community, wellbeing, safety and cohesion has focused primarily on threats posed by the attitudes and behaviour of the least powerful – for example, welfare dependants, feral youth and recalcitrant immigrants – leading to a disproportionate emphasis in social policy on measures aimed at the surveillance and control of these individuals and communities (particularly pre-Second World War and since the late 1970s). Moreover, it is clear that this focus has served to distract attention away from more serious social harms caused by the anti-social and criminal acts of private corporations and government.

Specifically in respect of the concept 'community', so often the way this has been used in mainstream policy discourse (and particularly under New Labour) has been to emphasise sameness, consent and the absence of conflict. Such usage, however, presents a misleading representation of social relations. As we illustrated in Chapter 1, and as Stuart Hall observes: 'Britain is not homogenous; it was never a society without conflict. The English fought tooth and nail over everything we know of as English political virtues – rule of law, free speech, the franchise' (cited in Adams 2007: 8). Yet despite this, the powerful continue to espouse an understanding of community as unity in the expectation that this will activate local people to engage responsibly, in civil society, and find solutions to the problems wrought by neo-liberal economic organising and social policies. By activating communities in this way, wellbeing, safety and cohesion will, claim the powerful, be restored. Meanwhile, social harms generated by their policies, practices and activities remain concealed, and the status quo (unequal power relations) remains intact.

However, as we saw in Chapter 2, communities possess agency and community as a concept provides a powerful symbol around which individuals can organise collectively in strategies of resistance. Throughout history, as we saw in Chapter 1, community has represented a site for mobilising solidarity and enhancing the capacity of people to engage in political activism aimed at realising alternative visions of social wellbeing. In this final chapter, we describe some of the tools available to academics and practitioners working with communities to help facilitate dialogue regarding how these alternatives might look and how they might be made to happen. In a way, this would require something similar to the critical CDP model described in Chapter 1 – with academics conducting research into perspectives on community wellbeing, and practitioners working with communities within and beyond the neighbourhood in the ways described above. Working in these ways would allow people to see beyond socially-constructed notions of local problems, and to identify and understand the wider social context shaping life chances and perspectives on social wellbeing. It would allow those explanations of neighbourhood problems emphasising dysfunctional behaviour to be challenged, and a refocus on the connections between difficult local circumstances and processes external to the area (including the influence of global forces) which determine these.

It is clear that realising community wellbeing for the many will not happen in a capitalist market system shaped in accordance with the neo-liberal paradigm. Therefore, leaving aside the desirability of a Marxist revolution, the priority must be greater regulation of the existing social system in the interest of the many. In contrast to the neo-liberal political discourse, 'free-market' capitalism is never entirely unfettered – free of regulation. At the time of writing (summer 2007), central banks around the world are stepping in with massive injections of cash to fend off the threat of a worldwide credit squeeze caused by a crisis in the US mortgage lending market (Teather et al. 2007). The risks (and incompetence) of powerful financial institutions – as with the case of Northern Rock in Britain – are overseen by the state. In contrast, the least powerful are left to devise their own coping strategies – individually, or through family or community.

Alternatively, researching and practising in ways suggested in this chapter offers the prospect of achieving more progressive social policies and enhanced community wellbeing for the many. Clearly, the dominant structural factors shaping social relationships in post-industrial capitalism are extremely forceful. However, as we have argued, using the tools set out above, there are real opportunities for academics, community workers and other welfare practitioners to generate public spaces for open democratic dialogue in a range of settings – thereby expanding the capacities of individuals and communities to critically examine how power is produced and applied, and under what conditions resistance and social transformation become a real possibility.

Bibliography

A World to Win (2005) 'Election 05' (email circulated 11 April, 21.38 hours).

Abdullah, D. (2006) 'Incitement to Violence', *The Guardian*, 17 October, p. 32.

Abel-Smith, B. and Townsend, P. (1965) *The Poor and the Poorest*, Occasional Papers on Social Administration, London: Bell.

Acheson, D. (1998) *Independent Inquiry into Inequalities in Health*, London: The Stationery Office.

Adams, T. (2007) 'Stuart Hall – The Interview', *The Observer Review*, 23 September, pp. 8–9.

Addley, E. (2003) 'It's Just a Lot of Suits and Faceless Men', *The Guardian*, 25 November, p. 7.

Ahmed, K. and Townsend, M. (2004) 'Exam Overload Harming Pupils', *The Observer*, 15 February, p. 2.

Alexiadou, N. (2001) 'Management Identities in Transition: A Case Study from Further Education', *The Sociological Review*, 49 (3), pp. 412–435.

Allen, J. and Massey, D. (eds) (1992) *The Economy in Question*, London: Sage.

Andalo, D. (2008) 'Poor Relations', *Society Guardian*, 19 March, p. 7.

Andersen, N.Å. (2003) *Discursive Analytical Strategies: Understanding Foucault, Koselleck, Laclau, Luhmann,* Bristol: Policy Press.

Appleton, J. (2002) 'Testing Britishness', *Spiked Politics*, 19 September, www.spiked-online.com/Printable/00000006DA58.htm [accessed 08/10/02].

Arnot, C. (2006) 'Ode to Joy – Interview with Andrew Oswald', *Education Guardian*, 6 June, p. 11.

Asthana, A. (2007) 'Call to Ban All School Exams for Under-16s', *The Observer*, 10 June, p. 1.

Atkinson, R. and Moon, G. (1994) *Urban Policy in Britain: The City, the State and the Market*, Basingstoke: Macmillan.

Back, L. (2004) 'Pale Shadows: Racisms, Masculinity and Multiculture', in J. Roche, S. Tucker, R. Thomson and R. Flynn (eds) *Youth in Society*, 2nd Edition, London: Sage, pp. 28– 41.

Back, G. and Hamnett, C. (1985) 'State Housing Policy Formation and the Changing Role of Housing Associations in Britain', *Policy and Politics*, 13(4), pp. 393–411.

Balakrishnan, A. (2008) 'Property Ladder Harder to Grasp than Ever', *The Guardian*, 12 March, p. 29.

Ball, S.J. (2008) *The Education Debate*, Bristol: Policy Press.

Bamber, J. and Murphy, H. (1999) 'Youth Work: The Possibilities for Critical Practice', *Journal of Youth Studies*, 2(2), pp. 227–242.

Barber, B.R. (2007) *Consumed: How Markets Corrupt Children, Infantilize Adults, and Swallow Citizens Whole*, New York: W.W.Norton & Company.

Barlow, J. and Duncan, S. (1994) *Success and Failure in Housing Provision: European Systems Compared*, Oxford: Pergamon.

Bauman, Z. (1998) *Work, Consumerism and the New Poor*, Buckingham: Open University Press.

Bauman, Z. (2001) *Community: Seeking Safety in an Insecure World*, Cambridge: Polity.

Bauman, Z. (2006) *Liquid Fear*, Cambridge: Polity Press.

BBC News (2004) 'So What Exactly is Multiculturalism?', 5 April, at: http://news.bbc.co.uk/mpapps/pagetools/print/news.bbc.co.uk/1/hi/uk/3600791.stm [accessed 1/2/08].

BBC News (2007a) 'In Full: Brown on Constitution', 4 July, at: http://news.bbc.co.uk/1/hi/uk_politics/6266526.stm [accessed 4/7/07].

BBC News (2007b) 'Johnson Rejects Tests Scrap Call', 11 June, at: http://news.bbc.co.uk/go/pr/fr/-/1/hi/education/6739363.stm [accessed 11/6/07].

BBC News (2008) 'Bid to Tackle "Sick-note Culture"', 20 February, at: http://news.bbc.co.uk/1/hi/health/7253577.stm [accessed 20/2/08].

BBC Radio 4 (2007) *You and Yours*, 27 July.

Beckett, A. (2004) 'The Making of the Terror Myth', *G2 – The Guardian*, 15 October, pp. 2–4.

Beckmann, A. and Cooper, C. (2004) '"Globalisation", the New Managerialism and Education: Rethinking the Purpose of Education in Britain', *The Journal for Critical Education Policy Studies*, 2(2), September, pp. 1–14, at: http://www.jceps.com/print.php?articleID=31 [accessed 26/6/07].

Beckmann, A. and Cooper, C. (2005a) '*Nous accusons* – Revisiting Foucault's Comments on the Role of the "Specific Intellectual" in the Context of Increasing Processes of *Gleichschaltung* in Britain', *Outlines: Critical Social Studies*, 7(2), December, pp. 3–22.

Beckmann, A. and Cooper, C. (2005b) 'Conditions of Domination: Reflections on Harms Generated by the British State Education System', *British Journal of Sociology of Education*, 26(4), pp. 475–489.

Behr, R. (2005) 'R-E-S-P-E-C-T', *The Observer*, 22 May, pp. 16–17.

Benjamin, A. (2001) 'Into the Fire', *Society Guardian*, 29 August, p. 48.

Bhattacharyya, G. and Gabriel, J. (2004) 'Racial Formations of Youth', in J. Roche, S. Tucker, R. Thomson and R. Flynn (eds) *Youth in Society*, 2nd Edition, London: Sage, pp. 61–73.

Blackburn, J. (2000) 'Understanding Paulo Freire: Reflections on the Origins, Concepts, and Possible Pitfalls of his Educational Approach', *Community Development Journal*, 35(1), January, pp. 3–15.

Blair, T. (2005) 'The Rights of the Many Come First', *The Observer*, 11 December, p. 30.

Blears, H. (2005) 'The Politics of Decency' in P. Collins (ed.) *Reform Works* London: The Social Market Foundation, pp. 12–20.

Bourdieu, P. (2004) *Acts of Resistance: Against the Myths of Our Time*, Oxford: Polity Press.

Braham, P., Rattansi, A. and Skellington, R. (eds) (1992) *Racism and Antiracism: Inequalities, Opportunities and Policies*, London: Open University Press/Sage.

Branigan, T. (2006) 'Challenging Ideology of Terrorists is Key to Foreign Policy', *The Guardian*, 22 March, p. 11.

Brecher, B. (2007) '"No" to Work in a Degree Factory', *The Times Higher Education Supplement*, 27 July, p. 42.

Bright, M. (2005a) 'Charity Pleads for Tolerance as Autistic Youngsters Face Asbos', *The Observer*, 22 May, p. 7.

Bright, M. (2005b) 'Blair Adviser: Stop Calling Children "yobs"', *The Observer*, 22 May, pp. 1–2.

Brown, C. and Morris, N. (2006) 'Blair Faces Torrent of Criticism on Human Rights', *The Independent*, 24 February, p. 2.

Brown, S. (2005) *Understanding Youth and Crime: Listening to Youth?*, 2nd Edition, Maidenhead: Open University Press.

Brunner, O., Conze, W. and Koselleck, R. (eds) (1990) *Geschichtliche Grundbegriffe, Historisches Lexikon zur politisch-sozialen Sprache in Deutschland*, Stuttgart: Klett-Cotta.

Bunting, M. (2004) 'Today's Youth: Anxious, Depressed, Antisocial', *The Guardian*, 13 September, p. 1.

Bunting, M. (2007) 'Yes, We Have Failed Rhys Jones, but We Have Also Failed His Killer', *The Guardian*, 27 August, p. 25.

Burden, T., Cooper, C. and Petrie, S. (2000) *'Modernising' Social Policy: Unravelling New Labour's Welfare Reforms*, Aldershot: Ashgate.

Burkett, I. (2001) 'Traversing the Swampy Terrain of Postmodern Communities: towards Theoretical Revisionings of Community Development', *European Journal of Social Work*, 4(3), pp. 233–246.

Byrne, D. (2006) *Social Exclusion*, 2nd Edition, Maidenhead: Open University Press.

Campbell, B. (1993) *Goliath: Britain's Dangerous Places*, London: Methuen.

Carter, H. (2005a) 'Third of Children in North-west Live in Poverty', *The Guardian*, 12 March, p. 11.

Carter, H. (2005b) 'Asian Inmate Attacked Weeks before Racist Death', *The Guardian*, 12 March, p. 12.

Carvel, J. (2004) 'Opposition to Immigrants Hardens under Blair', *The Guardian*, 7 December, p. 6.

Carvel, J. (2006) 'NHS Told: Put Money before Medicine', *The Guardian*, 23 January, p. 1.

Cassidy, S. (2005) 'Efforts to End Class Divide at Universities are Failing', *The Independent*, 20 January, p. 23.

Cassidy, S. (2006) 'Universities Struggle to Fill Places as Thousands of Students are Put Off by £3,000 Top-up Fees', *The Independent*, 19 August, p. 5.

Charlton, J. (2000) 'Class Struggle and the Origins of State Welfare Reform', in M. Lavalette and G. Mooney (eds) *Class Struggle and Social Welfare*, London: Routledge, pp. 52–70.

Christensen, K. and Levinson, D. (eds) (2003) *Encyclopedia of Community: From the Village to the Virtual World*, Vols. 1–4, London: Sage.

Clarke, J. (2004) *Changing Welfare, Changing States: New Directions in Social Policy*, London: Sage.

Clarke, J. (2005) 'New Labour's Citizens: Activated, Empowered, Responsibilized, Abandoned?', *Critical Social Policy*, 25:4, pp. 447–463.

Cohen, A.P. (1985) *The Symbolic Construction of Community*, London: Routledge.

Cohen, N. (1997) 'Profile: Totally Wonkers', *The Observer*, 9 March, at: http://politics.guardian.co.uk/print/0,4232190-108685,00.html [accessed 4/2/08].

Cohen, S. (2004) *Folk Devils and Moral Panics*, 4th Edition, Oxford: Blackwells.

Collinson, P. (2006) 'Study Reveals Financial Crisis of the 18–40s', *The Guardian*, 28 March, p. 1.

Collishaw, S., Maughan, B., Goodman, R., et al. (2004) 'Time Trends in Adolescent Mental Health', *Journal of Child Psychology and Psychiatry*, 45(8), pp. 1350–1362.

Conn, D. (2007) 'Supermarket Sweep up', *Society Guardian*, 25 July, pp. 1–2.

Cooper, C. (1998) 'Democratising Social Housing: Building the "People's Home"', in C. Cooper and M. Hawtin (eds) *Resident Involvement and Community Action: Theory to Practice*, Coventry: Chartered Institute of Housing/Housing Studies Association, pp. 97–124.

Cooper, C. (2002) *Understanding School Exclusion: Challenging Processes of Docility*, Nottingham: Education Now Books.

Cooper, C. (2004) 'Surviving the British School System: A Toolbox for Change', in R.Meighan (ed.) *Damage Limitation: Trying to Reduce the Harm Schools do to Children*, Nottingham: Educational Heretics Press, pp. 14–22.

Cooper, C. (2005) 'Places, "Folk Devils" and Social Policy', in P. Somerville and N. Sprigings (eds) *Housing and Social Policy: Contemporary Themes and Critical Perspectives*, pp. 69–102.

Cooper, C. (2006) 'Community Involvement in Community Safety – But Whose "Community"? and Whose "Safety"?' in A. Dearling, T. Newburn and P. Somerville (eds) *Supporting Safe Communities – Housing, Crime and Communities*, Coventry: Chartered Institute of Housing/Housing Studies Association, pp. 219–234.

Cooper, C. and Hawtin, M. (eds) (1997) *Housing, Community and Conflict: Understanding Resident 'Involvement'*, Aldershot: Arena.

Cooper, C. and Hawtin, M. (eds) (1998) *Resident Involvement and Community Action: Theory to Practice*, Coventry: Chartered Institute of Housing/Housing Studies Association.

Cooper, C. and Wyatt, S. (1997) 'The Pugilist's Guide to Tenant Participation: A "Sisyphean" Task or a Question of Tactics?', *Community Development Journal*, 32:1, January, pp. 96–99.

Cooper, K. (2007) 'Landlords Race to 100k', *Inside Housing*, 26 October, p. 1.

Corkey, D. and Craig, G. (1978) 'CDP: Community Work or Class Politics?', in P. Curno (ed.) *Political Issues and Community Work*, London: Routledge & Kegan Paul, pp. 36–66.

Corrie, C. and Corrie, C. (2005) 'Rachel Was Bulldozed to Death, but Her Words are a Spur to Action', *The Guardian*, 8 October, p. 28.

Corston, Baroness (2006) 'Reasonable Redress – Interview', *The Guardian*, 3 May, p. 5.

Craig, G. (1989) 'Community Work and the State', *Community Development Journal*, 24:1, pp. 3–18.

Craig, G., Dawson, A., Hutton, S., Roberts, N. and Wilkinson, M. (2004) *Local Impacts of International Migration: The Information Base*, Working Papers in Social Sciences and Policy, Hull: University of Hull.

Crawford, A. (2007) 'Crime Prevention and Community Safety', in M. Maguire, R. Morgan and R. Reiner (eds) *The Oxford Handbook of Criminology*, 4th Edition, Oxford: Oxford University Press, pp. 866–909.

Creed, G.W. (2006a) 'Community as Modern Pastoral', in G.W. Creed (ed.) *The Seductions of Community: Emancipation, Oppressions, Quandaries*, Santa Fe and Oxford: School of American Research Press and James Currey Ltd, pp. 23–48.

Creed, G.W. (2006b) 'Reconsidering Community', in G.W. Creed (ed.) *The Seductions of Community: Emancipation, Oppressions, Quandaries*, Santa Fe and Oxford: School of American Research Press and James Currey Ltd, pp. 3–22.

Crouch, C. (2004) *Post-democracy*, Cambridge: Polity.

Crow, G. and Allan, G. (1994) *Community Life: An introduction to Local Social Relations*, New York: Harvester Wheatsheaf.

Curtis, P. (2008a) 'Tuition Fees Favour the Rich – New Study', *The Guardian*, 14 February, p. 1.

Curtis, P. (2008b) 'To Have and Have Not', *Education Guardian*, 29 January, p. 5.

Curtis, P. and Cowan, R. (2006) 'Children's Groups Warn Punishment not a Panacea', *The Guardian*, 11 January, p. 7.

Daunton, M.J. (1987) *A Property-Owning Democracy? Housing in Britain*, London: Faber and Faber.

Delanty, G. (2005) *Community*, London: Routledge .

Democracy Now! (2005) 'Before London Bombing, Leaked UK Memo Warned Iraq War a Key Cause for Growth of "Extremism" in Britain', 13 July, at: http://www.democracynow.org/article.pl?sid=05/07/13/1357230 [accessed 11/11/05].

(DfCLG) Department for Communities and Local Government (2008) *Unlocking the Talent of our Communities*, London: DfCLG.

Dillon, R.S. (2007) 'Respect', entry in *Stanford Encyclopedia of Philosophy*, http://plato.stanford.edu/entries/respect/ [accessed 11/01/07].

Dodd, V. and Travis, A. (2005) 'Muslims Face Increased Stop and Search', *The Guardian*, 2 March, p. 1.

Dominelli, L. (1995) 'Women in the Community: Feminist Principles and Organizing in Community Work', *Community Development Journal*, 30(2), pp. 133–143.

Dominelli, L. (2006) *Women and Community Action*, 2nd Edition, Bristol: Policy Press.

Donnison, D. (1982) *The Politics of Poverty*, Oxford: Martin Robertson.

Doward, J. (2004) 'Charles Reaches Out to a "Lost Generation" of Aimless Youth', *The Observer*, 29 February, p. 13.

Downes, D. and Hansen, K. (2006) 'Welfare and Punishment: The Relationship between Welfare Spending and Imprisonment', *Crime and Society Foundation Briefing 2*, November.

Doyal, L. and Gough, I. (1991) *A Theory of Human Need*, Basingstoke: Macmillan.

Durkheim, E. (1933/1893) *The Division of Labour in Society*, New York: Macmillan.

Durkheim, E. (1952/1897) *Suicide: A Study in Sociology*, London: Routledge.

Durkheim, E. (1976/1915) *The Elementary Forms of the Religious Life*, London: George Allen & Unwin.

Eagleton, T. (2007) 'Those in Power are Right to See Multiculturalism as a Threat', *The Guardian*, 21 February, p. 32.

Edwards, D. and Cromwell, D. (2006) *Guardians of Power: The Myth of the Liberal Media*, London: Pluto Press.

Engels, F. (1987) *The Condition of the Working Class in England*, London: Penguin.

Esping-Andersen, G. (1990) *The Three Worlds of Welfare Capitalism*, Cambridge: Polity Press.

Fanshawe, S. (2007) 'Risky Business', *Society Guardian*, 1 August, p. 2.

Fernandez, C. (2006) 'Tesco Condemned for Selling Pole Dancing Toy', *Daily Mail*, 25 October, at: http://www.dailymail.co.uk/pages/live/articles/news/news.html?in_article_id=412195&in_page_id=1770 [accessed 10/01/2007].

Foley, P. and Martin, S. (2000) 'A New Deal for the Community? Public Participation in Regeneration and Local Service Delivery', *Policy & Politics*, 28(4), pp. 479–491.

Foord, M. and Young, F. (2006) 'Housing Managers Are from Mars, Social Workers Are from Venus: Anti-social Behaviour, "Respect" and Inter Professional Working – Reconciling the Irreconcilable?', in A. Dearling, T. Newburn and P. Somerville (eds) *Supporting Safer Communities: Housing, Crime and Neighbourhoods*, Coventry: Chartered Institute of Housing/ Housing Studies Association, pp. 169–184.

Foot, M. (2005) 'A Triumph of Hearsay and Hysteria', *The Guardian*, 5 April, p. 20.

Foucault, M. (1976) *Discipline and Punish*, London: Allen Lane.

Foucault, M. (1979) *The History of Sexuality, Vol. 1, An Introduction*, London: Allen Lane.

Foucault, M. (1988) 'Technologies of the Self', in L. Martin (ed.) *Technologies of the Self*, London: Tavistock, pp. 15–44.

Foucault, M. (2005) *The Archaeology of Knowledge*, London: Routledge.

France, A. (2007) *Understanding Youth in Late Modernity*, Maidenhead: Open University Press.

Freedland, J. (2006) 'If This Onslaught was about Jews, I Would be Looking for My Passport', *The Guardian*, 18 October, p. 31.

Freire, P. (1996) *Pedagogy of the Oppressed*, London: Penguin Books.

Freud, S. (1919) *Totem and Taboo: Resemblances between the Psychic Lives of Savages and Neurotics*, London: Routledge.

Garner, R. (2007) 'White Working-class Boys are the Worst Performers in School', *The Independent*, 22 June, p. 26.

Giddens, A. (2006) *Sociology*, 5th Edition, Cambridge: Polity Press.

Giles, H. (2002) 'The Battle of Orgreave, 18 June 1984', at: http://www.historicalfilmservices.com/orgreave_account.htm [accessed12/01/07].

Gilling, D. (1999) 'Community Safety: A Critique', in M. Brogden (ed.) *The British Criminology Conferences: Selected Proceedings*, Vol.2, available at: http://www.britsoccrim.org/bccsp/vol02/07GILLLHTM [accessed15/06/06].

Gilling, D. (2005) 'Partnership and Crime Prevention', in N. Tilley (ed.) *Handbook of Crime Prevention and Community Safety*, Cullompton: Willan Publishing, pp. 734–756.

Giroux, H.A. (2000) *Stealing Innocence: Youth, Corporate Power, and the Politics of Culture*, New York: St. Martin's Press.

Glass, R.D. (2001) 'On Paulo Freire's Philosophy of Praxis and the Foundations of Liberation Education', *Educational Researcher*, 30(2), pp. 15–25.

Goffman, E. (1963) *Stigma*, Englewood Cliffs, NJ: Prentice-Hall.

Goffman, E. (1968) *Asylums*, Harmondsworth: Pelican.

Goldblatt, D. (2006) *The Ball is Round: A Global History of Football*, London: Penguin.

Goodwin, N. (2005) 'The Making of the "Operation Solstice" Film', in A. Worthington (ed.) *The Battle of the Beanfield*, Teignmouth: Enabler Publications, pp. 166–180.

Gordeon, C. (1980) (ed.) *Power/Knowledge – Selected Interviews and Other Writings*, Brighton: Harvester Press.

Gordon, D. (2004) 'Poverty, Death and Disease', in P. Hillyard, C. Pantazis, S. Tombs and D. Gordon (eds) *Beyond Criminology: Taking Harms Seriously*, London: Pluto Press, pp. 251–266.

Gott, R. (2005) 'The Prime Minister is a War Criminal', *The Guardian*, 26 April, p. 25.

Gould, C.C. (1990) *Rethinking Democracy: Freedom and Social Co-operation in Politics, Economy and Society*, Cambridge: Cambridge University Press.

Graham, P. and Clarke, J. (2002) 'Dangerous Places: Crime and the City', in J. Muncie and E. McLaughlin (eds) *The Problem of Crime*, 2nd Edition, London: Sage, pp. 151–190.

Gramsci, A. (1971) *Selections from the Prison Notebooks*, trans. & ed. by Q. Hoare and G. Nowell Smith, New York: International Publishers.

Grass, G. (2005) 'The High Price of Freedom', *The Guardian Review*, 7 May, pp. 4–5.

Grayson, J. (1997) 'Campaigning Tenants: A Pre-history of Tenant Involvement to 1979', in C. Cooper and M. Hawtin (eds) *Housing, Community and Conflict: Understanding Resident 'Involvement'*, Aldershot: Arena, pp. 15–65.

Gregory, F. and Wilkinson, P. (2005) 'Riding Pillion for Tackling Terrorism is a High-risk Policy', in C. Browning (ed.), *Security, Terrorism and the UK*, ISP/NSC Briefing Paper 05/01, London: Chatham House/Economic & Social Research Council, pp. 2–4.

Guardian Unlimited (2007) 'Exam-factory Schools Prompt Crime', 1 May, at: http://www.guardian.co.uk/uklatest/story/0,,-6599997,00.html [accessed 8/5/07].

Habermas, J. (1981) *Theory of Communicative Action*, Vol. 1, Cambridge: Polity Press.

Hall, S. (2007) 'Living with Difference', *Soundings*, 37, Winter, pp. 148–158.

Hamnett, C., McDowell, L. and Sarre, P. (eds) (1989) *The Changing Social Structure*, London: Sage.

Hardt, M. and Negri, A. (2005) *Multitude: War and Democracy in the Age of Empire*, London: Penguin Books.

Harloe, M. (1995) *The People's Home? Social Rented Housing in Europe & America*, Oxford: Blackwell.

Hasan, R. (2000) 'Riots and Urban Unrest in Britain in the 1980s and 1990s – A Critique of Dominant Explanations', in M. Lavalette and G. Mooney (eds) *Class Struggle and Social Welfare*, London: Routledge, pp. 173–198.

Haydon, D. and Scraton, P. (2000) ' "Condemn a Little More, Understand a Little Less": The Political Context and Rights' Implications of the Domestic and Euopean Rulings in the Venables-Thompson Case', *Journal of Law & Society*, 27(3), pp. 416–448.

Hayek, F. (1944) *The Road to Serfdom*, London: Routledge & Kegan Paul.

Hilditch, M. (2007) 'No End to Salary Surge', *Inside Housing*, 21 September, p. 1.

Hill, D. (2003) '69% of 3-year-olds Know This 🐴 Symbol. Half of 4-year-olds Don't Know Their Own Name. Should We Worry?', *G2 – The Guardian*, 11 November, pp. 2–4.

Hillary, G.A. (1955) 'Definitions of Community: Areas of Agreement', *Rural Sociology*, 20, pp. 86–118.

Hills, J. (1998) *Income and Wealth: The Latest Evidence*, York: Joseph Rowntree Foundation.

Hillyard, P. and Tombs, S. (2004) 'Beyond Criminology', in P. Hillyard, C. Pantazis, S. Tombs and D. Gordon (eds) *Beyond Criminology: Taking Harms Seriously*, London: Pluto Press, pp. 10–29.

Hoffman, J. (2004) *Citizenship beyond the State*, London: Sage.

Hoffman, J. (2007) 'Antonio Gramsci', in J. Scott (ed.) *Fifty Key Sociologists – The Formative Theorists*, Abingdon: Routledge, pp. 54–58.

Home Office (2001a) *Building Cohesive Communities: A Report of the Ministerial Group on Public Order and Community Cohesion Chaired by John Denham*, London: Home Office.

Home Office (2001b) *Community Cohesion: A Report of the Independent Review Team Chaired by Ted Cantle*, London: Home Office.

Home Office (2007) *Anti-social Behaviour Orders – Statistics*, at: http://www.crimereduction.gov.uk/asbos/asbos2.htm [accessed 13/09/07].

Hughes, G. (2007) *The Politics of Crime and Community*, Basingstoke: Palgrave Macmillan.

Hughes, G. and Edwards, A. (2005) 'Crime Prevention in Context', in N. Tilley (ed.) *Handbook of Crime Prevention and Community Safety*, Cullompton: Willan Publishing, pp. 14–34.

(HRW) Human Rights Watch (2005), 'Briefing on the Terrorism Bill 2005', at: http://hrw.org/backgrounder/eca/uk1105/index.htm, [accessed 11/11/05].

Illich, I. (1977) *Limits to Medicine. Medical Nemesis: The Expropriation of Health*, London: Marion Boyars.

Imrie, R. and Raco, M. (2003) 'Community and the Changing Nature of Urban Policy', in R. Imrie and M. Raco (eds) *Urban Renaissance? New Labour, Community and Urban Policy*, Bristol: Policy Press, pp. 3–36.

Inman, P. and Balkrishnan, A. (2007) 'Crisis of Confidence Could Engulf Banking Sector after Northern Rock's Emergency Loan', *The Guardian*, 14 September, p. 31.

(IRR) Institute of Race Relations (2005) 'The Anti-Muslim Backlash Begins', 14 July, *IRR News Team*, at: http://www.irr.org.uk/2005/july/ak000008.html [accessed 12/08/05].

James, O. (2006) 'Workaholic Consumerism is Now a Treadmill and a Curse', *The Guardian*, 2 May, p. 28.

James, O. (2007) 'Infected by Affluenza', *The Guardian*, 24 January, p. 30.

Jeffs, T. and Smith, M.K. (1996) '"Getting the Dirtbags Off the Streets" – Curfews and Other Solutions to Juvenile Crime', *Youth and Policy*, 52, pp. 1–14.

Johnson, A. (2007) '200 Failed by the System: The Suicide Victims Who Shame Britain', *The Independent on Sunday*, 12 August, pp. 8–9.

(JISC) Joint Intelligence and Security Committee (2003) *Iraqi Weapons of Mass Destruction – Intelligence and Assessment*, London: The Stationary Office.

Jones, C., Ferguson, I., Lavalette, M. and Penketh, L. (2006) 'Forward Thinking', *Society Guardian*, 22 March, p. 3.

Jones, C. and Novak, C. (2000) 'Class Struggle, Self-help and Popular Welfare', in M. Lavalette and G. Mooney (eds) *Class Struggle and Social Welfare*, London: Routledge, pp. 34–51.

Jordan, B. (2005) 'New Labour: Choice and Values', *Critical Social Policy*, 25(4), pp. 427–446.

Jordan, B. (2006) *Social Policy for the Twenty-First Century: New Perspectives, Big Issues*, Cambridge: Polity Press.

Kant, I. (1785/1964), *Grundlegung zur Metaphysik der Sitten*, trans. by H.J. Paton, New York: Harper and Row.

Kearns, A. (2003) 'Social Capital, Regeneration and Urban Policy', in R. Imrie and M. Raco (eds) *Urban Renaissance? New Labour, Community and Urban Policy*, Bristol: Policy Press, pp. 37–60.

Kellner, D. (1991) 'Introduction to the Second Edition', in H. Marcuse, *One-Dimensional Man*, 2nd Edition, London: Routledge, pp. xi–xxxviii.

Kelly, A. (2004) 'Parent Trap', *Society Guardian*, 8 September, pp. 2–3.

Kelly, A. (2008) 'Interview: Andy Benson', *Society Guardian*, 19 March, p. 5.

Kennedy, M. (2006) 'How Does the £85 Sandwich Taste? In a Word: Rich', *The Guardian*, International edition, 11 April, p. 15.

Kettle, M. (2005) 'Society is Disintegrating, and Single-issue Politics is Back', *The Guardian*, 19 April, p. 22.

Kingsnorth, P. (2004) *One No, Many Yeses: A Journey to the Heart of the Global Resistance Movement*, London: The Free Press.

Klein, N. (2007) *The Shock Doctrine: The Rise of Disaster Capitalism*, London: Allen Lane.

Klein, R. (2005) 'Transforming the NHS: The Story in 2004', in M. Powell, L. Bauld and K. Clarke (eds) *Social Policy Review 17: Analysis and Debate in Social Policy, 2005*, Bristol: The Policy Press, pp. 51–68.

Kumar, M. S. (2003) 'Urbanization', in K. Christensen and D. Levinson (eds) *Encyclopedia of Community: From the Village to the Virtual World*, Vol. 4, London: Sage, pp. 1433–1437.

Kundnani, A. (2002) 'The Death of Multiculturalism', Institute of Race Relations online resources, www.irr.org.uk/cantle/ [accessed 08/10/02].

Laclau, E. and Mouffe, C. (2001) *Hegemony and Socialist Strategy: Towards a Radical Democratic Politics*, 2nd Edition, London: Verso.

Laing, R.D. (1960) *A Divided Self: An Existential Study in Sanity and Madness*, Harmondsworth: Penguin.

Lansley, S., Goss, S. and Wolmar, C. (1989) *Councils in Conflict: The Rise and Fall of the Municipal Left*, Basingstoke: Macmillan.

Laurance, J. (2006) 'Abused. Bullied. Confined. Drugged: The Scandal of How Britain Cares for its Most Vulnerable People – the Mentally Disabled', *The Independent*, 5 July, pp. 1–2.

Lea, J. (2002) *Crime and Modernity*, London: Sage.

Ledwith, M. (2005) *Community Development: A Critical Approach*, Bristol: Policy Press.

Levitas, R. (2005) *The Inclusive Society? Social Exclusion and New Labour*, 2nd Edition, Basingstoke: Palgrave.

(LCC) Lincolnshire County Council (2008) *Children and Young People Plan 2007–2010 – 1st Review June 2008*, Lincoln: LCC.

Lister, R. (1997) 'Citizenship: Towards a Feminist Synthesis', *Feminist Review*, 57, Autumn, pp. 28–48.

Little, A. (2002) 'Community and Radical Democracy', *Journal of Political Ideologies*, 7(3), pp. 369–382.

Logan, C. (2005) *Risk Assessment and Management in Sexual and Violent Offending: Final Report*, July, Liverpool: Liverpool University.

Lombroso, C. (1968) *Crime: Its Causes and Remedies*, Montclair: Patterson Smith.

Löwith, K. (1982) *Max Weber and Karl Marx*, London: George Allen & Unwin.

Lucas, C. (2005) 'Unearthly Silence', *The Guardian*, 2 May, p. 16.

Luhmann, N. (1995) *Social Systems*, trans. by J. Bednarz and D. Baecker, Palo Alto, CA: Stanford University Press.

MacLeod, D. and Curtis, P. (2005) 'Whose Line is it Anyway?', *Education Guardian*, 4 October, p. 12.

Malpass, P. (2000) *Housing Associations and Housing Policy: A Historical Perspective*, Basingstoke: Macmillan.

Malpass, P. (2005) *Housing and the Welfare State: The Development of Housing Policy in Britain*, Basingstoke: Palgrave.

Marcuse, H. (1991) *One-Dimensional Man*, 2nd Edition, London: Routledge.

Marshall, T.H. (1950) *Citizenship and Social Class*, Cambridge: Cambridge University Press.

Marx, K. (1844) 'Introduction to A Contribution to the Critique of Hegel's Philosophy of Right', in *Deutsch-Französische Jahrbücher*, February, at: http://www.marxists.org/archive/marx/works/1843/critique-hpr/intro.htm [accessed10/01/08].

Marx, K. (1976) *Capital: Volume 1: A Critique of Political Economy*, Harmondsworth: Penguin.

May, T. (2001) *Social Research: Issues, Methods and Process*, 3rd Edition, Buckingham: Open University Press.

Mayhew, H. (1861/1967) *London Labour and the London Poor: A Cyclopaedia of the Condition and Earnings of Those That Will Work, Those That Cannot Work, and Those That Will Not Work*, New York: A.M. Kelley.

McGhee, D. (2005) *Intolerant Britain? Hate, Citizenship and Difference*, Maidenhead: Open University Press.

Meikle, J. (2005) 'Lack of Care Costs Stroke Victims' Lives', *The Guardian*, 15 March, p. 8.

Miller, D. (2004) 'Introduction', in D. Miller (ed.) *Tell Me Lies: Propaganda and Media Distortion in the Attack on Iraq*, London: Pluto Press, pp. 1–11.

Mitchell, A. (2005) 'Sold for the Sake of it', *The Guardian*, 15 March, p. 23.

Modood, T. (2007) *Multiculturalism*, Cambridge: Polity.

Monbiot, G. (2003) *The Age of Consent: A Manifesto for a New World Order*, London: Flamingo.

Monbiot, G. (2004) 'Extreme Measures', *The Guardian*, 2 March, p. 23.

Monbiot, G. (2005a) 'Protest is Criminalised and the Huffers and Puffers Say Nothing', *The Guardian*, 4 October, p. 27.

Monbiot, G. (2005b) 'Behind the Phosphorus Clouds are War Crimes within War Crimes', *The Guardian*, 22 November, p. 31.

Monbiot, G. (2006) 'Routine and Systematic Torture Is at the Heart of America's War on Terror', *The Guardian*, 12 December, p. 27.

Monbiot, G. (2007) 'London is Getting into the Olympic Spirit – by Kicking Out the Gypsies', *The Guardian*, 12 June, p. 31.

Monbiot, G. (2008) 'How Britain became Party to a Crime That May Have Killed a Million People', *The Guardian*, 1 January, p. 24.

Morgan, R. and Newburn, T. (2007) 'Youth Justice', in M. Maguire, R. Morgan and R. Reiner (eds) *The Oxford Handbook of Criminology*, 4th Edition, Oxford: Oxford University Press, pp. 1024–1060.

Morley, D. and Chen, K-H. (1996) *Stuart Hall: Critical Dialogues in Cultural Studies*, New York: Routledge.

Morris, N. and Brown, J. (2006), 'Helen and Sylvia, the New Face of Terrorism', *The Independent*, 6 April, pp. 1–2.

Morrison, W. (2006) *Criminology, Civilisation and the New World Order*, Abingdon: Routledge-Cavendish.

Muir, H. (2005) 'Anger as Equality Chief Questions Taboo on the Word "Coloured"', *The Guardian*, 5 October, p. 7.

Murie, A. (2007) 'Housing Policy, Housing Tenure and the Housing Market', in K. Clarke, T. Maltby and P. Kennett (eds) *Social Policy Review 19: Analysis and Debate in Social Policy, 2007*, Bristol: The Policy Press, pp. 49–65.

Murray, C. (1990) *The Emerging British Underclass*, London: Institute of Economic Affairs and Welfare Unit.

Murray, K. (2007) 'Battle Chargers', *Inside Housing*, 27 July, pp. 18–20.

Myers, J.C. (2004) 'Marx v. Weber: Uno Mas!' in M.S. Prelinger and J. Schalit (eds) *Collective Action: A Bad Subjects Anthology*, London: Pluto Press, pp. 78–83.

Newman, J. and Mahony, N. (2007) 'Democracy and the Public Realm: Towards a Progressive Agenda?', *Soundings*, 36, Summer, pp. 56–66.

Newman, M. (2008) 'Nottingham Scholar Held for 6 Days under Anti-terror Law', *Times Higher Education*, 29 May–4 June, p. 16.

Norton-Taylor, R., Dodd, V. and Muir, H. (2005) 'Ministers Warned of Iraq Link to UK terror', *The Guardian*, 20 July, p. 8.

Offer, A. (2006) *The Challenge of Affluence: Self-Control and Well-Being in the United States and Britain since 1950*, Oxford: Oxford University Press.

Orum, A.M. (2003) 'Industrial Revolution', in K. Christensen and D. Levinson (eds) *Encyclopedia of Community: From the Village to the Virtual World*, Vol. 2, London: Sage, pp. 651–653.

Parkin, F. (1992) *Durkheim*, Oxford: Oxford University Press.

Peckham, S. (2007) 'One, or Four? The National Health Service in 2006', in K. Clarke, T. Maltby and P. Kennett (eds) *Social Policy Review 19: Analysis and Debate in Social Policy, 2007*, Bristol: The Policy Press, pp. 33–48.

Pemberton, S. (2004) 'A Theory of Moral Indifference: Understanding the Production of Harm by Capitalist Society', in P. Hillyard, C. Pantazis, S. Tombs and D. Gordon (eds) *Beyond Criminology: Taking Harms Seriously*, London: Pluto Press, pp. 67–83.

Pickering, M. (1993) *Auguste Comte: An Intellectual Biography*, Vol. 1, Cambridge: Cambridge University Press.

Pierson, J. and Worley, C. (2005) 'Housing and Urban Regeneration Policy: Citizen and Community under New Labour', in P. Somerville and N. Sprigings (eds) *Housing and Social Policy: Contemporary Themes and Critical Perspectives*, Abingdon: Routledge, pp. 217–241.

Pilger, J. (2004a) 'The Case for Civil Disobedience', in D. Miller (ed.) *Tell me Lies: Propaganda and Media Distortion in the Attack on Iraq*, London: Pluto Press, pp. 23–28.

Pilger, J. (2004b) 'Crime Against Humanity', in D. Miller (ed.) *Tell Me Lies: Propaganda and Media Distortion in the Attack on Iraq*, London: Pluto Press, pp. 29–33.

Pinter, H. (2005) 'Pinter v the US', *g2 The Guardian*, 8 December, pp. 9–13.

Pope, W. (1998) 'Emile Durkheim', in R. Stones (ed.) *Key Sociological Thinkers*, Basingstoke: Macmillan, pp. 46–58.

Popkewitz, T.S. and Brennan, M. (eds) (1998) *Foucault's Challenge: Discourse, Knowledge, and Power in Education*, New York & London: Teachers College Press.

Popple, K. (1995) *Analysing Community Work: Its Theory and Practice*, Buckingham: Open University Press.

Porter, H. (2006) 'Only a Constitution Can Save Us from This Abuse of Power', *The Observer*, 2 April, p. 23.

Price, J. (1983) 'A Piece of Patchwork?', *City Limits*, 102, 16–22 September, p. 21.

Prior, D. (2005) 'Civil Renewal and Community Safety: Virtuous Policy Spiral or Dynamic of Exclusion', *Social Policy & Society*, 4(4), pp. 357–367.

Purdy, D. (2007) 'Citizen's Income: Sowing the Seeds of Change', *Soundings*, 35, Spring, pp. 54–65.

Putnam, R. (1999) *Bowling Alone*, New York: Simon and Schuster.

Pyke, N. and Dillon, J. (2001) 'Stop Jailing Your Asylum Seekers, UN tells Britain', *The Independent on Sunday (European Edition)*, 12 August, p. 1.

Race in Britain Special Edition (2001) 'Inside Our Changing Land', *The Observer*, p. 1.

Rawls, J. (1971) *A Theory of Justice*, Cambridge, MA: Harvard University Press.

Reiner, R. (2007) 'Political Economy, Crime, and Criminal Justice', in M. Maguire, R. Morgan and R. Reiner (eds) *The Oxford Handbook of Criminology*, 4th Edition, Oxford: Oxford University Press, pp. 341–380.

Respect Task Force (2006) *Respect Action Plan*, London: Home Office.

Revill, J. (2005) '£184m a Day, 7m Operations a Year. But Is the NHS Good Value?', *The Observer*, 6 March, pp. 8–9.

Revill, J. and Hinsliff, G. (2005) 'Top Hospital Forced to Turn Away Ill Children', *The Observer*, 6 March, p. 1.

Ridge, T. (2003) *Childhood Poverty and Social Exclusion: From a Child's Perspective*, Bristol: The Policy Press.

Robb, M. (2007) 'Gender', in M.J. Kehily (ed.) *Understanding Youth*, London: Sage, pp. 109–145.

Robinson, L. (2004) 'Black Adolescent Identity', in J. Roche, S. Tucker, R. Thomson and R. Flynn (eds) *Youth in Society*, 2nd Edition, London: Sage, pp. 153–159.

Robson, T. (2000) *The State and Community Action*, London: Pluto Press.

Rock, P. (2007) 'Sociological Theories of Crime', in M. Maguire, R. Morgan and R. Reiner (eds) *The Oxford Handbook of Criminology*, 4th Edition, Oxford: Oxford University Press, pp. 3–42.

Rodger, J.J. (2006) 'Antisocial Families and Withholding Welfare Support', *Critical Social Policy*, 26(1), pp. 121–143.

Rogers, E. (2008) 'Associations Cash It in', *Inside Housing*, 29 February, p. 1.

Rowe, M. and Devanney, C. (2003) 'Partnership and the Governance of Regeneration', *Critical Social Policy*, 23(3), pp. 375–397.

Ruane, S. (2005) 'The Future of Healthcare in the UK: Think-tanks and Their Policy Prescriptions', in M. Powell, L. Bauld and K. Clarke (eds) *Social Policy Review 17: Analysis and Debate in Social Policy, 2005*, Bristol: Policy Press, pp. 147–166.

Rustin, M. (2007) 'What's Wrong with Happiness?', *Soundings*, 36, Summer, pp. 56–66.

Rustin, M. and Chamberlayne, P. (2002) 'Introduction: From Biography to Social Policy', in P. Chamberlayne, M. Rustin and T. Wengraf (eds), *Biography and Social Exclusion in Europe: Experiences and Life Journeys*, Bristol: Policy Press, pp. 1–21.

Rutherford, J. (2007a) 'New Labour, the Market, and the End of Welfare', *Soundings*, 36, Summer, pp. 40–54.

Rutherford, J. (2007b) *After Identity*, London: Lawrence and Wishart.

Sales, R. (2002) 'The Deserving and the Undeserving? Refugees, Asylum Seekers and Welfare in Britain', *Critical Social Policy*, 22(3), pp. 456–478.

Salman, S. (2007) 'Where do We Go from Here?', *Society Guardian: Caring Communities Supplement*, 4 July, p. 1.

Shah, H. and Rutherford, J. (2006) 'This Vision of a Good Society Can Lift the Nation Out of Social Recession', *The Guardian*, 20 September, p. 28.

Shaw, M. and Martin, I. (2000) 'Community Work, Citizenship and Democracy: Re-making the Connections', *Community Development Journal*, 35(4), pp. 401–413.

Shelter (2005) *Homelessness Statistics: Shelter Response*, 12 December, at: http://england.shelter.org.uk/home/home-624.cfm/pressreleaselisting/1/pressrelease/191 [accessed 5/02/2007].

Shepherd, J. (2007) 'Aim, Shoot... Miss Again', *Education Guardian*, 12 June, p. 1.

Shepherd, J. (2008) 'Park Life', *Education Guardian*, 19 February, p. 3.

Simms, A. (2007) *Tescopoly: How One Shop Came Out on Top and Why it Matters*, London: Constable.

Smart, B. (2003) *Economy, Culture and Society: A Sociological Critique of Neo-liberalism*, Buckingham: Open University Press.

Smith, M.K. (2001) *Richard Henry Tawney, Fellowship and Adult Education*, at: infed encyclopaedia, [accessed 12/12/2005].

Smith, M.K. (2005) 'Youth Matters – The Green Paper for Youth 2005', at: www.infed.org/youthwork/green_paper.htm [accessed 22/2/2008].

Smithers, R. (2005) '175,000-strong Hidden Army of School-age Carers', *The Guardian*, 13 April, p. 13.

(SEU) Social Exclusion Unit (2000) *National Strategy for Neighbourhood Renewal: A Framework for Consultation*, London: The Stationery Office.

(SEU) Social Exclusion Unit (2001) *A New Commitment to Neighbourhood Renewal: National Strategy Action Plan*, London: The Stationery Office.

Solomos, J. (2003) *Race and Racism in Britain*, 3rd Edition, Basingstoke: Palgrave Macmillan.

Squires, P. (2006a) (ed.) *Community Safety: Critical Perspectives on Policy and Practice*, Bristol: Policy Press.

Squires, P. (2006b) 'New Labour and the Politics of Antisocial Behaviour', *Critical Social Policy*, 26(1), pp. 144–168.

Squires, P. and Stephen, D.E. (2005) 'Rethinking ASBOs', *Critical Social Policy*, 25(4), pp. 517–528.

Stacey, M. (1974) 'The Myth of Community Studies', in Bell, C. and Newby, H. (eds) *The Sociology of Community – A Selection of Readings*, London: Frank Cass, pp. 13–26.

Steele, J. (2007) 'Children Hardest Hit by Humanitarian Crisis in Iraq', *The Guardian*, 31 July, p. 16.

Stewart, A. (2001) *Theories of Power and Domination: The Politics of Empowerment in Late Modernity*, London: Sage.

Stewart, H. (2005) 'Class Divisions Bar Students from University', *The Observer*, 16 January, p. 7.

Stewart, J.H. (1951) (ed.) *A Documentary Survey of the French Revolution*, New York: Macmillan, cited in S. Kreis, 'The History Guide', at: http://www.historyguide.org/intellect/cahiers.html [accessed 21/03/07].

Stoker, G. (1991) *The Politics of Local Government*, 2nd Edition, Basingstoke: Macmillan.

Taylor, M. (2003) *Public Policy in the Community*, Basingstoke: Palgrave Macmillan.

Taylor, M. (2006) 'Failed Asylum Seekers Forced to Sleep Rough, Says Report', *The Guardian*, 7 November, p. 8.

Teather, D., Seager, A., Allen, K. and McCurry, J. (2007) 'Central Banks Pour in Billions – but Global Slide Continues', *The Guardian*, 11 August, p. 38.

Temko, N. and Doward, J. (2006) 'War on Youth Crime is "Demonising Teens"', *The Observer*, 20 August, p. 4.

The National Archives (2007) 'Spotlights on History Website: Demobilisation in Britain, 1918–20', at: http://www.nationalarchives.gov.uk [accessed 17/06/07].

The New York Times (2003) 'J.P. Morgan Selected to Run New Trade Bank in Iraq', 30 August, at: http://query.nytimes.com/gst/fullpage.html?res= 9A04E0DA1638F933A0575BC0A9659C8B63 [accessed 14/01/08].

The Primary Review (2007) *Community Soundings: The Primary Review Regional Witness Sessions*, Cambridge: University of Cambridge.

Thompson, E.P. (1991/1963) *The Making of the English Working Class*, London: Penguin.

Thoreau, H. (1849) 'Resistance to Civil Government', The Thoreau Reader Website [accessed 12/12/2005].

Tilley, N. (2005) 'Introduction: Thinking Realistically about Crime Prevention', in N. Tilley (ed.) *Handbook of Crime Prevention and Community Safety*, Cullompton: Willan Publishing, pp. 3–13.

Tombs, S. and Hillyard, P. (2004) 'Towards a Political Economy of Harm: States, Corporations and the Production of Inequality', in P. Hillyard, C. Pantazis, S. Tombs and D. Gordon (eds) *Beyond Criminology: Taking Harms Seriously*, London: Pluto Press, pp. 30–54.

Tomlinson, S. (2001) *Education in a Post-welfare Society*, Buckingham: Open University Press.

Tönnies, F. (1955/1887) *Community and Association*, London: Routledge & Kegan Paul.

Townsend, M. (2006) 'Official: Iraq War Led to July Bombings', *The Observer*, 2 April, pp. 1–2.

Townsend, P. (1962) 'The Meaning of Poverty', *British Journal of Sociology*, 13(3), pp. 210–227.

Townsend, P., Davidson, N. and Whitehead, M. (1992) *Inequalities in Health: The Black Report and the Health Divide*, Harmondsworth: Penguin.

Travis, A. (2005a) 'Community Relations Hit by Terror Laws, Say MPs', *The Guardian*, 6 April, p. 12.

Travis, A. (2005b) 'Testing Passport to UK Citizenship', *The Guardian*, 1 November, p. 3.

Travis, A. (2006) 'Blair Spells Out His Masterplan for a Safer, Fairer Society', *The Guardian*, 11 January, p. 6.

Trombley, S. (1988) 'Sterilization and Informed Consent: The 1960s', *Women of Colour Website*, at: http://www.hsph.harvard.edu/Organizations/healthnet/ WoC/reproductive/trombley.html [accessed20/05/05].

(Unicef) The United Nations International Children's Emergency Fund (2007) *Child Poverty in Perspective: An Overview of Child Well-being in Rich Countries*, Florence: Unicef.

Verkaik, R. (2007) 'MPs Condemn Asylum System as "Inhumane"', *The Independent*, 30 March, p. 26.

Verkaik, R. and Grice, A. (2004) 'Day 1: Resignation, Day 2: Humiliation', *The Independent*, 17 December, pp. 1–2.

Vidal, J. and Pidd, H. (2007) 'Police to Use Terror Laws on Heathrow Climate Protestors', *The Guardian*, 11 August, p. 1.

Vulliamy, E. (2007) 'Blood and Glory', *Observer Magazine*, 4 March, pp. 20–31.

Wainwright, M. (2005) 'Police Accused of Manslaughter after Dumping Addict at Roadside', *The Guardian*, 8 April, p. 11.

Walter, A. (2004) 'Let us Decide', *The Guardian*, 29 June, p. 20.

Ward, L. (2005a) '"Child-unfriendly" England Served Notice', *The Guardian*, 2 March, p. 7.

Ward, L. (2005b) 'Designer Clothes, Five Properties – and £20,000 Debt', *The Guardian*, 5 April, p. 5.

Wazir, B. (2001) 'Hate Dies Hard in Oldham', Race in Britain Special Edition, *The Observer*, p. 4.

White, M. (2007) 'Straw Backs Black Mentors for Youths', *The Guardian*, 21 August, p. 12.

Whyte, D. (2004) 'All That Glitters Isn't Gold: Environmental Crimes and the Production of Local Criminological Knowledge', *Crime Prevention and Community Safety: An International Journal*, 6(1), pp. 55–63.

Wilkinson, R.G. (2005) *The Impact of Inequality: How to Make Sick Societies Healthier*, Abingdon: Routledge.

Williams, F. (1989) *Social Policy – A Critical Introduction*, Cambridge: Polity Press.

Williams, F. (1996) 'Racism and the Discipline of Social Policy: A Critique of Welfare Theory', in D. Taylor (ed.) *Critical Social Policy: A Reader*, London: Sage, pp. 48–76.

Williams, H. (2006) 'Britain's Ruling Elites Now Exercise Power with a Shameless Rapacity', *The Guardian*, 11 April, p. 23.

Williams, R. (1958) *Culture and Society*, London: Chatto and Windus.

Wintour, P. (2007) 'Voters to Get Direct Say on Local Spending', *The Guardian*, 5 July, p. 1.

Wintour, P. (2008a) 'I'll be President of Europe If You Give Me the Power – Blair', *The Guardian*, 2 February, p. 1.

Wintour, P. (2008b) '2.6m on Incapacity Benefits Face Tough "Back to Work" Tests', *The Guardian*, 14 March, p. 15.

Wintour, P. and Travis, A. (2007) 'Rules to Make Migrants Integrate', *The Guardian*, 5 June, p. 1.

Woodward, W. (2006) 'Radical Muslims Must Integrate, Says Blair', *Guardian Unlimited*, 9 December, at: www.guardian.co.uk/religion/Story/0,,1968074,00.html [accessed 15/12/06].

Woodward, W. (2008) 'The Smile That Says: I'm in the Money', *Guardian Unlimited*, 11 January, at: http://www.guardian.co.uk/guardianpolitics/story/0,,2238969,00.html [accessed 14/01/08].

Woolcock, M. (2003) 'Social Capital', in K. Christensen and D. Levinson (eds) *Encyclopedia of Community: From the Village to the Virtual World*, Vol. 4, London: Sage, pp. 1258–1262.

(WCML) Working Class Movement Library (2005), 'Community Development Projects 1969–1977', *WCML Website*, at: http://www.wcml.org.uk/group/cdp.htm [accessed29/04/05].

Worley, C. (2005) ' "It's Not about Race. It's about the Community": New Labour and "Community Cohesion" ', *Critical Social Policy*, 25(4), pp. 483–496.

Wright, E.O. (2007) 'Guidelines for Envisioning Real Utopias', *Soundings*, 36, Summer, pp. 26–39.

Young, M. and Wilmott, P. (1962) *Family and Kinship in East London*, Harmondsworth: Pelican.

Younge, G. (2005) 'Riots Are a Class Act – and Often They're the Only Alternative', *The Guardian*, 14 November, p. 31.

Index

Abdullah, D., 167–8
Abel-Smith, B., 51
Abu Ghraib, 209
Aliens Order 1905, 41
Aliens Order 1920, 42
Aliens Restriction (Amendment) Act 1919, 41
Aliens Restrictions Act 1914, 41
Amnesty International, 164
Andersen, N.Å., 224–7
Anti Nazi League, 69
anti-psychiatry movement, 14
anti-racism/anti-racist policies, 54, 67, 69, 84
anti-sexist policies, 67
'anti-social behaviour'/anti-social behaviour orders (asbos), 2–3, 5, 7, 19, 28, 98–9, 128, 133, 135–6, 140–1, 145, 148, 170–3, 175, 183–4, 212
    see also young people/youth, young people and asbos
Anti-social Behaviour Act 2003, 133
Anti-Terrorism, Crime and Security Act 2001, 167–8
asylum seekers, 134, 162–5, 171, 220

Basic Citizen's Income (BCI), 20
'Battle of the Beanfield', 65
    see also travellers
Bauman, Z., 19, 82, 89, 104, 116–17, 140, 173–4, 212–13
Beck, U., 214
Benson, A., 16
Black nationalists, 119
Blair, T., 12, 62, 96–7, 99–100, 106, 121, 127–8, 136, 147, 156, 160, 166–7, 181, 184, 189, 207, 209–11
Blears, H., 135, 138, 167, 184
Blunkett, D., 128, 152, 158
Booth, Charles, 38
Bourdieu, P., 113, 121, 214–15
Bowie, David, 69

Boyes, Sylvia, 211
Briggs, A., 40
British Crime Surveys, 68, 138
Broadwater Farm, 70
Brown, G., 2–3, 10, 18, 23, 121, 157, 181
Bulger, James, 181
Bunglawala, I., 167
Byrne, D., 12, 49, 60, 75–6, 79–81, 83, 93–4, 102–3, 142, 144, 171, 188, 199

cahiers de doléances, 233
Callaghan, James, 11, 60–1, 68
    Ruskin College Speech, 23, 188–9
Calouste Gulbenkian Foundation, 47, 51
Cameron, David, 3
Cantle review, report, 151, 155
Cathy Come Home (1966), 52
Catt, John, 211
CCTV, 74, 129, 145, 149, 184
Centre on Housing Rights and Evictions, 149
Chakrabarti, S., 211
Charity Organisation Society, 34, 139
Chartism, 40
    Chartist schools and reading rooms, 36
    Chartist tradition, 37
Chatham House, 210
Chicago School, 45
children
    child poverty, 63, 79, 187
    Children and Young People's strategic partnerships, 182
    Death of Childhood theories, 204
    in Iraq, 207, 209
    see also young people/youth
Chomsky, N., 9
'citizenship', 21, 73, 92–7, 103, 108, 116, 129, 152, 160–1, 164, 170, 200, 222
    citizenship test, 161

City Challenge, 75
Civil Contingencies Act 2004, 169
civil disturbances 2001: Burnley,
    Oldham and Bradford,
    127, 150
civil liberties, 99, 122–3, 133, 137,
    167–8, 210–11, 235
Clapton, Eric, 69
Clarke, J., 19, 34, 40, 45–6, 71, 76–8,
    82–3, 96–9, 229–30
Clash, The, 69
class, 17, 25, 30, 32, 36, 38, 44, 46, 49,
    55, 57, 63, 76–81, 84–5, 103, 107,
    120, 123, 148, 158, 180, 188–9,
    198, 219, 226, 234
  class and 'masculinities'/
      'femininities', 44, 180–1
  the divisive impact of the
      right-to-buy on working-class
      communities, 62, 191
  gentrification and the displacement
      of poor working-class people,
      144
  impact of industrialisation on
      social relationships, 31–4
  and inequality, 57, 63, 79–80, 148,
      188–9
  influence of working-class
      education systems on class
      consciousness in the
      nineteenth century, 36–7
  influence of Methodism on the
      working class, 34–5, 90
  as a source of conflict, 25, 38–9,
      46–8, 63, 65, 85, 103, 107,
      118–20, 123, 219
  the 'underclass', 27, 75–8, 84–5, 94,
      141, 163–4, 171, 182, 219
  working-class gains from the
      Keynesian welfare state, 49, 80,
      84, 93, 180, 191, 219
climate change, 8, 205–6
Clough, Brian, 69
Cohen, S.
  moral panics, 76
commodification of public services,
    174
Commonwealth Immigrants Act
    1962, 53

communitarian/-ism, 3, 25, 27–8, 88,
    94–8, 100–4, 106–7, 126–8, 140,
    144, 149, 162, 170–1, 216–18, 220,
    224, 229–30
community
  as agency, 2, 25, 29–30, 111, 230, 236
  definitions of/(re)defining, 3, 87,
      100, 117
  empowerment, 3, 75, 96, 106, 143,
      171
  gated, 81–2, 101, 145, 149, 185
  involvement/participation, 2–3, 17,
      75, 92–3, 95–6, 103–4, 108,
      128–30, 132, 143–4, 154, 171,
      174, 200, 217–18, 223–4, 230
  means/site of governance/
      managing social tensions, 3, 87,
      95–6, 107, 132, 171, 229
  moral communities, 89–90
  rural, 33, 91–2
  self-determination, 3, 115, 216
  sites for social action/resistance, 4,
      17, 25, 27, 29–30, 38, 58, 84,
      87–8, 103, 119, 123–5, 226, 229,
      236–7
  symbolic construction/
      representation of, 83, 101
  'world community', 105–6
community cohesion, 4–6, 10, 19, 21,
    88–9, 98, 102, 106
  see also New Labour, and
      community cohesion
Community Cohesion Task Force, 152
community development, 10, 18, 21,
    47, 49–51, 55, 58–9, 72, 92, 96,
    110, 113–14, 117, 140
Community Development Projects
    (CDPs), 48, 51, 54–9, 236
community safety, 2, 4–7, 10, 23, 25,
    28, 68, 73–5, 87, 99, 117, 175,
    206, 210, 212–13, 215, 225–7, 235
  see also New Labour, and
      community safety
community wellbeing, 12, 28, 76, 79,
    83, 87, 131, 138, 159, 170–2, 175,
    205, 217–23, 226, 228, 231–2,
    235–7
  see also social wellbeing; subjective
      wellbeing

community work/workers, 10, 45–8, 50–1, 56, 58–9, 66, 72, 95, 98, 227, 237
'in and against the state', 58, 230
conflict(s), 2–3, 10, 25–31, 33, 37–8, 40, 42, 45–6, 48–9, 52–3, 57–8, 60–1, 63, 68, 71, 83–8, 92–3, 97, 101–4, 106–8, 111, 116, 118–21, 125–6, 128, 131, 139, 145, 153–4, 158, 161, 171, 210, 213, 216, 219–20, 227, 230, 232, 235
  anti-globalisation protests/ protestors, 3, 123
  direct action/civil disobedience, 47, 123–4
  'militant non-violence', 123–5
  social activism, 29, 126
  struggles, 17, 29, 31, 39, 44, 55, 87, 107–8, 118–19, 123–5, 234
  is violent conflict legitimate?, 118–21
conscientisation, 112, 114, 116, 216
consumerism/consumer society, 6, 81, 102, 175, 199–206, 215–16
  'flawed consumer(s)', 82, 149
Corrie, Rachel, 124
Counter Terrorism Bill 2008, 167
crime and disorder, 128, 131–2, 134, 139, 145, 173, 212
  fear of, 127
  prevention/strategies, 2, 6, 130, 145
Crime and Disorder Act 1998, 130, 135, 183
Crime and Disorder Reduction Partnerships (CDRPs), 130, 132–4, 144–5
  Community Safety Partnerships (CSPs) in Wales, 130
  see also partnership(s)
Criminal Justice Act 1994, 7
Criminal Justice Act 2003, 7, 168
criminalisation of social policy, 78, 140
critical pedagogy, 110, 112, 114–16, 224
Crosland, A., 51
culture(s)/cultural, 3, 15–16, 20–1, 26, 28, 32, 44–6, 50, 67–8, 70–1, 82,

89–91, 94, 97, 104–5, 110, 115–18, 124–5, 136, 151–2, 154–63, 165, 170–1, 177–9, 182, 185, 187–9, 200–1, 220–2, 224, 226, 229
  'alien', 5
  'culture of silence/domination', 111–13
  diversity, 53
  see also multiculturalism
curfews, 135, 138–9, 149, 183–4

Davis, Angela, 53
Defend Council Housing (DCH), 17, 193–4
deindustrialisation, 63, 180
Department for Children, Schools and Families, 23
Department for Innovation, Universities and Skills (DIUS), 23
'dependency culture', 62, 75, 98, 141
Dickens, Charles, 36
disabled people/disability, 103, 148, 171, 192–3, 216, 219
  and benefits, 148, 175–9
  rights for, 54
  and social care, 198
dispersal orders/powers, 138–9, 149, 183–4
doli incapax, 183
domestic violence, 14
Dominelli, L., 44, 66
Doncaster Women's Aid/women's refuge, 11, 13
Donnison, D., 14
Douglass, F., 120
Doyal, L., 109, 174, 222–3
Durkheim, E., 6, 11, 45, 86, 88–92, 95, 106–7, 200

Eagleton, T., 160–1
economic development, 2, 72, 106
education, 6, 12, 17, 21–3, 25, 32, 35–8, 43–4, 46, 49, 62, 67, 71, 77, 81, 84, 90, 119, 121, 124, 141–2, 147–8, 151, 164, 173, 175, 180, 182, 185–6, 190–1, 199, 212, 216, 219, 223, 226, 228–9, 233–4
  adult education, 50
  and 'choice', 96

education – *continued*
    and 'citizenship', 92–3
    exacerbating the class divide, 174,
        188–9
    informal/democratic education,
        180, 183
    its utility for the production of
        'docile bodies', 21–2
    a *Pedagogy of the Oppressed*, 111–18
    and 'social justice', 99–100, 189
    therapeutic education, 157
    see also Chartism, Chartist schools;
        Methodism; miners, schools;
        schools
Elementary Education Act 1870, 37
Employment and Support Allowance,
    178
End Child Poverty coalition, 187
Engels, F., 36, 79–80
Esping-Andersen, G., 18
Etzioni, A., 95–6, 102
eugenics, 40
Evans, Maya, 211

Fabian tradition, 93
Falluja, 121–2
Female Reform Societies (FRSs), 43
feminism/feminist thinking, 11, 13, 66
    anti-pornography, 66
    'Reclaim the Night' marches, 66
football
    influence on community relations,
        34–6
Fordism, 49
Foucault, M., 21, 27, 98, 113, 170,
    224–6, 228
Franklin, Aretha, 136
Freire, P., 18, 21, 88, 110–18, 121,
    124–5, 160, 224, 228–9
French Revolution, 31

Gandhi, M., 123
Gaskell, E., 36
Gaza strip, 124
gender, 17, 25, 30, 43–4, 49, 63, 76,
    79, 81, 84–5, 103, 148, 162, 180,
    219, 226, 234
General Agreement on Trade in
    Services (GATS), 199, 234

General Strike 1926, 60
gentrification, 73, 81, 144
Giroux, H., 23, 185, 229, 235
globalisation, 7, 57
    global capitalism, 23, 60, 105, 119,
        234
    global market(s), 4, 199
    neo-liberal, 61, 231–2
Goffman, E., 14, 180
Gough, I., 109, 174, 222–3
Gramsci, A., 88, 103, 107, 110, 228
Grass, G., 214–15
Greater London Council (GLC),
    13, 67
Greenham Common Women's Peace
    Movement, 66
Guantánamo Bay, 209–10

Habermas, J., 88, 109–10, 117–18, 160,
    224
    'ideal speech situation(s)', 109–10,
        117, 171, 224
Hall, S., 31, 229, 235
Hardt, M., 109–10, 122–3, 232–4
Hayek, F. von, 94
health, 2, 6, 10, 25, 44, 49, 51, 62, 72,
    81, 84, 92–3, 96, 98, 141–2, 163,
    173, 175, 177–80, 182, 185, 187,
    191, 195–9, 207, 212, 219, 223,
    228, 234
    Black Report, 177
    inequalities/divisions, 142, 174, 177,
        196, 198
    mental health, 14, 149, 163–4, 176,
        178, 197, 212
    National Health Service (NHS), 52,
        176, 178, 196–8
    National Institute for Health and
        Clinical Excellence (Nice), 197
    'self care agenda', 197
    women's health, 54
Heath, Edward, 60
hegemonic masculinity 'in crisis', 180
hegemony, 107, 113, 226, 228
    counter hegemony, 59, 107, 110,
        216, 226–8
    definitions of 'gender', 44
    neo-liberal/capitalist, 12, 117
    'White Supremacist', 44

Home Office, 51, 54, 56, 58, 74, 102–3, 129–30, 133, 139, 143, 151–3, 156, 162, 164–5
homeless(ness), 14, 52, 149–50, 171, 195–6, 207
housing, 2, 6, 10, 12–19, 23, 25, 39–40, 44–5, 47, 49–54, 57, 59, 67, 71–4, 76, 79, 81, 84, 92–3, 120, 128, 135, 142, 148–50, 163, 175, 180–1, 191–6, 203, 212, 219, 221, 228–9
    activists/campaigns, 17–18, 38–9, 46–7, 54, 84, 194
    council housing, 17, 39–40, 49, 62, 67–8, 80, 191–5
    privatisation of council housing/ right to buy/stock transfer, 17, 62, 67–8, 191–5
    residualisation, 15, 62, 81, 191, 196
    'social housing', 16, 62, 81, 142, 148, 191, 193–6
    see also social exclusion
Housing Act 1988, 15
Housing and Town Planning Act 1919, 39
housing associations/Registered Social Landlords, 13–15, 17, 19, 192–5
Housing Corporation/Homes and Community Agency, 13–14, 193–4
Housing Finance Act 1972, 58
housing studies, 10, 17–18
Howard, Michael, 181, 184
Human Rights Watch (HRW), 169
Huntington, S., 105

Illich, I., 14
Immigration and Asylum Act 1999, 163
immigration/immigrants, 3, 5, 35, 40–3, 45, 52–3, 68–9, 71, 152, 154–7, 159, 161–5, 220, 235
Incapacity Benefit (IB), 175–8
industrial revolution, 30–2, 35–6
    social consequences of, 30–2
Institute of Economic Affairs, 76
Institute of Race Relations (IRR), 155, 165

International Criminal Court of Justice (ICC), 12, 209–10, 233
International Monetary Fund (IMF), 9, 57, 60–1, 84, 105, 146, 231
International Solidarity Movement, 124
Iraq, 8–9, 11–12, 121–4, 151, 166, 168, 207–11, 220, 231
Islamic Human Rights Commission, 167
Islamophobia, 166
    see also 'war on terror'

James, Oliver, 202
John, Helen, 211
Joint Intelligence and Security Committee (JISC), 207, 210
Joseph, Keith, 77

Kant, I., 136–7
Kautsky, K., 35
Keynes, J.M., 48, 60–1, 146
Keynesian welfarism/welfarist principles, 11, 30, 48–9, 62, 78–80, 84–5, 93–4, 97, 170, 173, 180, 219
    'in crisis', 59–62
    and full-employment, 51
    see also welfare state
Klein, N., 231
Koselleck, R., 224–5
Kundnani, A., 155, 158, 168
Küng, 49
Kwesi Johnson, Linton, 119

labour market(s), 1, 19–20, 23, 75, 100, 147, 175, 181, 195–6, 219
Laclau, E., 224, 226
Laing, R.D., 14
Lane, R.E., 25, 206
Layard, R., 25, 206
Levitas, R., 94, 141, 158, 174
Local Government, Planning and Land Act 1980, 67
Local Government Finance Act 1982, 68
London bombings, 7 July 2005, 156, 165

Luhmann, N., 224, 226–7
Luther King, Martin, 55, 123, 136

Major, John, 75
Malpass, P., 15, 191–6
managerialism/-ist, 15–16, 22,
    131–2, 171, 180, 182, 189, 194,
    198
Marcuse, H., 113–14, 200–1
market populism, 174
Marshall, T.H., 92, 222
Marx, Eleanor, 37
Marx, K., 31, 35–7, 86, 88, 107,
    110–11, 116, 174, 200, 211
Marxism/-ist(s), 35, 37, 57–8, 83, 107,
    120, 200, 236
Mayhew, H., 33
media, 3, 9, 29, 53, 63, 65, 70–1, 74,
    83, 110, 128, 151, 159, 167–8, 179,
    184, 186–7, 220, 226, 232
Methodism/-ist(s), 35, 37, 57–8, 83,
    107, 120, 200, 236
  Methodist schools, 34–5, 180
miners, 34, 36–7
  schools, 36
  strikes (1973), 60, (1984), 63–5
  see also trade unions
Monbiot, G., 7–8, 12, 121–2, 124,
    149–50, 208–9, 232
monetarism/-ist, 11, 60–1
'moral indifference', 175, 207, 212–13,
    215
Morgan Report 1991, 74, 129–30
Morris, William, 37
Mouffe, C., 108–9, 224, 226
Mubarek, Z., 213
multiculturalism, 152, 155–6,
    158–62, 170
  see also culture(s)/cultural
Murray, C., 76, 94, 186
Muslim Council of Britain, 167

National Coalition for Independent
    Action (NCIA), 16
National Housing Federation (NHF),
    194
National Intelligence Model (NIM),
    134
Negri, A., 109–10, 122–3, 232–4

neighbourhood management, 141
neighbourhood renewal, 142–3
  National Strategy for
      Neighbourhood Renewal, 142,
      146
  Neighbourhood Renewal Unit, 142,
      154
neo-liberal/liberalism/New Right, 1,
    6–7, 12, 18–19, 24–6, 30, 59–62,
    66, 68, 75–6, 78–9, 82, 84–5,
    94–8, 101, 105, 127–8, 140, 146,
    170–1, 174–6, 180–1, 194, 196,
    206–7, 212, 215, 218, 230–2,
    234–6
New Deal, 98, 147, 174, 182
New Deal for Communities (NDC),
    142–3
New Economics Foundation, 205
New Labour
  and community cohesion, 27–8,
      126–7, 150–60, 162, 165–6,
      168–9, 171, 175, 200, 207, 209,
      211, 213, 235
  and community safety, 27, 126–34,
      136, 138, 140, 142–4, 158,
      171–3, 216
  and the 'third way', 19, 49, 108, 147,
      162, 181, 199
  and urban regeneration, 27, 73,
      126–7, 141–5, 147–8, 205
  see also community cohesion
  see also community safety
  see also urban regeneration
new urban Left, 66–7
Nuremberg International Military
    Tribunal, 12, 209

Olympics
  and mass purification, 149
Orgreave coking plant
  the battle of, 63–5

Palestinian homes
  demolition of, 124
Pankhurst, S., 44
parenting programmes, 183
partnership(s), 6, 13, 28, 68, 75
  in crime control, 73, 129–31,
      141–2, 183

partnership(s) – *continued*
  Local Strategic Partnerships, 142
  see also Crime and Disorder
    Reduction Partnerships
    (CDRPs)
Patchwork Community, 13–14, 54
Peach, Blair, 69
Pilger, J., 124, 209–10
Pinter, H., 210
planning, 10, 18, 51, 72, 81, 130, 142,
    205, 229
Police Reform Act, 133, 135
policing
  'community policing', 96, 128
  a 'crisis in legitimacy', 73
  miners' strike and use of colonial
    riot tactics, 63–4
  Operation Swamp, 81, 70
  paramilitary policing, 65, 84
  police officers in schools, 183
  police-led community safety
    strategies, 129–30, 145
  and Respect Action Plan, 136
  snatch squad tactics, 64
  stop and search, 8–9, 167
  'sus' law, 70
  use of police riot gear, 69
  zero tolerance, 149
poll tax demonstration(s), 65, 121
poverty, 32, 38, 48, 51–2, 56–7, 63,
    68, 76, 79, 94, 104, 112–13, 119,
    122, 140–3, 147–8, 158, 162, 164,
    173, 187, 207, 215, 219, 233–4
Powell, Enoch, 53–4, 68–9
Prevention of Terrorism Act 2005, 168
Protection from Harassment Act 1997,
    7, 168
Public Choice theory, 61
public health, 33–4
Public Order Act 1986, 65
Public Service Agreement (PSA)
    targets, 142
Pusey, Michael, 206
Putnam, R., 102, 151

Queer Nation, 123

'race', 17, 25, 30, 33, 40, 44, 49, 52–4,
    68, 70–1, 76, 79, 81, 103, 120,
    148, 150, 152, 155, 159–60, 165,
    213, 219, 226, 234
Race Relations Act 1965, 53
racism(s)/racists, 43, 59, 68–70, 84,
    155, 157–8, 162–3, 167, 213,
    219–20, 228
  anti-racism campaigns, 54, 67, 69,
    84
  racist violence: Cardiff, Liverpool,
    Glasgow, 41–2; struggles
    against, 119
  Rock Against Racism (RAR), 69
radical democracy theory, 107–8
Rawls, J., 137, 222
Redding, Otis, 136
Refugee Council, 164
refugees, 134, 220
Regulation of Investigatory Powers
    Act 2000, 168
rendition, 210
Rent and Mortgage Interest Freeze Bill
    1915, 39
'Respect' agenda, 134–40
  see also young people/youth, and
    'Respect' agenda
riots/rioting, 38, 53–5, 63–4, 68–71,
    73, 76, 120–1, 126, 155, 158, 181
  as a class act, 120–1
Robinson, Tom, 69
Roma communities
  evictions of, 149–50
Rose, N., 96, 106
Rowntree, S., 51
Ruts, The, 119

Scargill, Arthur, 63
Scarman Report, 70–1
schools, 17, 21–3, 37, 51, 96, 141, 182,
    182–5, 187–90, 195, 199, 201,
    204, 229
  divisions within the school system,
    21
  exclusions from, 22
  extended schooling, 182–3
  production of 'docile bodies', 113
  and 'Respect' agenda, 135–6
  safer schools partnerships, 183
  truancy and disruptive behaviour,
    182

schools – *continued*
    twinning, 152–3
    see also education; Chartism,
        Chartist schools; Methodism;
        miners, schools
Seebohm Report 1968, 51, 54
Serious Organised Crime and Police
    Act 2005, 8, 168, 211
sexuality/-ies, 25, 44, 53–4, 103, 180,
    219
Shadjareh, M., 167
Shelter, 52, 196
single parent(s), 14, 79, 81, 177, 192
Single Regeneration Budget (SRB),
    75, 142
situational crime prevention, 145, 184
Skeffington Report 1969, 51
Smart, B., 61–2, 200–2, 214
social capital, 59, 102–3, 138, 151,
    153, 170
social care, 2, 14, 25, 54, 186, 196,
    198–9
    school-age carers, 186
social democracy/democratic, 21, 48,
    59–60, 71, 88, 94, 99–100, 119,
    170, 199
    perspectives on community, 92–4
Social Democratic Federation
    (SDF), 37
social exclusion/socially excluded, 23,
    27, 75, 78, 82, 120, 141, 147, 158,
    166, 181–2, 186, 221
    and housing policy choices, 191–5
    moral underclass discourse, 141,
        182
    social integrationist discourse, 141,
        182
Social Exclusion Unit (SEU), 141–3,
    146, 174, 182
social inclusion, 19, 21, 147, 158, 182,
    200
'social harm', 10
    from the actions of the powerful/
        neo-liberalism, 5–6, 25–6, 29,
        75, 83, 172, 174–5, 196–7, 200,
        202–3, 214–16, 219, 230, 235–6
    environmental pollution, 130
    human rights violations, 122, 163,
        167–9, 207–12, 215–16

poverty/social deprivation as
    sources of social harm, 130,
    187
social protection/security, 6, 24, 49,
    51, 84, 97, 128, 174–5, 180, 212,
    219, 222, 228, 231
Social Security Act 1986, 63
Social Security (Incapacity for Work)
    Act 1994, 175
social wellbeing, 4–6, 9–10, 13,
    18–20, 23–5, 28, 43, 85, 87–8,
    111, 126, 128, 175, 177, 191, 196,
    202, 214–16, 218–20, 222, 224–5,
    228, 231, 235–6
    see also community wellbeing;
        subjective wellbeing
socialism, 30, 33, 40, 67
    Gramsci's socialist ideals, 107
    municipal socialism, 13, 66,
        72, 129
    Tawney's socialism, 99
Solon Wandsworth Housing
    Association (SWHA), 14, 16, 54
Special Restrictions (Coloured Alien
    Seamen) Act 1925, 42
squatting, 13, 17, 47
Statewatch, 234
Steel Pulse, 69, 119
Straw, J., 128, 157, 168, 211
structural causes of social problems/
    social inequality, 83, 101, 113,
    116, 126, 128, 132, 144, 148, 157,
    173, 177, 220
structural change(s)
    acknowledge the need for, 12, 123
    political ramifications of, 29, 57, 79,
        107
structural context for social relations,
    30, 57, 59, 112, 138, 140, 155, 187,
    217, 222, 226, 235, 237
structural perspective on community
    cohesion, 158, 162
structuralist critique of social policy,
    144
student demonstrations, 7, 55
subjective wellbeing, 185, 206
    see also community wellbeing;
        social wellbeing
Suffragettes, 44

Sure Start, 142, 182
'sustainable enterprise', 142
Sutton Trust, 188–9

Tawney, R.H., 99–100
Teddy boys, 53
tenant participation/involvement,
    17–18, 50, 57
'terrorism', 5, 7, 9, 165–7, 169, 206–7,
    209–12, 231
Terrorism Act 2000, 168
    stop and search, 8–9
    used against free speech and
        protest, 8, 211
Terrorism Act 2006, 169
Thatcher/Thatcherism, 30, 61–3,
    65–9, 71–3, 75, 79, 81, 94–5, 142,
    147, 191
Thompson, E.P., 31–2, 34–5, 40,
    43–4, 90–1
Tönnies, F., 86, 88, 91–2, 95
Townsend, P., 51, 177, 198
trade unions, 32, 36–8, 40, 49–50, 80,
    84, 90–1, 119, 228
    conflict with government
        1970s/1980s, 60–1, 63–4
    weakening of powers, 1, 24,
        180, 233
    and women's activism, 43
    see also miners
travellers, 3, 65, 134, 150
    see also 'Battle of the Beanfield'

UN Convention on the Rights of the
    Child, 183–4
Unicef's 2007 assessment of children's
    and young people's wellbeing,
    185
University of Nottingham
    arrest and detention without
        charge of Rizwaan Sabir, 169
Urban Aid, 13
Urban Aid Programme (UAP), 51,
    54, 56
Urban Development Corporations, 67,
    72
Urban Programme, 55, 62, 71–2
urban regeneration, 6, 171
urbanisation, 31–3, 50, 86

Venables, Terry, 69

'war on terror', 9, 165–8, 175, 205,
    207, 210–11, 231, 234
    assaults on Muslims, 165–8
    see also Islamophobia
Weber, M., 86, 88, 107
Welfare Reform Act 1999, 176
Welfare Reform Bill 2006, 177
welfare state, 31, 48–9, 51–2, 62, 76,
    96, 119, 140–1, 174, 194, 196
    see also Keynesian welfarism/
        welfarist principles
Wesley, J., 35
White Paper 2008 *Putting
    Communities in Control*, 2
Wilkinson, R., 6, 138, 173, 213, 215
Williams, F., 44–5, 52, 157
Williams, R., 50, 90
Wilmott, P., 50
Wilson, Harold, 56, 60
Winter of Discontent 1978–1979, 61
Wolfgang, Walter, 211
Women's Housing Association, 39
workers collectives, 13, 54
Workers' Educational Association
    (WEA), 50
work-life balance, 147
World Bank (WB), 10, 105, 146, 231,
    234
World to Win, A, 123, 234
World Trade Organisation (WTO), 9,
    105, 199, 231, 234

Young, J., 128
Young, M., 50
young people/youth
    'anti-social'/'feral' youth, 3, 220,
        235
    demonisation of young people,
        184–5
    'disaffected' black youth, 157
    fear of youth crime, 2
    French youth, 120
    harmed by the education system,
        22, 190
    lack of social opportunity, 227
    loss of manufacturing jobs, 180
    policing black youth, 70

young people/youth – *continued*
  and 'Respect' agenda, 135, 140
  'yob' culture, 184, 227
  young people and asbos, 133,
    138–9
  youth (sub)culture(s), 69, 76, 149
  youth justice, punitive turn in, 181,
    183–5
  youth offending teams, 182
  youth policy, 175
  youth unemployment, 71

  see also 'anti-social behaviour'/
    anti-social behaviour orders
    (asbos)
  see also children
  see also 'Respect' agenda
Younge, G., 120–1
Youth Justice Board, 184
youth work, 2, 10, 34, 84, 180, 182–3,
    212, 227–8
  detached youth work, under threat,
    182–3